A. G. Ford

Professor of Economics, University of Warwick

Income, Spending and the Price Level

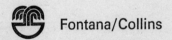 Fontana/Collins

First published in Fontana 1971
Reprinted October 1973

Copyright © A. G. Ford 1971

Printed in Great Britain
for the Publishers Wm. Collins Sons & Co Ltd,
14 St James's Place, London S.W.1,
by Richard Clay (The Chaucer Press), Ltd,
Bungay, Suffolk

Contents

Introduction

Aims and Methods

The aim of this book is to provide an introduction to macroeconomic analysis and its uses for policy purposes. It is designed not only for the first year of degree courses in economics but also for professional examinations involving economics, and for the second year of A Level courses.

Before beginning the book it would be a definite advantage to have read the introductory volume in this series, *An Introduction to Economic Behaviour*, by C. D. Harbury, especially Chapters 6 and 7. However, the present book assumes no prior knowledge of economics and is self-contained.

Chapters 1 to 8 comprise Part One and provide an introductory course in Keynesian macroeconomics and its application to the short-run management of the economy. Chapters 9 to 12 form Part Two. They cover more advanced material dealing with the incorporation of the economic analysis of international and governmental economic activities, the equilibrium of the economic system as a whole, and include some discussion of economic growth. This Part may be omitted at a first reading.

Chapter 8 which deals with the short-run macroeconomic management of the economy has been placed deliberately at the end of Part One of this volume and in advance of detailed and more complex economic analysis of the foreign-trade and governmental sectors, even though it does draw on such analysis. However, it is hoped that sufficient guide-lines to these matters are provided in this chapter to enable it to be intelligible to the reader who has mastered the preceding chapters. The reason for this unusual order is the desire of the author that Chapters 1 to 8 should form Part One and give the reader a grasp of short-run macroeconomic analysis *and policy*. Part Two is more difficult and beyond the syllabus of certain courses but does deal with very important issues, particularly for the university or polytechnic undergraduate. Re-reading Chapter 8 after Part Two will certainly be found to be worth while by them.

To reach a wide public the mathematical content has been kept to a bare minimum, although it is the author's belief that mathematical analysis is a powerful tool in modern economics. However, the effective use of such a tool does presuppose a background knowledge which most readers will not have. Hence geometric and numerical methods are used in preference to algebraic methods. The interested reader is referred to Morley's *Mathematics for Modern Economics*, which is listed along with the other volumes in the Fontana Introduction to Economics inside the front cover.

The economic analysis in the present book is illustrated by, and supported with, evidence and examples mainly from British economic experiences and the reader is encouraged to pursue these matters further. A select reading list is given at the end.

Acknowledgements

The following books have provided the sources for the statistics underlying the figures and tables: *National Income and Expenditure 1969*, H.M.S.O., 1969; B. R. Mitchell and P. Deane (ed.), *Abstract of British Historical Statistics*, Cambridge, 1962; *National Institute Economic Review* (statistical Appendix) and *The British Economy: Key Statistics 1900–1964*, London and Cambridge Economic Service, 1966.

PART ONE

Chapter 1

Income and Output

Introduction

One feature of the economic life of a country which concerns us all is unemployment. It could happen to any of us, to be thrown out of our current employment through no fault of our own—or in polite language to be made redundant. To gain some measure of the extent of unemployment in a country we can express the numbers of those registered as unemployed as a percentage of the total labour force. Let us see how this percentage has behaved in Britain in the twentieth century.

Between 1900 and 1914 the annual average percentage of the labour force unemployed fluctuated between 8 per cent and 2 per cent. Between 1921 and 1939 it never diminished below 10 per cent, and it reached an all time high of 22 per cent in 1932, in the depths of the world depression. Since 1945 it has never been above 4 per cent of the labour force, and on occasions it has even been below 1 per cent. We may well ask 'Why'. Further, if we look at Figure 1.1 we notice distinct fluctuations in unemployment which are matched by fluctuations in industrial production and gross domestic product.[1] When unemployment is low, production of goods is high: when

1. These are expressed as index numbers, which can be explained as follows. We choose a base period and express production in any year as a percentage of production in the base year. The series of percentages thus derived for a span of years are known as index numbers. Suppose in 1958 a colliery produced 800,000 tons of coal and in 1959 it produced 900,000 tons of coal. Choose 1958 as base year. The index number for coal production at this colliery in 1958 would be 100: in 1959 it would be 1959 production expressed as a percentage of 1958 production, or $\frac{900,000}{800,000} \times 100 = 112 \cdot 5$. Similarly, a price index would compare the general level of prices in any year with the level in a base year. This is perforce a very crude and simple explanation. There are difficulties which are discussed elsewhere in this series.

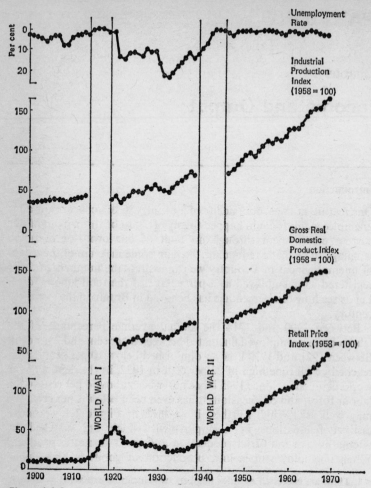

Figure 1.1 Growth and fluctuations in the United Kingdom economy

unemployment is high, production is relatively low. Again, the curious will want to know why. In each war period—1914–18 and 1939–45—it will be noticed that unemployment has fallen to very low levels and remained low. Does this mean that we need to be at war before enforced idleness of workers can be eliminated?

In each of the periods for which we have discussed the behaviour of unemployment in Britain, production grows despite the varied unemployment picture. However, the behaviour of prices shows striking differences. Before 1914 retail prices showed an amazing stability. After a sharp fall from 1920 to 1922 prices sagged slowly to 1935. However, since the end of the Second World War in 1945, they have risen relentlessly. Why? If we want steady prices, must we endure higher unemployment than we might like otherwise? Again, in the First World War they doubled in four years: in the Second World War they rose by only 40 per cent in six years. Why have these different patterns occurred?

These are some of the major questions which macroeconomics investigates and seeks to answer. Macroeconomics deals with the economy as a whole. It is not concerned primarily with how the individual or firm behaves, but how—collectively or in aggregate—households or firms behave. It seeks to explain why unemployment is high or low; why production is high or low; why prices are rising or falling; why interest rates or the cost of borrowing are high or low.

To achieve these objectives we need to develop a macroeconomic analysis, or theory. This not only will help us to explain, but may also help us to avoid some undesirable situations by suggesting suitable economic policies for us to adopt. Any theory needs to be well-based in fact and to yield predictions which are not falsified by events. In fact, one aim of this work is to enable the reader to suggest some answers to the questions arising from British experiences which were posed earlier, and to appraise the performance of the economy and the policies propounded by economists. It will concentrate on the short run and will only touch on the problems of growth. The task of this chapter is to describe in a highly simplified form the economy as a whole and to classify the many transactions being undertaken. This will provide a framework for analysis and policy-making.

Production

In any description of an economy the chief factor to emphasise is the economy's *production* of finished goods and services per year or per month. Remember that we are concerned not only with physical goods but also with services such as medical care, banking facilities, and hair-cuts. The provision of transport services is just as much a productive activity as the manufacture of motor cars, the provision of education as the manufacture of desks and chalk.

As a basic picture an economy has land of varying qualities, labour of various skills, and real capital of varying kinds such as machines, factories, aeroplanes, roads, and gas-works. They are known as *factors of production* and at any one time they will be limited in size. There will be a given amount of land, a given labour force, and a given stock of real capital. To produce a flow of output per year these factors of production must be combined together in appropriate ways in factories, or in offices, or on farms, or in mines.

In macroeconomics we are particularly concerned with the behaviour of total national output of *finished* (or final) goods and services. We must express this in monetary terms as the value of national output because we cannot add together tons of coal mined, gallons of beer brewed, and the number of bus journeys. We must multiply the amount of any product in a year by the price charged for it to the final purchaser to obtain the money value of its output. We can add such money values together as they are all expressed in the same units and thus obtain the value of total annual output of finished goods and services for any economy for any year. This is known as *gross national product*.[2]

But are there other forms of output than finished goods and services? Are we neglecting the output of sheet steel which is sold to the motor industry, the output of flour sold to bakers, the tobacco sold to cigarette manufacturers, the hops sold to brewers? For men, land, and machines are clearly employed in producing these raw materials and intermediate (or semi-finished) goods. Should we not add these on to the value of total finished output?

The answer is that we should be 'double-counting' if we did this. For the flour sold to the bakers has been counted *already* in the loaves he sells to the public. The value of the output of the motor industry includes the sheet steel which it has purchased from rolling mills. The steel is embodied in the final product—the new car in the show room. Thus the value of total output of finished goods and services includes already the value of the raw materials and semi-finished goods used in their production. To add the value of raw materials and semi-finished goods produced to total output of finished goods and services would be double-counting and would be grossly misleading by providing an inflated impression of the country's capacity to produce.

2. The term 'gross' will be explained in the text later. Briefly, in the productive process capital goods (e.g. machines) wear out and need replacing. Some portion of output has to be used for this purpose. *Gross* national product is the total value of final output *before* making such replacement provision, and *net* national product is the total value of final output *after* making such replacement.

National product and national income

In producing output, factors of production receive income. Labour receives wages and salaries, while the owners of capital receive profit, landowners receive rent. The aim of this section is to show that the total value of final goods and services produced is equal to the total value of incomes received by factors of production.

Let us assume a very simple economy with no international economic transactions and no governmental transactions. Let us suppose that the prices which are used to value the flow of output do not change over the time-period in question, and that we can treat the economy as one enormous firm which produces all the final output and provides for itself all the raw materials and semi-finished goods required. These are very unrealistic assumptions and will be relaxed as the chapter progresses. However, they will enable us to show simply the basic accounting relationships, and the process will show how economics operates by proceeding from the simple and unrealistic to the complex and more realistic.

In any one year our 'firm' will produce a particular pattern of output, and we assume that it sells it in entirety. Hence the total value of its output, or gross national product, will be the same as its sales receipts. These proceeds will be used by the firm to pay (a) wages and salaries to labour, (b) rent to landowners, and (c) the remnant accrues to the owners of the real capital assets as gross profits. In this way sales receipts are entirely used up in income payments, which are distributed to the suppliers of productive services. The role of gross profits as a 'residual legatee' should be noted.

We have[3]

Gross national product ≡ total sales receipts ≡
$$\left.\begin{matrix} \text{wages and salaries} \\ + \text{ rent} \\ + \text{ gross profits} \end{matrix}\right\} \equiv \text{gross national income}$$

Further, total sales receipts are equivalent to total spending on gross final output, which we call gross national expenditure. Hence gross national expenditure, gross national product, and gross national income are all the same size, and are three different ways of looking at

3. In these accounting relationships the sign ≡ is used to denote 'identically equal' or 'equal by definition'. The relationship holds whatever is the value of gross national product. It must be distinguished from the use of the sign = later in the book to denote equality under some particular condition.

the same thing—the value of final output of goods and services in the year.

The same conclusion will hold if the assumption of one enormous firm is relaxed by introducing a raw material sector and semi-finished product sector in addition to the final product sector. These new sectors sell their output to other firms for further processing until they emerge as final output. (This finding is demonstrated in the appendix to this chapter.)

Consumption and investment

When we consider the flow of final output of goods and services, it is clear that some are purchased by households for immediate use such as food, clothing, and fuel. These are known as *consumer goods*. It is likewise clear that some are purchased for the purpose of adding to real capital assets. For example, the owners of a firm may purchase a new machine tool in order to increase their capacity to produce, or a household may purchase a newly constructed house. These are known as *investment goods* and it is by their production that the factor of production, capital, can be expanded in size. Classifying the flow of final goods and services into (*a*) consumption and (*b*) investment goods is useful in economics. As in all classifications, the division may at times seem arbitrary, although it is clear that beer is a consumer good and a drop-forge is an investment good.

Consumption as an activity can be thought of as the enjoyment of the results of current production by the people of an economy and is usually accompanied by some degree of destruction. For accounting purposes, we assume that products are consumed as soon as they are obtained by the consumer. While this is clearly sensible for services and for foodstuffs, it is not so sensible a method when dealing with durable consumer goods such as cars, refrigerators, television sets which supply a flow of services over several years and which can be resold. Consumption may take the form of private purchase by individuals, or of public provision. Certain needs such as health, defence, internal security, education are met collectively by the state by the free supply of public goods rather than by individual purchases.

Investment as an activity occurs to the extent that production in any time period is not fully consumed, so that goods are available either for adding to the stock of real capital assets for use in future production or for adding to the stocks of goods for future consumption. If consumption goods produced in a time period exceed sales, then stocks of these goods rise; and this rise in stocks is treated as investment in that time period. If sales exceed production, stocks of goods fall and this is treated as disinvestment, that is, negative investment.

Not all the output of investment goods in any year can go to increase the stock of real capital in the economy. Some portion must be used to replace worn-out existing capital goods and to make good wear and tear. Machines, bridges, buildings, and power stations do not last for ever. It is a fact of life that capital goods are (slowly) worn out in productive processes, and we cannot ignore this when evaluating the addition to real capital stock by investment in any year. We must allow for depreciation, and the devotion of some of our current output of investment goods to maintaining real capital intact. What is then left of the output of investment goods is available for increasing the stock of capital, and is known as net fixed investment, whereas *gross* fixed investment is the output before making provision for depreciation.

In practice the calculation of depreciation is very difficult, for we may well replace an old machine with an improved version. Have we maintained capital 'intact' thus? Again, some machines may gradually wear out, while others may suddenly collapse. We shall skate over this problem and adopt the following definitions: (a) *realised gross investment* in any time period is output of investment goods *plus* any change in stocks of goods, while (b) *realised net investment* is gross investment minus depreciation and includes of course any change in stocks.

We can view the total output of final goods and services in an economy in two ways: (1) as *gross national product* (i.e. before making any depreciation provisions) and this provides a measure of production in the economy. We can view it (2) as *net national product* (that is, after making provision for depreciation). This provides a measure of goods and services available for consumption or investment purposes once real capital stock has been maintained intact.

In summary, we can express gross national product as the value of consumption goods and services produced and sold, *plus* the value of investment goods produced, *plus* any stock changes. Hence we can say:

(*a*) Gross national product $\equiv$
  consumption sales + gross investment (including stock changes)

$$Y_g \equiv C + I_g$$

where Y_g stands for gross national product, C for consumption expenditure, and I_g for gross investment.

(*b*) Net national product ≡
consumption sales + net investment (including stock changes)

$$Y \equiv C + I$$

where Y stands for net national product and I for net investment.

Consumption and saving

Let us consider how the recipients of national income dispose of it. As seen earlier, national income is the sum of all incomes accruing to owners of productive services as a result of the use of the various productive services they have supplied to produce a flow of finished goods and services. It is, indeed, another way of looking at this flow of output. The recipients dispose of their annual income on consumption purchases and what part of income remains is their savings for the year.

Savings are therefore unconsumed income and national income is divided up into total consumption and total savings of the country. If we are discussing the disposal of *gross* national income, depreciation provisions are included in *gross* savings. If the concept of net national income is used, we have net savings with depreciation provisions excluded. One difficulty should be mentioned. Firms frequently set aside some of their net profits, and distribute to shareholders (the owners of the firm) only part of the profits accruing to them. These undistributed profits, which belong to the shareholders, are clearly unconsumed income, and thus are treated as part of total savings made by the recipients of national income.

In explicit form we have:

Gross national income ≡ consumption expenditure *plus* gross savings

$$Y_g \equiv C + S_g$$

or Net national income ≡ consumption expenditure *plus* net savings

$$Y \equiv C + S$$

where savings included both personal savings by households and undistributed profits (or company savings), if any. From now onwards we shall drop the terms of 'net' and 'gross' and just talk in terms of national income, investment, savings, and so on, bearing in mind that they will either be all 'net' or all 'gross' consistently.

The circular flow of income

If we put together the 'production and spending' and 'disposal' aspects of our accounting relationships we get:

Consumption by households of 1,850 ⎫ ≡ national product ≡
plus investment by firms of 150   ⎭   of 2,000

> national income ≡ ⎧consumption of households of 1,850
> of 2,000   ⎩savings by households of 150

For the time being we assume that household savings flow into the 'finance market' from which firms acquire financial resources to enable them to purchase investment goods.

In symbolic form

$$C + I \equiv Y \equiv C + S$$

Subtracting C from each part

$$I \equiv Y - C \equiv S$$

That is, investment ≡ unconsumed output ≡ saving.

These relationships are also illustrated in Figure 1.2 which clearly

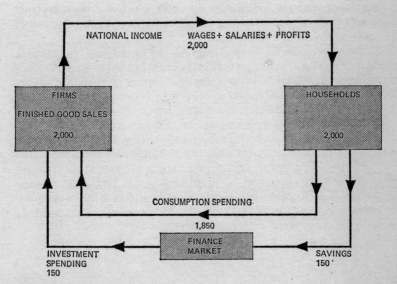

Figure 1.2 The flow of income and spending. The arrows denote direction of flow of money payments

demonstrates the circular flow of income from firms to households and back to firms via consumption spending, with savings forming a 'leakage' from this flow, a leakage that is the same size as investment spending, which forms an injection into this flow. Actual investment spending is the same size as actual saving because of the definitions adopted. These make both equivalent to unconsumed output, even though they may well have been undertaken by different groups.

Again, if we assume that the economy is operating at maximum output, it is clear that it is only to the extent that we are prepared to increase saving—to reduce our consumption claims on this output— that goods and resources can be released to expand investment in factories, roads, hospitals ... while it is by investment that our capacity to produce goods in the future may be expanded. (However, if resources released by saving are not taken up for investment but lie idle, then a tragic waste will occur.)

Can we show how investment spending by firms is financed in more detail? Consumption spending is financed by the income receipts of households,[4] but we have shown our 'firm' using its sales receipts to pay out wages and salaries and rent, and leaving gross profits as a residual for distribution to shareholders. How, then, will it acquire finance in order to purchase investment goods? The answer is that we need to develop for firms a capital account which receives loans from households' savings (including undistributed profits) and disposes of them on investment spending.

Households employ their savings directly or indirectly through the finance market. Through it they make loans to firms or acquire claims on firms. Table 1.1 illustrates this relationship of firms and households. It provides a simple double-entry system incorporating the fact that every transaction has a dual aspect. For example, sales of consumption goods and services constitute a receipt item from the point of view of firms and are entered thus. They are a payment item from the point of view of households, and are so entered in the households' current account. Or take the capital account. This concerns itself with the purchase of investment goods and their finance. Receipts into it come from savings (a payment item in the households' current account). Payments to it are made for investment goods (a receipt item in firms' current account).

4. Hire-purchase finance is ruled out at present.

Intended and realised values

These relationships that we have developed between spending, production, and income have referred to *realised* values. They have in fact provided us with a way of looking at the operation of the

Table 1.1

Current accounts

FIRMS

Receipts		*Payments*	
Sales of consumption goods and services	1,850	Wages and salaries, rent	1,500
Sales of investment goods	150	Profits (including undistributed profits)	500
	2,000		2,000

HOUSEHOLDS

Income from wages and salaries, rent	1,500	Consumption purchases	1,850
Income from profits	500	Savings (including undistributed profits)	150
	2,000		2,000

Capital account

FIRMS

Receipts of savings from households	150	Purchase of investment goods	150

---

economic system and they enabled us to set up the following analytical framework which we can employ to handle *planned*, *intended*, or *expected* values as follows:

Consumption expenditure by households *plus* investment spending by firms ⟩ generate output and incomes which are disposed of on ⟨ consumption purchases by households *plus* savings made by households

Consumption spending goes on to maintain the circular flow of income by sending a flow of payments back to generate incomes. Savings form a leakage—they do not reappear as income. Investment forms an injection into this flow and offsets the savings leakage.

In *realised* (that is, in *actual*) terms investment always equals savings, by definition. In practice, it would seem unlikely that we would find *planned* or *intended* investment just equal to *planned* or *intended* savings. We could hardly expect that in planned terms the numerical values of Figure 1.2 represent a likely situation in a real economy—planned investment of 150, planned consumption of 1,850, and planned saving of 150. The plans and intentions of economic units and their outcomes will be our concern in subsequent chapters, for we want to know *why* realised values are what they are. For example, if the desire to invest were to increase and exceed the desire to save, planned injections into the flow of income would exceed planned leakages from it. In that case, the flow of spending and incomes would rise. On the other hand, if the desire to save exceeded the desire to invest, the flow of income would fall, for planned leakages would then exceed planned injections.

Furthermore, this framework suggests important results for economic policy-making. These will be justified later. Here they can be briefly summarised, as follows.

If planned spending is high in relation to capacity to produce, and if spending plans are realised, then output and employment will be high and boom conditions will prevail. Prices will tend to rise, especially if planned spending exceeds the maximum output that can be produced. The economy would be facing inflationary conditions. If, however,—to take the contrary case—planned spending is low in relation to capacity to produce, then output and employment will be low and prices may tend to fall. Deflationary or slump conditions will result. It is not enough to produce goods and services and assume they will be sold. For there is no guarantee that planned spending will be just sufficient to purchase all the output produced.

International transactions

It is unrealistic to ignore international economic transactions which may affect directly the flow of spending, output, and income, for it is hard to think of any actual economy which is so self-sufficient that it can do without other countries' products. International trade in goods and services is widespread, and enables much gainful exchange of produce to take place through exporting and importing. For example, Britain is able to acquire tropical produce, raw materials, and oil from abroad by exporting manufactured products of all kinds. Without our imports of raw materials our industry would virtually collapse. Without our food imports, which form roughly half of our total food consumption, we would starve. By trade we are also able to acquire a greater variety of products.

Sales of our products abroad—our merchandise exports—provide another source of sales revenue for our firms besides domestic sales to consumers or other firms. The sale of a Jaguar XJ6 car to a foreigner generates sales receipts and incomes in Coventry in just the same way as the sale of one to a Birmingham bookmaker. And it is not only the sales of our goods abroad which generate incomes, but also the sale of our services abroad, such as overseas shipping services or financial services rendered to foreigners. Further, the spending of foreign tourists in Britain generates incomes for British factors of production. Hence exports of goods and services form another constituent of spending and so they go on to generate incomes.

International economic transactions give rise to another source of incomes. British-owned firms operate in Australia and earn profits, which they remit to Britain as dividends from abroad. Again, British residents own foreign governmental bonds from which they receive interest income from abroad. Income received from abroad may thus be added to exports of goods and services when considering the generation of income.

The world market presents an area from which our firms can purchase goods and services to form our imports. Thus, some portion of the sales receipts of our 'enormous firm' will be devoted to purchases of other countries' products, and this will form their exports. Imports of goods and services will thus constitute a leakage from the flow of spending and incomes in our economy. Furthermore in so far as foreigners own firms in Britain, some portion of profits will accrue as incomes paid abroad to them and not to British residents. Income paid abroad can be included with imports of goods and services.

Let us place our single firm representing the whole economy in an international setting[5]. We have in realised terms:

$$
\left.\begin{array}{l}
\text{Export sales} \\
plus \text{ domestic consumption} \\
\text{spending} \\
plus \text{ domestic investment} \\
\text{spending}
\end{array}\right\} \equiv \text{sales receipts} \equiv \left\{\begin{array}{l}
\text{wages and salaries} \\
plus \\
\text{rent} \\
plus \\
\text{profits} \\
plus \\
\text{import purchases}
\end{array}\right.
$$

This yields:

Export sales + consumption + investment
$$\equiv \text{national income} + \text{import purchases}$$

$$X + C + I \quad \equiv Y + F$$
$$X + C + I - F \equiv Y$$

5. The same conclusions follow if we have many firms and inter-firm transactions involving raw materials and semi-finished goods.

Export sales + consumption + investment — imports
$$\equiv \text{national income}$$
while national income $\equiv$ consumption + savings
$$Y \equiv C + S$$

Note: X, C, I, F are all valued at market prices for them.
These relationships are illustrated graphically in Figure 1.3.

The effect of including international transactions in our picture is this. National spending at market prices ($= X + I + C$) no longer equals national income because some portion of spending is devoted to import purchases. To arrive at home incomes, final goods and services have an 'import content' which has to be deducted. Besides, home consumers do not buy final good imports directly but through the agency of domestic firms (wholesalers, agents, distributors, retailers as well as manufacturers) who process them to a greater or a lesser extent.

No longer can we talk of the necessary equality of realised savings and investment. Instead we must talk in terms of realised injections and realised leakages. We have:

$$X + C + I - F \equiv Y \equiv C + S$$

Subtract C from each side

$$X + I \equiv F \equiv S$$

Whence $X + I \equiv S + F$

Or realised injections $\equiv$ realised leakages

This can also be demonstrated in Figure 1.3. Suppose the rectangle representing imports is slid to the right under saving. The whole block of savings plus imports clearly equals exports plus investment.

Governmental transactions

To ignore governmental transactions would be as unrealistic as to ignore international trade. However we will initially consider their incorporation in an economy with no international transactions, for the sake of simplicity.

The government (covering both central and local authorities) can be regarded as a 'collective person', one which purchases goods and services from firms to provide services which it normally does not sell—public goods such as education, defence, health. Further, the government also carries out real capital formation such as road and bridge construction, the building of new schools, universities, hospitals, and public buildings. The former services—defence, education, and health—are valued as a contribution to gross national product in terms of what has been spent on their provision. For instance, pay of civil servants or teachers is regarded as a purchase of administrative or educational services from 'firms', who then pay these sums out of factor incomes to the relevant civil servants or teachers. This is stretching the meaning of 'firm' almost to breaking point but

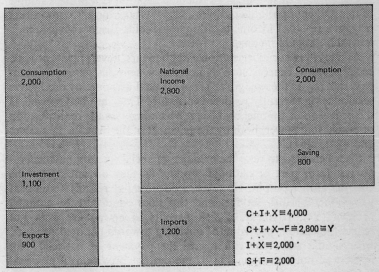

$$C+I+X \equiv 4,000$$
$$C+I+X-F \equiv 2,800 \equiv Y$$
$$I+X \equiv 2,000$$
$$S+F \equiv 2,000$$

Figure 1.3. National income and trade

it does seem the best way to incorporate unsaleable public goods into the flow of output and spending.

To finance these 'purchases' the government may impose taxation on households and firms. In addition, it may acquire financial resources by borrowing from the general public to whom it issues bonds. This would have the effect of increasing its indebtedness, the total of which is known as the national debt.

Taxation can be divided into two kinds.

(*a*) Taxation on expenditure, or 'indirect' taxation, whose receipts accrue to the government only when the product on which taxation has been levied is purchased. Examples are purchase tax on motor cars in Britain, and excise duty on beer, tobacco, wines, and spirits, and this form of taxation causes the market price of the product to exceed the cost of producing and marketing it by the amount of tax levied.

Again, the government may pay subsidies to producers to encourage them to produce output which otherwise would be unprofitable. These have the effect of allowing costs of production and marketing to exceed the market price without bankruptcy for producers. They are best treated as negative indirect taxation.

(b) Direct taxation which is imposed on the household or firm, irrespective of their purchases. Income taxation is a prime example of this. Other important examples are profits taxation and corporation tax. As a result of income taxation households' disposable income is less than national income.

As a result of social legislation over the years, governments provide social security benefits such as retirement pensions, unemployment pay, sick pay to those eligible. These are paid without any productive service being currently rendered in return. These are best viewed as the provision of a monetary benefit which involves the redistribution of purchasing power, both by the payment of the benefits themselves and by taxation.

Such benefits—to take the example of social security payments—do not form part of national product as they do not reflect the creation of new output. However, a doctor's pay reflects his current provision of health services and this does contribute to national product. Yet, payment of sick benefits to his patient does not reflect the current provision of anything towards national product. In a similar way, one can regard the payment of national debt interest as not corresponding to the current provision of any real services to be embodied in gross national output. All such payments are called *transfer payments*: they do not involve the creation of any contribution to national product, only the redistribution of money incomes. In this respect they add to the disposable incomes of households available for spending or saving, and can be regarded as a negative direct (or income) tax.

Lastly, the nationalised industries in this book will be regarded as equivalent to ordinary firms, and all government capital formation will be included as part of the domestic investment expenditure of the economy.

Clearly, governmental spending will constitute an injection into the flow of spending and incomes, while taxation in its various forms will constitute a leakage from this circular flow. It is therefore possible to draw up accounting relations as was done for households and firms.

(It should be noted that we are assuming that taxation on expenditure is paid by firms from their current sales receipts.)

We have, assuming one firm and the government:

Consumption spending at market prices *plus* investment spending at market prices *plus* governmental spending at market prices $\}$ $\equiv$ sales receipts at market prices $\{$ taxes on expenditure *plus* wages and salaries *plus* rent *plus* profits

This yields

Consumption + investment + governmental spending $\equiv$ national income + taxes on expenditure

$$C + I + G \equiv Y + T_e$$

Hence $\qquad C + I + G - T_e \equiv Y$

(This is illustrated in Figure 1.4.)

Note that $C + I + G$ equal the value of national product assessed

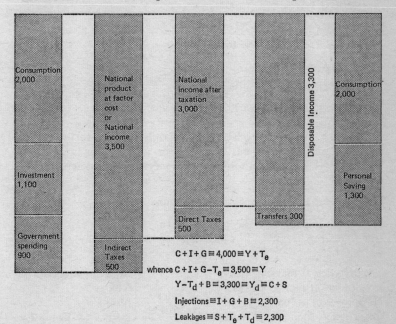

$C + I + G \equiv 4{,}000 \equiv Y + T_e$

whence $C + I + G - T_e \equiv 3{,}500 \equiv Y$

$Y - T_d + B \equiv 3{,}300 \equiv Y_d \equiv C + S$

Injections $\equiv I + G + B \equiv 2{,}300$

Leakages $\equiv S + T_e + T_d \equiv 2{,}300$

Figure 1.4. National income and government

at *market prices*. Because of taxation on expenditure, national product at market prices is not equal to what the same national product has cost to produce in terms of income payments to factors of production, which is national income. To yield national product valued *at factor cost* which is another way of looking at national income, taxation on expenditure (net of any production subsidies) must be subtracted from national product at market price. Alternatively, not all the flow of spending on goods and services at market prices goes on to generate incomes, because taxation on expenditure leaks away from the flow of spending into the governmental accounts. The same results will follow if we have many firms.

On the disposal of income side we have:

National income — direct taxation + transfers
$$\equiv \text{disposable income} \equiv \text{consumption} + \text{saving}$$
$$Y - T_d + B \equiv Y_d \qquad\qquad \equiv C + S$$
Hence $\qquad Y \equiv Y_d + T_d - B \qquad \equiv C + S + T_d - B$

$\therefore$ National income $\equiv$ consumption + savings + direct taxation — transfers

Now: $C + I + G - T_e \equiv Y \equiv C + S + T_d - B$

Subtract C from each side to get

$$I + G + B \equiv S + T_d + T_e$$

Realised injections $\equiv$ realised leakages

(See illustration in Figure 1.4.)

Once again the simple economy identity between realised investment and realised saving has to be modified. We have introduced another source of injections and leakages, and these indicate possibilities for the public authorities to influence economic activity.

International and governmental transactions

By combining together the previous two sections we can arrive at the following framework which can be used for any real-world economy:

Export sales at market prices investment at market prices consumption at market prices government spending at market prices	$\Biggr\} \equiv$ sales receipts $\equiv$	wages and salaries rent profits taxes on expenditure import purchases

$$X + I + C + G \equiv Y + T_e + F$$

whence $X + I + C + G - T_e - F \equiv Y \equiv$ national income at factor cost

and $Y \equiv C + S + T_d - B$

whence $X + I + G + C - T_e - F \quad \equiv C + S + T_d - B$

$$X + I + G + B \quad \equiv S + F + T_d + T_e$$

realised injections $\quad \equiv$ realised leakages

This is illustrated in Figure 1.5.

In Figure 1.5 the various stages are incorporated from spending at market prices to the use of disposable income by households for consumption and personal saving.

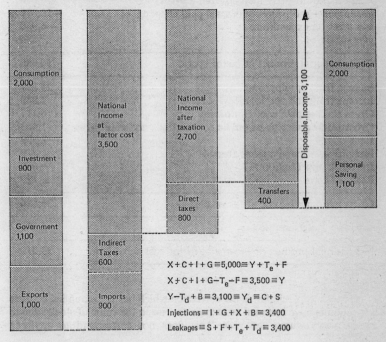

$X + C + I + G \equiv 5{,}000 \equiv Y + T_e + F$

$X + C + I + G - T_e - F \equiv 3{,}500 \equiv Y$

$Y - T_d + B \equiv 3{,}100 \equiv Y_d \equiv C + S$

Injections $\equiv I + G + X + B \equiv 3{,}400$

Leakages $\equiv S + F + T_e + T_d \equiv 3{,}400$

Figure 1.5 National income, trade, and government

U.K. national income

National income statistics provide a picture of the structure of the economy for the year in question, which is very important when considering the behaviour of the economy and policy measures. In Figure 1.6 and Table 1.2 are presented the 1968 figures for U.K. national income and product, together with one or two points not dealt with in the text. Note how gross national product at factor cost of £36,686 million has been made up either from the expenditure side or the income side. Of total gross spending at market prices, exports

Table 1.2   **U.K. gross national product 1968, £ million**

Consumers' expenditure	27,065
Public authorities' current expenditure on goods and services	7,702
Gross domestic fixed capital formation	7,798
Value of physical increase in stocks and work in progress	204
Exports and property income from abroad	10,670
less imports and property income paid abroad	−10,679
less taxes on expenditure	−6,960
plus subsidies	886
Gross national product at factor cost	**36,686**
Income from employment	25,267
Income from self-employment	2,840
Gross trading profits of companies	5,117
Gross trading surplus of public corporations and enterprises	1,463
Rent	2,359
Net property income from abroad	419
less stock appreciation (1)	−650
Residual error (2)	−129
Gross national income at factor cost	**36,686**
less capital consumption (depreciation)	3,375
Net national product or income at factor cost	**33,311**

Notes:

(1) Stock appreciation is the correction which has to be applied because accountants have included as income the rise in the value of stocks due to rising prices within the year. This does not correspond to anything produced.

(2) Logically the two totals should be identical but because of statistical errors they differed by £129 million. They have been calculated from different materials, and it is reassuring to find them so close together. They are still subject to revision.

Source: *C.S.O., National Income and Expenditure 1969*, H.M.S.O., 1969, pp. 2, 3.

of goods and services formed 20 per cent, gross investment 15 per cent, public current spending 14·5 per cent, and consumer spending 50·5 per cent. Imports of goods and services amounted to 20 per cent of total spending at market prices.

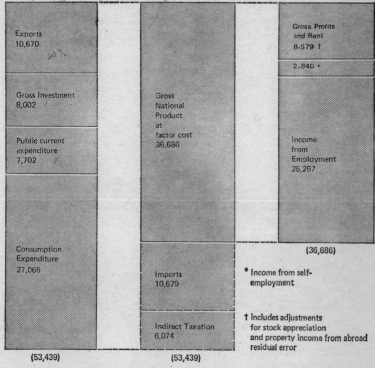

Figure 1.6 United Kingdom gross national product, 1968 (£ million)

Figure 1.7 provides an impression of the growth of U.K. gross national product at factor cost (expressed in current values), and its constituents on the income side. It shows gross national product as rising steadily over the period, but this does not necessarily mean that the *quantity* of output rose in this fashion. Prices could have risen sufficiently to account for it. For example, the money value of gross national product in 1968 was some 80 per cent greater than in 1958, but the price index rose in the same period by 33 per cent. When we compare the values of gross national product at constant (1963) prices for 1958 and 1968, the rise becomes 33 per cent. This gives a measure of the percentage rise in the volume of output, which is all-important for living standards, when adjusted for population growth.

The volume of output is all-important for living standards, for it is the output of finished goods and services distributed among the population which determines whether people are well-fed, clothed, and housed; or whether they are starving, ill-clothed, and living in shanties. Hence it is important to distinguish between money values of national product (evaluated at actual prices) and real values of

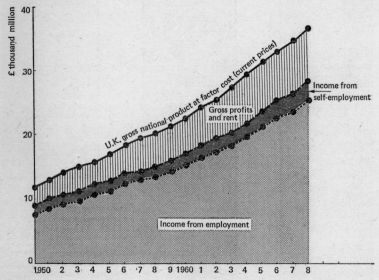

Figure 1.7 United Kingdom gross national income

national product (evaluated at constant prices) when looking at the course of national product over time.

In this chapter the flows of individual goods and services have been evaluated by multiplying volumes produced by prices to yield monetary values, which can be added together to yield gross national product. Within any accounting period the set of prices used over the whole range of output has been assumed to remain constant. While this is a reasonable thing to do within a year, say, it becomes less reasonable over longer time spans, when prices can change more significantly. Gross national product, valued in the prices prevailing in each year, may well rise from one year to another, but this may be because the price-level (or the set of prices used) has risen, rather than the quantity of goods and services produced.

A rise in the latter is what is important in producing an increase in economic activity, living standards, and employment, assuming an unchanged population. Hence economists tend to conduct their introductory macroeconomic analysis in terms of the behaviour of output evaluated at constant prices, consumption at constant prices, investment at constant prices, or as is sometimes said in *real* terms. 'Unchanged prices' is a common, simplifying assumption and it enables us to talk in 'real' terms or in 'volume' terms which can be linked directly with employment. Like all assumptions in economics, it must be relaxed if it outlives its usefulness.

Summary

This chapter has attempted to present a simplified description of the economic system and to develop accounting or realised relationships, showing how the various elements in a macroeconomic system fit together. This provides a framework within which we can go on to consider economic units' plans and intentions to see how and why realised values have adopted certain sizes as compared with others.

One major point in the approach to macroeconomics in this book must be stressed: planned spending and its realisation are vitally important in determining the scale of production and the intensity of economic activity in an economy. This distinction is of crucial importance, and we must constantly watch for it, the distinction between planned, intended, expected (or *ex ante*) investment, consumption, savings, etc., and actual, realised (or *ex post*) investment, consumption, savings. Hence in succeeding chapters we shall try to discover, if we can, what forces influence the spending plans of various economic units.

Money has scarcely been mentioned, except by implication. Money is essentially a stock, comprising the total of coin, notes, bank deposits at any one time. It serves as a unit of account in which receipts, payments, and prices are expressed; as a financial asset to be held; and as a medium of exchange, permitting the easy exchange of productive services for final goods and services, without all the inconvenience of barter. So far, it has been allotted a rather passive role but this will be remedied later.

APPENDIX TO CHAPTER 1

The relaxation of the 'enormous firm' assumption

Let us suppose we have a raw-material sector and a semi-finished good sector which sell their outputs to other firms for further processing and eventual production of finished goods and services. Before gross profits can be arrived at, some portion of sales receipts of the finished goods and services sector must be devoted to paying for raw materials and semi-finished products as well as for wages, salaries, and rent. This leaves the basic relationships unchanged, as will now be demonstrated. The numbers in brackets behind each item relate to its money value.

(a) Sales receipts from finished goods and services (100) ≡
- wages and salaries (60)
- rent (5)
- profits (15)
- raw material purchases (12)
- semi-finished purchases (8)

(b) Sales receipts from semi-finished goods (8) ≡
- wages and salaries (3)
- rent (1)
- profits (1)
- raw material purchases (3)

(c) Sales receipts from raw materials (15) ≡
- wages and salaries (9)
- rent (2)
- profits (4)

Adding (a) + (b) + (c)

Sales receipts from finished goods and services (100) ≡
+ Sales receipts from semi-finished goods (8)
+ Sales receipts from raw materials (15)

- total wages and salaries (72)
- total rent (8)
- total profits (20)
- total raw material purchases (15)
- total semi-finished purchases (8)

Cancelling out raw materials and semi-finished goods from each side

Sales receipts from finished goods   (100) ≡ national income (100)
and services

i.e. National product   ≡ national income

Hence the identity of national product and national income still holds when we have various sectors in the economy and, by implication, when we have many firms. It also enables us to develop a different way of looking at national product—as the sum total of *value added* in the various sectors of the economy.

Value added by a sector is defined as receipts from the sale of its output *minus* payments for inputs of raw materials and semi-finished goods; or, alternatively, as value of output leaving a sector *minus* value of products entering it. We have then:

$$\text{Value added in } (a) \equiv \text{sales receipts of } (a) \text{ (100)}$$
$$- \text{ raw material purchases of } (a) \text{ (12)}$$
$$- \text{ semi-finished purchases of } (a) \text{ (8)}$$
$$\equiv \text{wages} + \text{salaries} + \text{rent} + \text{profits in } (a)$$
$$\equiv 80$$

$$\text{Value added in } (b) \equiv \text{sales receipts of } (b) \text{ (8)}$$
$$- \text{ raw material purchases of } (b) \text{ (3)}$$
$$\equiv \text{wages} + \text{salaries} + \text{rent} + \text{profits in } (b)$$
$$\equiv 5$$

$$\text{Value added in } (c) \equiv \text{sales receipts of } (c) \text{ (15)}$$
$$\equiv \text{wages} + \text{salaries} + \text{profits in } (c) \equiv 15$$

$$\therefore \text{ Total value added} \equiv \text{total wages} + \text{salaries} + \text{rent} + \text{profits}$$
$$\equiv \text{national income} \equiv 100$$

It is thus possible to regard national product at the value of finished goods and services as built up from the individual amounts of 'value added' in the various sectors of firms in the economy. These amounts correspond to the incomes derived in the relevant individual sectors.

Although the terms 'net' and 'gross' have not been employed, the above relationships can be prefixed appropriately.

Chapter 2

Consumption and Saving

Introduction

This chapter marks the start of economic *analysis* in this book and seeks to explain the various forces influencing the decisions of households to spend on consumption and to save. Furthermore, it presents simplified behaviour relationships, in which the prime force determining the value of total consumption expenditure and saving is the level of income. Such simplifications in economics, if they are well based in fact, enable us to concentrate our analysis on essentials and to develop convincing explanations of past economic events as well as making worthwhile future predictions and forming the basis of a coherent and useful economic policy.

Consumption spending

What, then, determines the value of consumer spending in an economy? Let us assume that prices are unchanged. Further, we shall assume that households make certain consumption plans and that they carry out these plans successfully in terms of spending on consumption. Many possible influences on consumption spending come to mind, but one great simplification of Keynesian economics was to place central importance on the level of real income as the key variable determining consumer spending in real terms.[1] This would enable the economist to make such predictions as: 'If the level of income is 600, then consumption spending by households will be 500. If income is 800, then consumption spending will be 650.'

Other forces, which we shall discuss later in this chapter, are thus considered insignificant in their quantitative effect or as slow-moving over time. More recent analysis and factual investigations have shown that this is an oversimplified view, especially over a long time-span.

---

1. Much of modern macroecnomics can be traced back to the path-breaking work of the late Lord Keynes in his *General Theory of Employment, Interest and Money* which was first published in 1936.

However, for our purposes it will provide a sound enough basis that when income is high, so is consumption expenditure ; and when income is low, so is consumer spending.

Evidence of the close linkage between consumption expenditure and income is presented in Figure 2.1a, where consumer spending in the United Kingdom is plotted against gross national product, both measured at constant (1958) prices, for the period 1958–68. Figure 2.1b shows, for the same period, consumption plotted against disposable income (which equals national income *minus* direct taxes plus transfer payments), both measured at 1958 prices. In both figures the plots of consumption and income for each year show a clear pattern of lying very closely along a *rising* straight line.[2] It would seem that we could make not only the *qualitative* statement that when income rises so does consumer spending, but also the quantitative statement that a given rise in gross national product (say £100) will bring a definite rise in consumption spending (£69).

However, some caution is necessary before concluding that these results support the theory that consumption expenditure is determined by income. Consumer spending forms some 70 per cent of gross national product in Britain, and the charts *might* merely reflect the fact that income is high when consumption expenditure is high, because consumption is such a large part of gross national product. Again, both income and consumption might rise together because some third (unmentioned) factor was causing each to rise. For example, population growth would increase incomes as the labour force grew, and would also increase consumption because there were more families to feed, clothe, and educate.[3] Economic statisticians, however, have been able to dispel some of these cautions, and at this stage we accept the evidence of Figures 2.1a and 2.1b and conclude that consumption spending is determined in a definite way by the level of national income.

The propensity to consume schedule

Economists have named this relationship between consumption and income as **the propensity to consume schedule** or **the consumption**

2. By fitting a line to these plots the following equations can be derived:

Consumption = 1,739 + 0·69 gross national product
Consumption = 1,498 + 0·85 disposable income
(Each expressed in £ million at 1958 prices)

3. This point can be dealt with by plotting consumption per head against income per head, and the same close rising relationship is found for Britain.

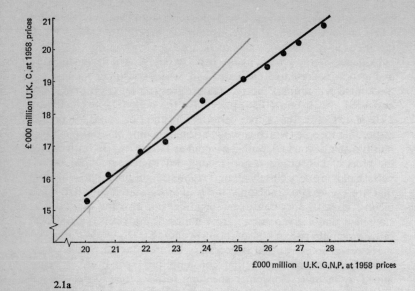

2.1a

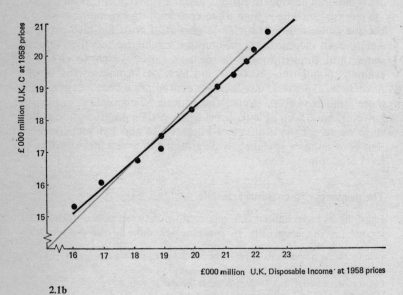

2.1b

Figure 2.1 United Kingdom consumption and income, 1958 to 1969 at 1958 prices

function. It is a behaviour relationship telling us, both at the household and the national level, what will be spent on consumption if income is at a certain value. As income changes so will consumer spending change, in the same direction and to a particular extent. Strictly speaking, we should have said 'disposable income', but in the simple economy with no governmental transactions this is the same as national income. Again, in this version of the propensity to consume schedule (or consumption function) we are relating consumption at constant prices (or in real terms) to income at constant prices (or in real terms). Real consumption depends on real income.

A consumption function of straight-line form is illustrated in Figure 2.2a with the corresponding numerical values listed in columns (1) and (2) of Table 2.1. Economists are interested in what proportion of income (Y) is spent in consumption (C), and have called the ratio

Table 2.1 **The derivation of the propensity to consume and the propensity to save schedules**

(1) If Y	(2) then C	(3) A.P.C. $\dfrac{C}{Y}$	(4) M.P.C. $\dfrac{\triangle C}{\triangle Y}$	(5) hence S	(6) A.P.S. $\dfrac{S}{Y}$	(7) M.P.S. $\dfrac{\triangle S}{\triangle Y}$
300	290	0·967	0·8	10	0·033	0·2
400	370	0·925	0·8	30	0·075	0·2
500	450	0·900	0·8	50	0·100	0·2
600	530	0·883	0·8	70	0·117	0·2

Notes:

(i) $S = Y - C$

(ii) Columns (1) and (2) form the consumption function or the propensity to consume schedule. The values of C have been derived by substituting the values of Y into the equation $C = 50 + 0.8Y$, which is the propensity to consume schedule.

(iii) Columns (1) and (5) form the savings function or the propensity to save schedule. This can be derived from the propensity to consume schedule as follows:

$S = Y - C = Y - 50 - 0.8Y = -50 + 0.2Y$

(iv) Observe that the coefficient of Y in the propensity to consume schedule equation is 0·8, which is the same as the marginal propensity to consume of column (4). Note also that the coefficient of Y in the propensity to save schedule equation is the same as the marginal propensity of column (7) at 0·2.

(v) These schedules are plotted in Figure 2·2.

of consumption to income the *average propensity to consume*. If we let Y stand for the size of income, and C for the size of consumption, then $\frac{C}{Y}$ is the average propensity to consume (A.P.C.). This ratio

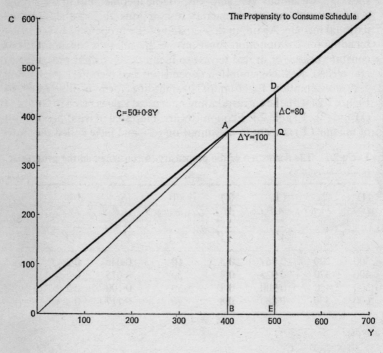

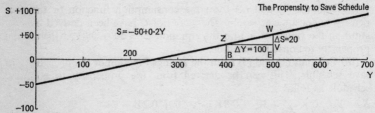

Figure 2.2 Straight-line consumption and savings schedules

is shown in column (3) of Table 2.1, and in Figure 2.2 is represented by the slope of a line drawn from O to the relevant point on the schedule. At point A the size of consumption is AB while income is

OB so that the average propensity to consume is $AB \div OB$ or the slope of AO.

Secondly, economists are particularly interested in the extent to which consumption expenditure changes in response to a given change in income, and for convenient short-hand have adopted the symbol $\triangle$ to mean 'change in', so that $\triangle C$ and $\triangle Y$ represent change in consumption and change in income respectively. The ratio of change in consumption to change in income ($\triangle C \div \triangle Y$) is known as *the marginal propensity to consume*. It is represented by column (4) of Table 2.1. Suppose at an income of 400 the marginal propensity to consume is 0·8. Then a rise in income of 100 will cause consumer spending to rise by 80. This is illustrated graphically in Figure 2.2 by the slope of the segment AD of the propensity to consume schedule, which is DQ divided by AQ, or $\triangle C$ divided by $\triangle Y$.

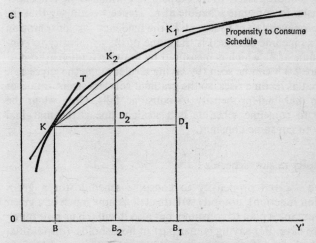

Figure 2.3 A curved propensity to consume schedule

It will be noticed from Table 2.1 that the marginal propensity to consume is constant at 0·8 while the average propensity to consume is falling towards that value. Further, it will be seen from Figure 2.2a that when the values of C from column (2) are plotted against the values of Y from column (1), they lie along a straight-line whose slope is constant at 0·8, and which cuts the C axis at 50. It can be shown that the slope of a line from O to any point on the propensity to consume schedule such as A will fall, the further is A out on the schedule as Y rises. (Try it with a ruler.) Hence Figure 2.2 yields the same results as Table 2.1, and makes it clear that a propensity to consume schedule with a constant marginal propensity to consume can be represented graphically by a straight line. Only if the straight line goes through the origin O, will the average propensity to consume remain constant as income changes and it will be equal to the marginal propensity to consume.

If the propensity to consume schedule has a curved shape as in Figure 2.3, we can proceed as follows to illustrate the marginal propensity to consume. Consider a change in income from OB to OB_1. The change in consumption is K_1D_1 and the slope of KK_1 measures change in consumption divided by change in income. If the change in income is smaller—say BB_2—the ratio of $\triangle C$ to $\triangle Y$ is greater as measured by the slope of KK_2. If we make the change in income yet smaller, K_2 moves towards K and the slope of KK_2 approximates more closely to the slope of KT which is the tangent to the propensity to consume schedule at K. Hence we can say that the marginal propensity to consume at K (the tendency for consumption to change as income changes) is the slope of the propensity to consume schedule at K, which is measured by drawing a tangent to it at K. In Figure 2.3 it can be seen (by laying a ruler along the curve as a tangent) that as income rises, so the gradient gets less steep—in other words, the marginal propensity to consume falls. Only when the propensity to consume schedule is a straight line is the marginal propensity to consume constant.

The propensity to save schedule

If we have a given propensity to consume schedule (or a given consumption function), not only will this tell us how much of a given income households plan to consume, but also it will tell us how much they plan to save. For saving is that part of households' (disposable) income which is not spent on consumption good purchases. If income is 400 and planned consumption is 370, then planned saving will be 30. Column (5) of Table 2.1 provides the various levels of savings corresponding to the levels of income of column (1) and these combined together provide the propensity to save schedule (or the savings function) which is plotted in Figure 2.2. If we know the consumption function, we know the savings function, and *vice versa*.

This is shown diagrammatically in Figure 2.4. In the upper portion (a), a given propensity to consume schedule CF is drawn. A line is drawn from O bisecting the right angle between the axes and this is called the 45° line, which has the property that for any point on it,

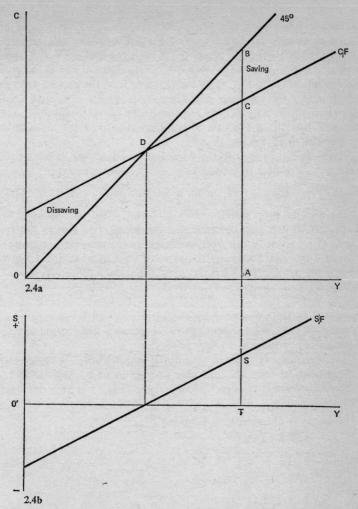

Figure 2.4 Derivation of savings schedule from consumption schedule

such as *B*, *OA* equals *AB*.[4] The 45° line would represent the position of the propensity to consume schedule if households spent all their income on consumption goods and saved nothing.

Consider the gap between the propensity to consume schedule *CF*

4. Triangle *OAB* is isosceles since $\lfloor BOA = 45° = \lfloor OBA.$

and the 45° line, which is BC at income level OA. This gap is the difference between consumption (AC) and income ($AB = OA$) and hence represents saving at income level OA. This can be transferred to part (b) of Figure 2.4 where $O'T$ equals OA and $TS = CB$, and S will be one point on the savings function corresponding to the given consumption function CF. At each income level the gap between the 45° line and CF measures planned saving, which is positive above D (where all income is spent) and negative (= dissaving) below D. These values of saving can be transferred to part (b) to yield the propensity to save schedule SF.

As with the propensity to consume schedule, the behaviour of saving with respect to income can be described in terms of 'propensities'. First, the ratio of saving to income at any income level $\left(\dfrac{S}{Y}\right)$ is the **average propensity to save** and is indicated in column (6) of Table 2.1. It can also be illustrated graphically (see Figure 2.4b) by the slope of a line drawn from the origin to the relevant point on the savings function. Secondly, the ratio of change in saving ($\triangle S$) to change in income ($\triangle Y$) is called the **marginal propensity to save** $\left(= \dfrac{\triangle S}{\triangle Y}\right)$ and is shown in column (7) of Table 2.1. Graphically it is indicated by the slope of the savings function at the relevant point. A constant marginal propensity to save means a straight-line savings function, or propensity to save schedule.

The observant reader will have noted that in Table 2.1 the average propensities to consume and save add up to unity, and so do the marginal propensities at each income level. This is not accidental, but follows logically:

(i) Income = consumption + saving
$$Y = C + S$$

Divide each side by income (Y)
$$1 = \frac{C}{Y} + \frac{S}{Y}$$
$$1 = APC + APS$$

(ii) Change in income = change in consumption + change in saving
$$\triangle Y = \triangle C + \triangle S$$

Divide each side by change in income ($\triangle Y$)
$$1 = \frac{\triangle C}{\triangle Y} + \frac{\triangle S}{\triangle Y}$$
$$1 = MPC + MPS$$

Hence if the marginal propensity to consume is 0·83, the marginal propensity to save is 0·17. If the marginal propensity to consume is constant as income changes, the marginal propensity to save remains constant. However, if the marginal propensity to consume falls as income rises, as in Figure 2.3, the marginal propensity to save will rise.

From empirical evidence it does seem to be the rule that the marginal propensity to consume of an economy is less than one and therefore the marginal propensity to save is greater than zero. Hence as income changes, both consumption expenditure and saving wil change in the same direction in definite proportions of the change in income. Furthermore, the use of straight-line schedules or functions proves justified in fact as well as convenient in analysis.

Individual households and consumption

Thus far our treatment has been in terms of aggregates. What can be said about the behaviour of *individual* households, whose actions underlie the behaviour of aggregate consumption? Empirical evidence indicates that at the individual household level there is the same close relationship between consumer spending and income, and that the marginal propensity to consume falls as income rises. Further, by studying the behaviour of an individual household we shall be able to discover forces other than income that influence consumption spending and the fraction of income consumed.

If we follow the usual practice in microeconomics, we can consider the individual household as seeking to maximise its utility, or to attain its most preferred position, by choosing the most appropriate pattern of consumption and saving with a given income and given prices. Some households will refrain from spending all their income on consumption and thus save, because they value the opportunity to spend *in the future* which savings confer more highly than extra consumption *now*. Others may save because they wish to accumulate financial assets with no thought of future spending, and they derive more utility from an addition to these assets than from the consumption spending which they have foregone. Again, other households may spend more than their income on consumption by running down their financial assets (for example, a household which in the past has saved to accumulate financial assets in order to supplement its pensions in retirement), or even by borrowing. In these cases each household is trying to attain its most satisfactory mix of consumption and saving, and different results occur because of different preferences and situations.

From a given real income an individual household's attitudes towards consumption spending and saving (its saving-consumption preferences) are conditioned by a mass of variables which may be slow-moving over time. Attitudes towards *present* as compared with *future* enjoyment can be crucial in determining the extent to which a household will refrain from spending now in order that it can spend in the future. Its *time preferences* will indicate whether £100 spent on consumption now is worth more or less than £100 available for consumer spending in, say, twenty years' time. Time preference underlies saving to acquire a pension or house property or indeed purely for a rainy day. Willingness to save for such purposes may well be enhanced if the saver has the opportunity to earn interest by lending out his accumulated savings. Indeed, a rise in the rate of interest might tempt him to save more.

Nowadays many households find these decisions to some extent taken out of their hands when contribution to a pension scheme is a condition of a particular job, when purchase of a house is so frequently financed by a mortgage with regular repayments, and when life assurance schemes on a personal basis are so widespread. Contractual savings of these kinds loom large in personal savings and can provide a major element of stability in saving-consumption preferences. Further they may make saving-consumption decisions less sensitive to changes in the rate of interest.

For one individual household as compared with another, social factors such as family size and the ages of family members are important in influencing the fraction of a given income consumed. A household with a large number of young dependants will tend to consume a larger fraction of a given income than one which has none. Another social factor is provided by the degree to which each household feels it necessary to emulate neighbouring households in consumption patterns, so that how much one household spends on consumption from a given income may depend on other households' actions. Advertising and its effects in creating wants may foster the strength of the emulation effect in raising the fraction of income consumed, as well as tending to raise directly this fraction over time.

Again, for one household as compared with another its holdings of financial or real assets (or wealth) may have important effects on the fraction of income consumed, even if savings-consumption preferences of the two households and their real incomes are identical. We can assert—if we dismiss miserly tendencies—that the household whose asset holdings are greater will tend to consume a greater fraction of the same income than the household whose assets are lower, since it will have a less urgent need to add to its assets by saving.

Given the pattern of these preferences among individual households, and the distribution of a given real national income and assets among them, it is possible to add up the individual savings and consumption decisions to derive savings-consumption preferences for the community as a whole. These preferences may be expected to be fairly stable in so far as they are based on reasonably steady behaviour patterns and habits at the household level.

Factors influencing aggregate consumption

Clearly, however, if changes take place in the distribution of income among households with different savings-consumption preferences, changes can be expected in the fractions of a given real national income consumed and saved at the national level. For example, suppose that £10,000 is transferred from the income of one rich household where the marginal propensity to consume is 0·6 and the marginal propensity to save is 0·4, to the incomes of ten poor households where each's marginal propensity to consume is 0·95 and marginal propensity to save is 0·05. The rich household's consumption will fall by £6,000 and the poor household's will rise by £9,500 so that in aggregate there would be a rise in consumption of £3,500 although total income was unchanged.

Likewise, the saving of the rich household would fall by £4,000 and the poor's expand by £500, making a fall in total savings of £3,500. Hence, if income distribution is thought of in terms of people in particular income brackets, an alteration in the distribution of a given income is likely to alter the proportions consumed and saved. A more equal distribution tends to raise the proportion consumed; and a less equal tends to lower the fraction consumed.

Alternatively, it is possible to think of the distribution of income in terms of the shares of profits on the one hand, and the shares of wages and salaries on the other. Provided that profit recipients have a higher marginal propensity to save than wage recipients, and a lower marginal propensity to consume, a redistribution of a given real income away from wages and salaries to profits would cause the fraction of real national income saved to rise, and the fraction consumed to fall. If every household had similar marginal propensities, redistribution would not affect the proportions nationally; but there is strong evidence that the rich consume a lower fraction of extra income than the poor, and that profit recipients save a higher fraction than wage and salary earners.

In each of these examples of redistribution the propensity to consume schedule would shift. In the former, the redistribution from rich to poor would cause the entire schedule to move upwards, while in the latter the fall in the share of wages and the rise in the share of profits would cause the schedule to move downwards.

The availability of finance and loans is an important influence on the purchasing of durable consumer goods such as motor vehicles, refrigerators, and television sets, which typically are bought in many cases by using borrowed funds whether from banks or hire-purchase finance companies. If credit and hire purchase finance are less readily available, this category of consumer spending will fall; but whether total consumption falls or merely alters in character will be dependent on the use which consumers make of that part of their income which they earmark for deposit and repayments. If lack of finance puts a new car out of reach, does the household save more or spend more on beer and cigarettes? Hence governmental measures to affect the availability of finance may bear much more heavily on the modern durable consumer good sector than on the food, drink, and clothing sectors of an economy.

Changes in taxation may also alter the fraction of real national income spent on consumer goods and the fraction saved, both directly and through their influence on income distribution. Expectations of alterations in prices, or in real income receipts, can also have short-period effects. If prices are expected to fall in the near future, many households will postpone consumer spending as much as possible (for example, waiting for the 'January sales'); and if a rise in incomes is confidently expected, households may well anticipate it by increasing consumer spending now, especially if the rise is believed to be permanent. On the other hand, a change in incomes which is believed temporary, may not affect consumer spending at all, and it may take time for some households to become accustomed to higher incomes and the greater consumption possibilities which they bring.

The above forces constitute the main determinants of consumption spending from a given real income. Given that some of the forces affecting saving-consumption preferences of individual households and the distribution of income change slowly over time—and there are good grounds for this—and that, quantitatively, changes in others have only slight influence, all these can be assumed constant in the short run at least. Then we can adopt and justify the simplification of a given propensity to consume schedule (or a given consumption function) by which the level of consumption spending depends on the level of income. We shall rely on this heavily in the following chapters.

Chapter 3

The Determination of Income

Introduction

In Chapter 1 it was shown that, in a simple economy with no governmental or international activities, realised consumption expenditure plus realised investment were equal by definition to realised national income and national product. These were accounting identities, and as such said little about what determined national income and why at some times spending and output were high and at others they were low.

For answers to these problems it is necessary to look especially at spending intentions, rather than production plans. Although one can produce as much or as little as one pleases, there is no guarantee that it will all be sold, and there may be only one output at which all can be sold. Indeed, the economic system can be viewed as one in which production responds and adjusts to spending plans and intentions, and as one in which spending plans are realised (provided that enough productive resources are available). The vital question can then be raised. Are spending plans (and hence production) determined haphazardly, or is there a certain logic to it so that the system has equilibrium possibilities?

In the previous chapter, the forces influencing consumer spending plans have been analysed, where one of the great simplifying assumptions in macroeconomics was made and justified: that planned consumption expenditure depended in a particular and definite way on income: that at least in the short run it was reasonable to say that consumption was determined by income and that the consumption function could be taken as a straight-line schedule on a graph or as an equation of the form of $C = 50 + 0.8Y$, for example. The importance of this simplification will become clear in this chapter, for it is one crucial part of the explanation why and how income is determined at any particular level and how an equilibrium can be reached in which planned expenditure just matches planned output.

Note that certain symbols are prefixed by an asterisk. This is to denote 'planned' or 'intended' magnitudes. E.g. $*C$ means planned consumption spending.

Income determination

The propensity to consume schedule (the consumption function) enables us to say what the level of income will be when there is a given amount of investment spending, or to answer the following questions. *What level of income (or output) will generate sufficient planned consumption expenditure which, when added to the planned investment spending, will produce planned effective demand equal to that income (or output) level? Or, what level of income (or output) will generate sufficient planned savings to equal the planned investment spending, so that such leakages from the flow of this income and expenditure are just matched by injections into it?* The answers to these questions will be presented in tabular form, and in figures or as graphs. Thereafter the interpretation of the determinate income position will be discussed.

Table 3.1

(1)	(2)	(3)	(4)	(5)	(6)
	then	then		Planned effective demand	
If income *Y	planned consumption *C	planned saving *S	Planned investment *I	= (2) + (4) *D = *C + *I	'Gap' (5) − (1)
350	330	20	50	380	+30
400	370	30	50	420	+20
450	410	40	50	460	+10
500	450	50	50	500	0
550	490	60	50	540	−10
600	530	70	50	580	−20
650	570	80	50	620	−30
700	610	90	50	660	−40

Note: Values for *C and *S have been derived from the propensity to consume schedule or consumption function *C = 50 + 0·8*Y and its associated savings function *S = −50 + 0·2*Y. The same functions are used for Figure 3.1.

Let us assume a given amount of planned investment (50) which is set out in column (4) of Table 3.1, and a given consumption function, which is set out arithmetically in columns (1) and (2), while columns (1) and (3) represent the associated savings function. Furthermore, we assume spending plans are successfully realised, and that output reacts immediately to effective demand.

At each income level, planned or intended effective demand is calculated by adding planned investment (of 50) to the appropriate amount of planned consumption spending to yield column (5). At income of 500, planned consumption is 450 and planned effective demand is 500. This is the determinate income level. If output and

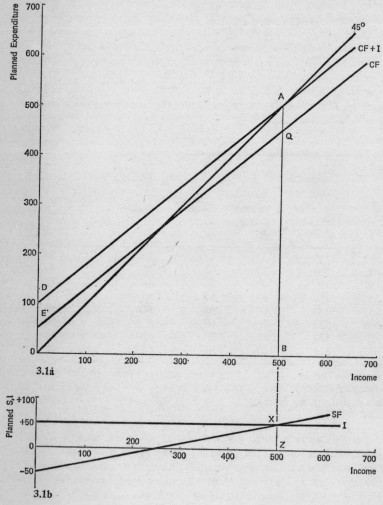

Figure 3.1 The determinate income position

income are 500, then sufficient planned effective demand is generated to purchase this output. If income and output were 450, then planned effective demand at 460 would be greater than this output, so that output would rise until 500 was reached. Likewise if income and output were each 650, planned effective demand would be 620, which would be inadequate to purchase this output so that output would fall. The gap between output and effective demand would be narrowed and finally eliminated at 500 (see column (6) of Table 3.1).

Precisely the same conclusions can be derived by considering saving and investment. At income and output of 500, intended or planned saving just equals planned investment. Below that figure, investment exceeds saving, so that more is being injected into the flow of spending than is leaking from it, and the flow will increase until 500 is reached. Above that figure, more is leaking from the flow than is being injected into it and the flow will slacken until 500 is reached.

These relations are illustrated graphically in Figure 3.1 where the savings and consumption functions are plotted. In Figure 3.1a investment of DE has been added to the propensity to consume schedule or consumption function to produce a graphical representation of column (5) in Table 3.1, and to show planned effective demand at each level of output and income. Then, from the origin, the 45° line is drawn to show all points at which expenditure equals income or at which the horizontal distance from the origin O is equal to the vertical distance from O. (Triangle OAB has $OB = AB$ and angle AOB is 45°.)

Where the planned effective demand line cuts this 45° line we will find the income position which generates enough planned consumption spending which, when added to investment, produces planned effective demand equivalent to that income. This occurs at A, where income and output is OB (= 500) and equal to effective demand of BA which is composed of consumption spending of BQ (= 450) and investment spending of QA (= 50). The excess of planned effective demand over income at income levels below OB is illustrated by the fact that the planned effective demand line lies above the 45° line, and contrarywise lies below it at income levels above OB.

In figure 3.1b planned investment is 50 and I is drawn horizontally at this level. The determinate income is at X, where planned savings (read off the saving function) just matches planned investment with income OZ (= 500 = OB). Below this figure, investment exceeds saving and income flow would rise until OZ was

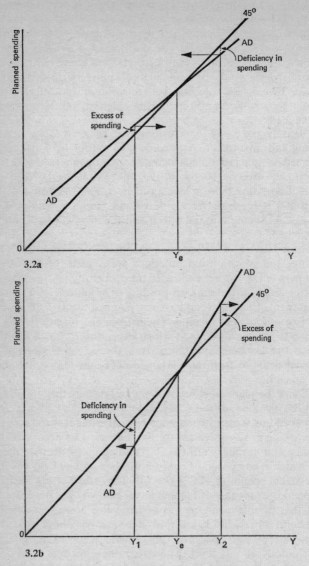

Figure 3.2 Stability of equilibrium

reached. Above OZ, saving exceeds investment and the flow would slacken until OZ was reached.

Equilibrium income

It has been shown in various ways how the assumptions of a given propensity to consume schedule, and a given amount of planned investment, produce a determinate income position at which planned or intended effective demand equals the value of income. Furthermore, it has been indicated from the examples in the text that if the value of Y exceeds or falls short of this determinate value, there are forces at work within the context of the realisation of spending plans to cause it to converge on this value. If in successive years or time periods businessmen keep investment spending constant, and the consumption function is unchanged, a constant income per time period will result. This determinate income position may be thought of as an equilibrium position, because if Y should be given any different value, there are these forces making it move to the determinate value.

Stability

The statement in the previous sentence needs closer attention. In the above examples we saw that the determinate income position was 500. If Y were below this at 450, then planned spending would be 460, so that Y would rise towards 500. Again, if it were above this at 600, then planned spending would be 580 and Y would fall towards 500. This is illustrated in Figure 3.2a, where it should be noted that the slope of $ADAD$ is less than that of the 45° line, whose slope is 1. This is necessary if there is to be an excess of planned spending over Y at income levels below the determinate position, and a deficiency of planned spending with respect to Y at income levels above the determinate position.

Consider now Figure 3.2b. Here $ADAD$ is drawn steeper than the 45° line, so that its slope exceeds unity. At income level Y_1 below the determinate position Y_e, planned spending *falls short* of Y_1 so that output *falls away from* Y_e. Likewise, if income exceeds Y_e as at Y_2, planned spending will exceed Y_2 and output will *rise away from* Y_e. In these circumstances, where the slope of $ADAD$ exceeds one and income is initially not at its determinate level, Y will diverge from Y_e.

Clearly the earlier suggestions of convergence of Y on the determinate position are valid only if the slope of the planned effective demand line $ADAD$ is less than one. What does the slope of $ADAD$ represent? Reference to Figure 3.2 indicates that $ADAD$ is the propensity to consume schedule, to which a fixed amount of planned investment has been added. Hence the slope of $ADAD$ is the same at any income level as the slope of the propensity to consume schedule. It is, thus, the marginal propensity to consume. So long as the marginal propensity to consume is less than one, and investment is unchanged, the slope of $ADAD$ will be less than the slope of the 45° line.

In this case, if Y is not at its determinate position, forces will be at work to cause Y to move towards the determinate position. There will be no explosive divergence, but there will be convergence. Y_e can be considered a stable position in the sense that if Y is temporarily displaced from this value it will return to it. The finding that the marginal propensity to consume is less than 1 is thus of great importance for stability, when investment is unchanged. More generally stability requires that a change in Y should bring a smaller change in planned spending, which could be read off the $ADAD$ line.

Interpretation of Y (This section may be omitted at a first reading. Recommence with *Equilibrium conditions*, p. 58.)

(i) How should we interpret Y, which we have used together with the given propensity to consume schedule to find planned consumption spending? It cannot be *realised* income of the year or time period in question, because that is settled by the end of the year, whereas consumption plans are surely made earlier in the year. Further, we have assumed that spending plans are successfully realised, so that they determine realised income.

What then? Let us recall from the real world that income is usually received at the end of a week or month for work done in that week or month, and is spent, or saved, in the forthcoming week or month. Hence Y can plausibly be interpreted as income actually received in the previous time period, on the basis of which households make their consumption and savings plans for the current time period. Their planned consumption spending of this time period, plus planned investment spending, will determine actual income of the current time period, which households will spend or save in the next time period.

Our determinate income position, where Y equals planned spending, means therefore that actual income of the previous time period just matches planned spending of the current time period. Now this determines actual income of the current time period. Hence at the determinate income position:

Actual income of previous time period = current planned
    spending = actual (realised) income of the current time period

Provided that planned investment and the propensity to consume schedule remain unchanged, a constant income level results over successive time periods if the determinate position has been attained. In this sense it may be thought of as an equilibrium position, but there are other aspects to consider.

(ii) Alternatively, Y may be interpreted as 'expected' income of the current time period. What, then, will govern the income expectations of households? One very plausible view is that households will expect income of the current time period to be the same as actual income of the previous time period. Equilibrium will require that their expectations of income should prove correct, and that they should actually receive the income they expect. This is satisfied by the determinate income position at which (with given planned investment and a given propensity to consume schedule):

Current expected income = current planned spending =
    actual income of current time period

Now, expected income of the next time period equals actual income of the current time period so that equilibrium will also mean that expected income will remain constant over successive time periods. In equilibrium a result similar to (i) above is found. For, since current expected income is equal to actual income of the previous time period, the equilibrium requirement that current planned spending equals current expected income, can be changed into current planned spending equals actual income of the previous period. But this formulation introduces also the part played by expectations of income.

If current expected income (or realised income of the previous period) within the context of Table 3.1 is 450, and thus falls short of equilibrium income of 500, current planned effective demand will be 460, so that actual income of the current period is 460, and exceeds expected income. In the next period, current expected income will be 460 and planned effective demand will rise to 468. This process of raising income will continue until it has reached the equilibrium value of 500.

(iii) Up to now nothing has been said about production plans and changes in stocks of goods. For production has been assumed to react passively, but it is undoubtedly true that firms make production plans. Equally it is true that if sales of goods exceed current output, then stocks of goods must fall, and if sales fall short of goods actually produced, then stocks of goods must rise. Our analysis must incorporate these points.

Let us assume that at the beginning of any time period producers make output or production plans to which they adhere during the period and which they revise, if necessary, at the beginning of the next time period, and that production plans are realised. Further, on the basis of these plans, suppose that producers pay out incomes to households equivalent to planned output in advance of production. Y, which determines planned consumption, is therefore to be interpreted as planned production.

Equilibrium occurs when current planned production is just matched by current planned spending, so that all output is sold with no *unexpected* changes in stocks of goods held by firms. This is a more satisfactory notion of equilibrium, in which spending plans equal production plans. If planned production (Y) is greater than the equilibrium value, then planned spending will be less than production (Y) so that stocks of goods rise *unexpectedly*. If stocks rise unexpectedly, it is reasonable to expect firms to reduce planned production in the next time period, and thus move down towards the equilibrium position. If planned production (Y) is less than its equilibrium value, then planned spending will exceed production, so that stocks fall *unexpectedly* in order that both spending and production plans can be realised. If stocks fall unexpectedly, firms will increase planned production in the next time period and move up towards the equilibrium position.

To what extent will firms alter their production plans in disequilibrium situations when current production and spending plans differ? The simplest approach is to suggest that they will alter production plans in the next period by the extent to which sales have differed from production in the current period, or in other words by the extent to which stocks have changed. For example, if in the current period planned production is 450 and sales are 460 so that stocks fall by 10, they will plan to produce 460 in the next period (see row three in Table 3.1). Likewise, if planned production is 600 and sales 580 so that stocks rise by 20, they will cut production by 20 to 580 in the next time period. This would lead to the equilibrium position.

(This approach implies that firms are neglecting their stock position. In the former case, stocks of goods, far from being replenished, will fall until the equilibrium position is reached. In the latter, stocks will keep rising until equilibrium is reached. Hence they might plausibly be expected to expand production yet faster to replenish stocks as well as to meet increased sales, or in the latter case to cut production yet faster to run down stocks. Such reactions may mean that equilibrium is approached more speedily.)

Table 3.2.

Time period	(1) Planned production *Y	(2) Planned consumption *C	(3) Planned savings *C	(4) Planned investment *I	(5) Planned aggregate spending and sales	(6) Gap (5) − (1)
1	200·0	150·0	50·0	100	250·0	50·0
2	250·0	175·0	75·0	100	275·0	25·0
3	275·0	187·5	87·5	100	287·5	12·5
4	287·5	193·8	93·7	100	293·8	6·2
5	293·8	196·9	96·9	100	296·9	3·1
6	296·9	198·4	98·5	100	298·4	1·5
Equilibrium	300	200	100	100	300	0

The process by which discrepancies between planned production and planned spending are eliminated is illustrated further in Table 3.2. Here planned investment is 100, and the given propensity to consume schedule yields the values of planned consumption of column (2) corresponding to the values of Y in column (1). Its equation is $C = 50 + 0.5Y$.

In time period 1, firms plan to produce 200 and pay out this sum to households as incomes. Hence planned consumption is 150 and planned saving 50, so that planned spending is 250 and exceeds planned production by 50. This gap is indicated by column (6), and represents the fall in stocks. In period 2, planned production is increased to 250 (the value of sales in period 1), and the gap is narrowed to 25. As time elapses the gap narrows between planned production and planned spending as they approach the equilibrium value of 300.

THE SCRIPT SYSTEM IS A LONG RUN PLAN. WE CAN LOCK PRICES AND SUBSIDISE THEM DOWN AND THEN SUBSIDISE FULL EMPLOYMENT. WE CAN THEN INTRODUCE A RIGHTS SYSTEM. IF THE PEOPLE HAVE A ONE CHILD FAMILY FOR 5 GENERATIONS THE POPULATION WILL FALL TO 3½ MILLION AND THIS WILL TAKE 175 YEARS AND WE CAN AFFORD TO BUILD EVERYBODY A HOUSE LIKE BUCKINGHAM PALACE EACH. THE SCRIPT SYSTEM IS A MILITARY SOCIAL CONTROL PLAN WHICH CONTROLS KNOWLEDGE, EDUCATION AND ECONOMICS AND IT IS STRUCTURED.

Equilibrium conditions

The determinate income position was formulated in terms of the Y, which equalled planned spending when planned investment was given and there was a given consumption function or a given propensity to consume schedule. It was the level of Y at which the planned spending line cut the 45° line. By interpreting Y as planned production, it was possible to convert the determinate income position into an equilibrium income position which had the satisfactory requirement of planned spending equal to planned production. At this position firms will find they have made the right production decisions since all output is sold with no *unexpected* stock changes, while purchasers will have been able to satisfy their plans.

The equilibrium condition has been formulated in the following terms:

Current planned spending = current planned production

i.e. Current planned investment
+ consumption = current planned production
$$*I + *C = *Y$$
whence $$*I = *Y - *C = *S$$

Current planned investment = current planned saving
$$*I = *S$$

Hence the equilibrium condition could equally well be phrased in terms of current planned investment being equal to current planned saving. If planned investment exceeds planned saving, more is being injected into the flow of spending than is leaking from it, so that spending and output rise. Planned saving then rises and gradually, as the gap between planned investment and saving narrows, spending. Output and income approach their equilibrium position.

All the above views of equilibrium (and the determinate income position) have had the common property that a dis-equilibrium position (planned spending *not* equal to planned output or planned investment *not* equal to planned saving) tends to correct itself. It provokes forces leading to a narrowing of the dis-equilibrium and a convergence on the equilibrium position. If there were a temporary disturbance in planned investment which disturbed an equilibrium and brought dis-equilibrium, and then investment returned to its former value, the economy would return to its old equilibrium position. The equilibrium position is thus *stable*, and, as we discussed earlier in this chapter, this requires that the planned effective demand line slopes less steeply than the 45° line. Or, if planned investment is unchanged, it requires that the marginal propensity to consume is less than 1. However, if the marginal propensity to consume were greater than 1, or if the planned effective demand line sloped more

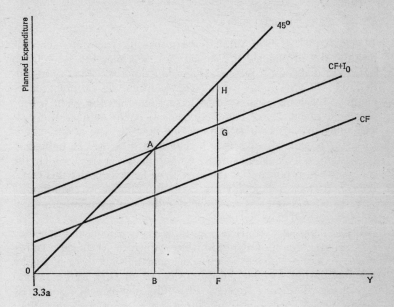

3.3a

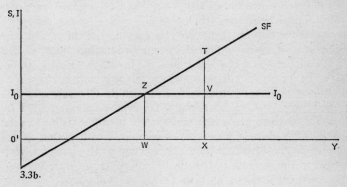

3.3b

Figure 3.3 The deflationary gap

steeply than the 45° line, then a temporary disturbance would touch off a divergent process with spending, income, and output moving away from the equilibrium position. This would be an *unstable* equilibrium, which economists must consider, however unlikely it might be.

Deflation and unemployment

We have seen that the position of the propensity to consume schedule and the size of planned investment will determine the equilibrium position for spending, income, and production. Now the size of production will govern how many people firms will be prepared to employ. The lower is production at any one time the lower will be the employment offered and the larger will be the number of people unemployed. Furthermore, at any one time the size of the labour force or the number of people prepared to work will be limited so that there will be a maximum output in any period which the economy can produce. For the time being let us consider this maximum output as 'full employment' output (although we shall modify this in a later chapter). Can we be sure that our equilibrium output will provide full employment?

Let us suppose we have a given propensity to consume schedule and a given amount of planned investment which are added together to produce the planned effective demand line $CF + I_o$ in Figure 3.3. Equilibrium income and output is OB, or $O'W$ in the saving-investment diagram. However, if 'full employment' output is $OF (= O'X)$, the equilibrium output and income position will be associated with unemployment of labour and undercapacity operation of plant. If businessmen were to produce full employment output OF, planned effective demand at GF would be inadequate to purchase all the output $(OF = HF)$. GH would remain unsold, and profit-seeking firms would speedily cut production back to OB where all output was sold. Only if planned investment rose by GH—assuming the propensity to consume schedule to remain unchanged—could full employment output be sold in entirety. The excess of output (FH) over planned spending (FG), which is represented by $GH (= TV)$ is known as a *deflationary gap*. It can be defined as the deficiency of planned expenditure as compared with output at full employment. Provided that there are no changes in planned investment and in the propensity to consume schedule in future periods, the unemployment associated with OB output will persist.

This analysis has provided the answer to the riddle of mass un-

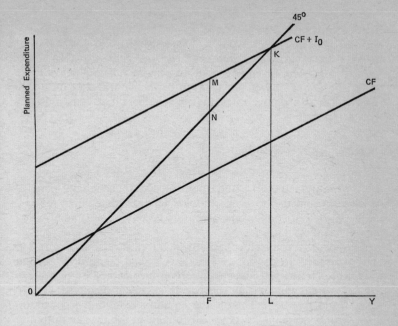

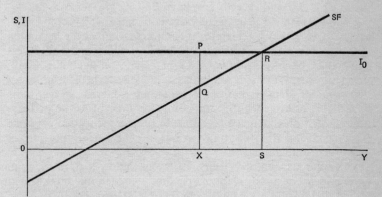

Figure 3.4 The inflationary gap

employment which had been unexplained by orthodox economics before the publication of *The General Theory of Employment, Interest and Money* by Keynes in 1936. *Unemployment occurs because planned spending is inadequate.* We have no guarantee that equilibrium output will be large enough to provide full employment. We must not assume full employment to be the natural state of affairs. Rather it is an objective which may have to be sought consciously by acts of policy.

Inflation and excess demand

In the previous section we discussed what would happen if equilibrium output fell short of full employment output. Equally, planned investment and the propensity to consume schedule could take up such values that equilibrium output exceeded the maximum or full employment output.

Consider this changed situation which is illustrated in Figure 3.4. The propensity to consume schedule (CF) and planned investment (I_o) are such as to produce equilibrium income and output of OL $(= OS)$. Full employment output is assumed again to be OF $(= OX)$ so that in real terms the equilibrium output is unattainable since the economy is physically unable to produce an output of OL in real terms. When full employment output is produced, planned spending is FM and exceeds output $(OF = FN)$ by NM.

Likewise planned investment exceeds planned (full employment) saving by $QP (= NM)$. Planned spending is too great for maximum output in real terms, and excess demand of NM exists. This excess demand of planned spending over maximum output (at constant prices or in real terms) is known as an **inflationary gap**. It indicates that spending plans cannot all be realised in real terms, so that some households or firms will be disappointed as their plans are perforce unfulfilled. Unless planned investment or the propensity to consume schedule change in future time periods, the inflationary pressure of excess demand will persist.

This analysis reinforces our earlier conclusion that there is no automatic necessity for planned spending to match full employment output and to produce equilibrium there.

Price changes

If we have a deflationary situation with a deficiency of planned spending and unemployment, then we might expect to find prices of goods and money wages tending to decline in the face of excess supply. Indeed, deflation is sometimes thought of as falling prices.

On the other hand, if we have an inflationary situation with excess demand for output and labour, then we could well find this excess demand forcing up money wages and prices in the face of shortages. Inflation is frequently thought of as rising prices.

These matters will be discussed more fully in Chapter 7.

Chapter 4

The Multiplier

What will happen to the equilibrium income and output position if planned investment changes?

In Table 4.1 there is set out the same propensity to consume schedule as in Table 3.1 (p. 49), but planned investment is now 70 instead of 50. The new equilibrium income position is 600, as compared with 500, so that a rise in planned investment spending of 20 has brought an increase in income and output of 100 between two equilibrium positions. The change in investment ($\triangle I$) has brought about a five-fold multiplied change in total spending, output, and income ($\triangle Y$).

This relationship is known as the **multiplier** and is defined as:

$$\text{The multiplier} = \frac{\text{change in } {}^*Y}{\text{primary change in spending}}$$

unit change in aggregate demand

$$= \frac{\triangle {}^*Y}{\triangle {}^*A}\left(= \frac{\triangle {}^*Y}{\triangle {}^*I}\text{here}\right)$$

where the change in ${}^*Y$ ($= \triangle {}^*Y$) refers to the difference between two equilibrium positions of income and output, the one corresponding to the old level of planned investment spending and the other to the new level of planned investment. The primary change is represented by $\triangle {}^*A$ as a general concept, the specific example of which is here $\triangle {}^*I$.

The multiplier process

By what process has a rise in investment spending produced a rise in total spending, income, and employment of a considerably greater size? Let us attempt to trace out the effects of a rise in investment spending of 100, when the marginal propensity to consume is 0·6 and the marginal propensity to save is 0·4.

This increase in planned investment spending (it could be the digging of irrigation channels by previously unemployed men who had been existing on charitable hand-outs) will increase output and incomes received by those working in the investment sector by 100.

Table 4.1

(1)	(2) then planned *C	(3) then planned *S	(4) Planned *I	(5) Planned effective demand = *C + *I	(6) 'Gap' (5) − (1)
If *Y					
350	330	20	70	400	+50
400	370	30	70	440	+40
450	410	40	70	480	+30
500	450	50	70	520	+20
550	490	60	70	560	+10
600	530	70	70 - 50	600 - 500	0
650	570	80	70	640 100	−10
700	610	90	70	680	−20

Note: Values for *C and *S have been derived from consumption function
*C = 50 + 0·8*Y and its associated savings function *S = −50 + 0·2*Y
as in Table 3.1.

Table 4.2

	(1) Increase in planned *I	(2) Increase in *Y	(3) Increase in planned *C	(4) Increase in planned *S
Round 1	100 ⟶	100 ⟶	60	40
2		60 ⟶	36	24
3		36 ⟶	22	14
4		22 ⟶	13	9
5		13 ⟶	8	5
6		8 ⟶	5	3
Totals after 6 rounds		239	144	95

Note: The figures have been rounded to nearest whole number.

The recipients will increase their planned consumption spending by 60 and their planned savings by 40. Increased consumption spending of 60 will cause output and incomes generated in the consumption sector to rise by 60, of which the recipients will spend 36 on extra consumption and save 24. This increased consumption will in like

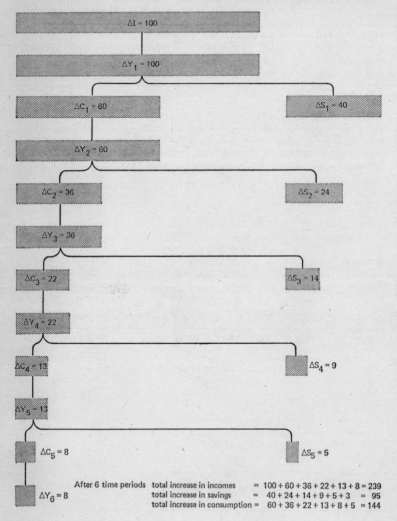

After 6 time periods total increase in incomes = $100 + 60 + 36 + 22 + 13 + 8 = 239$
total increase in savings = $40 + 24 + 14 + 9 + 5 + 3 = 95$
total increase in consumption = $60 + 36 + 22 + 13 + 8 + 5 = 144$

Figure 4.1 The multiplier process

manner increase incomes by 36. . . . After these three 'rounds' of extra spending, the total extra spending and incomes will amount to $100 + 60 + 36 = 196$. This is greater than the initial change in investment spending *because consumption spending has risen as well.*

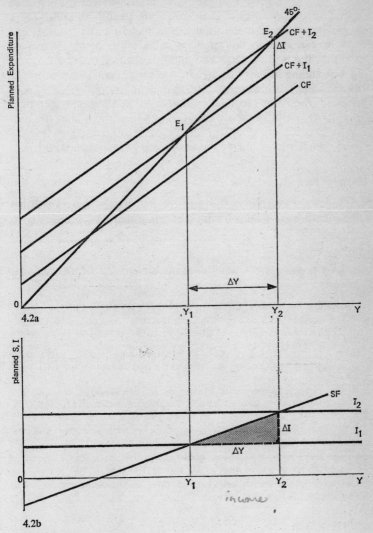

Figure 4.2 The multiplier

Furthermore, we are assuming that businessmen react immediately to these changes in spending by changing production to the same extent.

This process is illustrated in Figure 4.1 and Table 4.2, where it will be noted that after 6 rounds the total increase in spending, incomes, and output has amounted to 239. Note also that the increases in spending and incomes of each round are steadily diminishing as time progresses, so that the total rise in spending and incomes can clearly be expected to converge on some given figure. It can be shown that this will be 250.[1] The multiplier would then be 2·5.

To repeat, the primary change in spending (here a rise in investment spending) brings a greater change in output and incomes because it stimulates secondary changes in consumption spending. Furthermore, we have tacitly assumed in our example that the economy is capable of supplying all the extra output which the increased spending calls forth. We shall stick to this assumption.

Multiplier formula

A straight-line consumption function and hence a straight-line saving function are assumed with a constant marginal propensity to consume $\left(c = \dfrac{\triangle C}{\triangle Y} \right)$ and a constant marginal propensity to save $\left(s = \dfrac{\triangle S}{\triangle Y} \right)$, and a given amount of investment (I_1) which yields an

1. Recall that the marginal propensity to consume is 0·6.
   i. The increase in income in round one is 100.
   ii. The increase in income in round two is the increase in consumption spending in round one which is $60 = 0·6\,(100)$.
   iii. The increase in income in round three is the increase in consumption spending in round two which is $36 = 0·6\,(60) = (0·6)\,(0·6)\,100 = (0·6)^2\,100$.
   iv. The increase in income in round four is the increase in consumption spending in round three which is $21·6 = 0·6\,(36) = (0·6)\,(0·6)\,(0·6)\,100 = (0·6)^3\,100$.

The pattern is clearly emerging that the total rise in spending, incomes and output can be written as:

(a) $100 + 60 + 36 + 21·6 + 12·96 + \ldots$

or (b) $100 + 0·6\,(100) + (0·6)^2\,(100) + (0·6)^3\,100 + (0·6)^4\,100 + \ldots$

(b) is the sum of a geometric series with first term 100 and common ratio of 0·6. The formula for the sum to infinity is

$$\frac{\text{First-term}}{1 - \text{common ratio}}$$ which here yields $\dfrac{100}{1 - 0·6} = \dfrac{100}{0·4} = 250$.

Hence total rise in incomes as the process is continued will amount to 250.

equilibrium income position of Y_1 as shown in Figure 4.2. Investment then rises to I_2, where $\triangle I = I_2 - I_1$, and a fresh equilibrium income position is established at Y_2, with $\triangle Y = {}^*Y_2 - {}^*Y_1$. The multiplier, which is the ratio of the change in income between two equilibrium positions divided by the primary change in spending ($\triangle Y \div \triangle I$ here), is more easily interpreted in Figure 4.2b. For $\dfrac{\triangle I}{\triangle Y}$ = slope of savings function = marginal propensity to save = s, so that $\dfrac{\triangle Y}{\triangle I} = \dfrac{1}{\text{marginal propensity to save}} = \dfrac{1}{s} = \dfrac{1}{1-c}$ since here marginal propensity to save + marginal propensity to consume = 1.

This multiplier formula can be derived more conveniently by some simple algebra. If we recall that between two equilibrium positions the change in planned spending must equal the change in expected income or the change in planned output, hence:

Change in planned spending = change in income (or output)

$$\triangle {}^*C + \triangle {}^*I = \triangle {}^*Y$$

$$But \ \triangle {}^*C = c \triangle Y \ \text{(given m.p.c.)}$$

$$\therefore \ c \triangle {}^*Y + \triangle {}^*I = \triangle {}^*Y$$

$$\triangle {}^*I = \triangle {}^*Y - c \triangle {}^*Y$$

Divide each side by $\triangle {}^*Y$ to get

$$\frac{\triangle {}^*I}{\triangle {}^*Y} = 1 - c$$

$$whence \ \frac{\triangle {}^*Y}{\triangle {}^*I} = \frac{1}{1-c} = \text{multiplier}$$

In various ways we have shown that in the circumstances of a simple economy with no international or governmental transactions, the multiplier is $\dfrac{1}{1-c}$ or $\dfrac{1}{s}$. Hence if the marginal propensity to consume is $0{\cdot}8$ the multiplier is 5, while if it falls to $0{\cdot}6$ the multiplier falls to $2{\cdot}5$. The multiplier has been developed here with respect to changes in investment spending, but the reader must guard against the somewhat prevalent impression among new students of economics that it is only a change in investment spending which has multiplier effects.[2]

2. The reader should demonstrate that a shift in the propensity to consume schedule up or down will have multiplier effects. This is best done on a 45° diagram.

Chapters 9 and 10 should dispel this impression by indicating that changes in exports and changes in public spending, for example, have multiplier effects, and also the other impression that the multiplier is always as in the simple formula above. With import and taxation leakages as well as savings leakages the formula becomes more complicated.

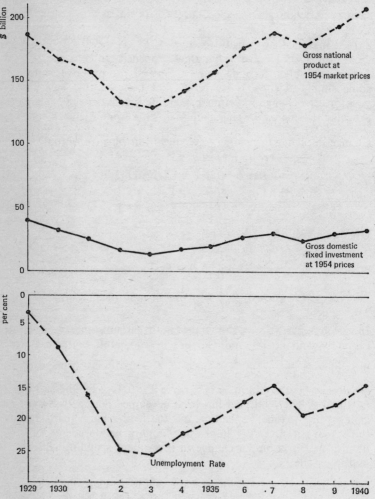

Figure 4.3 United States 1929–40. Slump and recovery

An illustration of the U.S. economy

Between 1929 and 1933 the American economy experienced the largest slump in its history and then partially recovered between 1933 and 1937. The annual unemployment rate rose sharply from

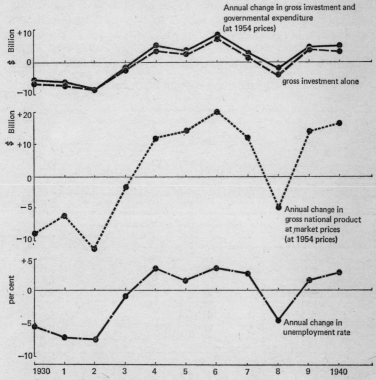

Figure 4.4 The multiplier process: United States, 1930–40

3·2 per cent of the labour force in 1929 to 25·2 per cent in 1933, and recovered to 14·3 per cent in 1937. The course of gross national product in real terms (at 1954 market prices) and unemployment are shown in Figure 4.3 to which is added the behaviour of gross fixed investment. (Governmental spending has been neglected because of its steadiness until 1936, and exports because of their relatively small size.)

This figure strongly suggests the multiplier influence of changes in investment. The fall in investment from 1929 to 1933 helped to bring a multiplied fall in output, while the rise in investment from 1933 to 1937 brought recovery. The influence would seem to have been felt in the same year.

In Figure 4.4, the annual changes in output, investment, investment plus governmental spending (the addition of this makes little difference), and in the unemployment rate, are plotted. A large change in I is accompanied by a large change in Y in the same direction: a small change in I is accompanied by a small change in Y. The similar pattern is striking. The average annual change in I is 4·82 billion dollars while the average annual change in Y is 14·13 billion dollars. This would suggest a crude 'average' multiplier of $\dfrac{14 \cdot 13}{4 \cdot 82} = 2 \cdot 93$ (say 3) for the U.S. economy in this period of time.

Table 4.3

Time period	(1) Change in planned investment $\triangle^* I_t$	(2) Change in planned consumption $\triangle^* C_t$	(3) Change in planned saving $\triangle^* S_t$	(4) Change in planned spending and income $\triangle^* I_t + \triangle^* C_t = \triangle\ Y_t$	(5) Change in realised saving $\triangle S_t$
			(as compared with initial values)		
1	100	0	0	100	100
2	100	60	40	160	100
3	100	96	64	196	100
4	100	118	78	218	100
5	100	131	87	231	100
6	100	139	92	239	100
7	100	143	96	243	100
8	100	146	97	246	100
Final equilibrium position	100	150	100	250	100

Notes: Column (3) is change in planned saving and in any time period is equal to the change in Y of the preceding time period *minus* the change in C of the same period, e.g. $\triangle^* S_5 = \triangle^* Y_4 - \triangle^* C_5$.

Column (5) is change in realised saving and in any time period is equal to the change in Y of that time period *minus* the change in consumption of that period, e.g. $\triangle S_7 = \triangle Y_7 - \triangle C_7$.

Figures are rounded to whole numbers.

The period multiplier (This section may be omitted at a first reading.)

Let us trace out the multiplier path in another way which recognises explicitly that time is necessary for extra incomes to be spent and to emerge as extra incomes elsewhere.

Suppose that spending plans are realised and that extra income generated in one time period is disposed of in the next time period on extra consumption and saving, so that the change in planned consumption in period 4 depends on the change in incomes in period 3. Suppose, further, that the marginal propensity to consume is 0·6, and that investment in time period 1 rises above its previous level by 100 and remains at this new level in succeeding time periods, thus destroying one equilibrium income position and developing a new one.

In time period 1 (see Table 4.3) the increase in investment causes income to exceed its old equilibrium level by 100, while consumer spending is unchanged. However, this increase in income of 100 makes itself felt on consumption spending in time period 2; and the latter rises by 60 above its old equilibrium level, while the change in planned saving in period 2 is 40. Planned spending in period 2, therefore, rises by 160 ($= \triangle * I_2 + \triangle * C_2$) above the old equilibrium level and causes income to rise by 160, so that in period 3 the rise in planned consumption is now 96 above the old equilibrium level, which with the rise in investment of 100 causes the income increase in period 3 to amount to 196. From the figures it is clear that $\triangle * Y$ is ceasing to rise so rapidly and is converging on its equilibrium value of 250, which can be deduced from the multiplier relationship:

$$\frac{\triangle * Y}{\triangle * I} = \frac{1}{1 - c} = \frac{1}{1 - 0·6} = 2·5$$

It will also be seen how the change in planned saving is gradually pulled up to equality with planned investment change by successive increases in incomes, while the change in realised saving (which equals change in realised income minus change in realised consumption for any period) always equals the change in investment.

The same method of analysis can be applied to the case where production plans are realised, and stocks of goods alter unexpectedly when planned spending does not equal planned production. It is assumed that producers increase or decrease planned production in the current period, as compared with the previous period, to the extent that stocks have fallen or risen unexpectedly. For example, if planned spending exceeds planned production by 50 in period 4, so that stocks fall unexpected by 50, then producers will plan to produce 50 more in period 5 than in period 4.

Let us consider an economy in equilibrium with planned spending equalling planned production. Planned investment then rises by 100 in time period 1 over equilibrium values, so that planned spending rises by 100. For planned consumption depends on planned production, which remains at old equilibrium values in period 1, and

Table 4.4

Time period	(1) Change in planned production $\triangle *Y$	(2) Change in planned consumption $\triangle *C$	(3) Change in planned saving $\triangle *S$	(4) Change in planned investment $\triangle *I$	(5) Change in planned spending $\triangle *D$	(6) Unexpected change in stocks $=$ $\triangle *Y - \triangle *D$
1	0	0	0	100	100	−100
2	100	60	40	100	160	−60
3	160	96	64	100	196	−36
4	196	118	78	100	218	−22
5	218	131	87	100	231	−13
6	231	139	92	100	239	−8
Final position	250	150	100	100	250	0

Notes:
(i) Figures are rounded to nearest whole number.
(ii) Production plans are realised, and so are spending plans, but stocks change unexpectedly in disequilibrium.
(iii) Planned production is increased between two periods by the extent to which stocks have fallen in the former period.
(iv) All changes are with respect to the initial equilibrium position.

hence shows no rise. Stocks fall unexpectedly, then, by 100 in time period 1, and planned production rises by 100 above the old equilibrium position in time period 2. Planned consumption then rises in time period 2 by the marginal propensity to consume (assumed 0.6) times the rise in planned production and income (100)—that is, by 60—while planned saving rises by 40.

Hence in time period 2 planned production has risen by 100, while planned spending has risen by 160, so that stocks fall unexpectedly by 60. Planned production in time period 3 will then be 60 greater than in period 2, and 160 greater than in the initial equilibrium position. (Period 2's planned production is 100 greater than

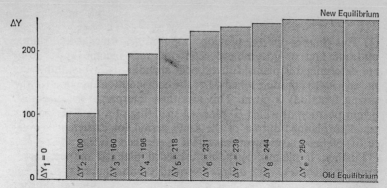

Figure 4.5 The multiplier process and convergence

in the initial equilibrium position.) The process is illustrated in Table 4.4, where it will be noted that the change in current planned production is the same as the change in planned spending of the previous period. (See also Figure 4.5 for a diagrammatic version of this form of multiplier.)

As in the previous case the change in planned production with respect to the old initial equilibrium position shows a slackening rate of increase and gradually converges on 250.[3] Planned saving is gradually brought up to equality with planned investment, while the difference between planned saving and planned investment of any period is easily seen as the same as the unexpected change in stocks.

3. This may be shown as follows:

In time period 1, the rise in planned production with respect to initial position $\triangle^* Y_1 = 0$.

In time period 2, the rise in planned production with respect to initial position $\triangle^* Y_2 = 100$.

In time period 3, $\triangle^* Y_3 = 160 = 100 + 60$.

In time period 4, $\triangle^* Y_4 = 196 = 100 + 60 + 36$.

In time period 5, $\triangle^* Y_5 = 218 = 100 + 60 + 36 + 22$

$$= 100 + 0.6 (100) + (0.6)^2 (100) + (0.6)^3 (100).$$

Hence in time period t $\triangle^* Y_t = 100 + (0.6) (100) + (0.6)^2 (100) + \ldots$
$$+ (0.6)^{t-2} 100$$

or the sum of a geometric series with first term of 100 and common ratio of 0·6.

As we continue the process indefinitely $\triangle^* Y_t$ becomes the sum of a geometric series to infinity. The formula for this sum to infinity is

$$\frac{\text{First-term}}{1 - \text{common-ratio}} = \frac{100}{1 - 0.6} = \frac{100}{0.4} = 250$$

Summary

(1) This chapter and the previous one have shown that in a simple no-trade and no-government economy, real income and output are determined if planned investment spending is given, and if the propensity to consume schedule or the consumption function (or the saving function) is given. This was then interpreted as an equilibrium position at which (i) planned spending of a time period was equal to planned output of the same period (or expected income) or (ii) planned investment was equal to planned saving.

Further, if planned spending exceeded planned output, forces were set to work to raise output to equality with planned spending at the indicated equilibrium level, while if planned spending fell short of planned output, the same forces would depress output to converge on the appropriate equilibrium level. If in an equilibrium situation there was a temporary disturbance in investment, which was then restored to its old level, equilibrium would be speedily restored so that it could be considered a stable equilibrium. (This is assuming the marginal propensity to consume is less than one.)

(2) There is, indeed, no necessity for this equilibrium to occur at a position of maximum or full-employment output. If equilibrium output happened to fall short of full-employment output, unemployment of capacity and unemployed labour result because of a deficiency in planned spending. Again, if equilibrium output exceeds full-employment output, the equilibrium is unattainable and inflation results because of the excess of planned spending over maximum output. This analysis will be of great use in the analysis of deflation and inflation and for the formulation of policy. (See Chapters 7 and 8.)

(3) It was demonstrated that, if investment changed, a new equilibrium income position would result, with the change in income some multiple of the change in investment. The multiplier was defined as the change in income or output between two equilibrium positions divided by the primary change in spending which had occasioned the former change. It was emphasised that in the process of successive rounds of spending changes, time must be allowed for income to converge on its new equilibrium. In this simple economy the multiplier was

$$\frac{1}{1 - \text{marginal propensity to consume}} \text{ or } \frac{1}{\text{marginal propensity to save}}$$

but this formula will perforce become more complex when account is taken of governmental and international transactions.

Chapter 5

Investment

Gross and net investment

This chapter examines the various forces influencing investment plans, or decisions in an economy. It helps us answer the question of how our given amount of investment spending in earlier chapters has been arrived at, and to see the circumstances in which investment plans are likely to change.

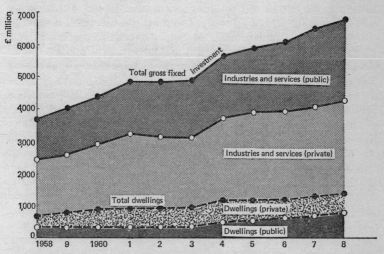

Figure 5.1 United Kingdom gross investment at 1963 prices

By *gross* investment we mean gross additions to real capital stock, or real capital formation, without taking account of subtractions from real capital stock as some equipment which is worn out or has become obsolete through the adoption of new methods is withdrawn from use. In a given year new houses may be constructed, new power stations completed, new factories built, new equipment installed—all gross investment. Figure 5.1 depicts the course of U.K. gross investment (expressed in 1963 prices), and its various subdivisions of (i) 'public' and 'private', and (ii) 'dwellings' and 'industries and services'. The size of public as compared with private investment should be noted.

All this has been in terms of gross investment. It is vital for us to discover how much of this investment is replacement. For, if we want to know by how much real capital stock has grown in the year, and our capacity to produce, assuming ample supplies of labour, we must know such things as how much slum clearance has been permitted by new residential construction, or how many inefficient or worn-out thermal power stations can be closed as nuclear power stations come into being.

Hence, economists are particularly concerned with *net* investment, which is net additions to real capital stock, or net real capital formation, after taking account of replacement or depreciation and obsolescence, and with what induces entrepreneurs and the public sector to undertake net additions to capital stock. Although we shall devote our attention to net investment in the main, it must be emphasised that replacement, or not, of worn-out machinery is a decision which firms must face in the same way as proposals to add to capital stock by net investment, and which they should take using the same principles.

Furthermore, with technical progress and better methods it is becoming less usual for like to be replaced with like. On British Railways, worn-out steam engines have been replaced by more efficient diesel and electric locomotives; on the roads the same can be seen with improved cars, trucks, buses—to say nothing of air transport. Thus some portion of replacement investment may well increase capacity to produce without there being apparently any net addition to capital stock. Again, investment in some projects may enforce obsolescence and retirement of other equipment before it is physically worn-out. For the time being, let us abstract from these important elements and consider replacement as being 'like with like', so that attention can be focused on net additions to capital stock.

Motivation of investment

Why, then, is net investment planned and undertaken in any time period? Presumably it is because the projects in question are *expected* by private firms or public authorities to be a *worthwhile* way of using scarce resources. From the private sector's point of view, 'worthwhile' is to be interpreted as 'profitable', although some projects may be undertaken for prestige purposes or for personal aggrandisement rather than in the expectation of profit.

It is more difficult or even impossible, and perhaps undesirable, some would argue, to interpret and evaluate 'worthwhile' in the same sense for public sector capital formation as for that in the private sector. On the one hand some projects (for example, roads, bridges, defence establishments, schools, and universities) provide services for which no prices are charged and no receipts are actually collected. Other projects which provide services for which prices are charged (for example, in Britain electricity generation, coal-mining, telephones and postal services, and transport) should not be subject, it is argued, to the profit maximisation calculus They should merely 'break even' or be supplied according to 'social need'. Yet it is important to attempt to judge whether resources are being used wisely in various public sector investment projects which are being undertaken in the context of particular political and social policies.

Many projects are socially worthwhile. But which are most worthwhile? Would resources be better employed in private sector investment projects? For prestige and aggrandisement projects are likely to be undertaken in the public sector just as much as in the private sector, and rather more so in the absence of any evaluative process. To this end there have been developed 'cost effectiveness' or 'cost-benefit' techniques which seek to appraise public sector projects and to help us judge whether they are worthwhile by providing what are essentially 'social profitability' estimates. These seek to evaluate in monetary terms the various benefits and costs of public sector projects, such as the time saved road users by a transport improvement which reduced congestion. Such techniques and their employment are still in their infancy in the public sector so that much public sector investment is planned on the basis of what is vaguely thought worthwhile or what is politically inescapable, while private sector investment is planned on the basis of expected private profitability.

Looked at in another way, if firms or the public sector desire to undertake new investment projects, this is the same as saying that at that particular moment in time, desired real capital stock is greater than actual capital stock, so that actual capital stock needs adjusting. In other words, planned investment in the time period $(*I_t)$ equals desired capital stock of that period $(*K_t)$ *minus* actual capital stock at the beginning of that period (K_{at}).

Why, then, should desired capital stock exceed actual capital stock? In the agricultural, commercial, and industrial sectors producers may expect a certain volume of sales and seek to supply planned output accordingly. If they were previously operating profitably at desired full-capacity positions, and if these expected sales are greater than before, then their current actual capacity and capital stock will be inadequate to produce the (higher) planned output without undesired overcapacity operation and strain. They will seek to expand their capacity and capital stock if the rise in sales is expected to be permanent. If they are currently operating profitably, mere duplication of plant with the same methods and the same prices will surely be equally profitable in satisfying the extra demand, and more profitable if economies of scale are realisable.

The expectation of growth in sales under the above circumstances provides the main reason here why desired capital stock exceeds actual capital stock, and why net investment is planned. If, of course, firms were operating at under-full-capacity positions, or believed the rise in sales purely temporary or seasonal, then no additions to capital stock would be needed or undertaken to meet the extra output.

Similar reasoning can be applied to planned investment in stocks of goods in various sectors of the economy. If businessmen desire to keep stocks of goods (whether raw materials, intermediate goods, or final products) as a constant fraction of production or sales, then if they expect a rise in production or sales they will want to hold higher stocks, assuming that previously stocks were correctly in proportion to sales. How much they plan to add to stocks (planned investment in stocks of goods) will depend on the size of the expected growth as well as the coefficient relating desired stocks to sales. As we shall suggest later, planned investment (both fixed and in stocks) will also be influenced by the cost and availability of finance.

Investment in residential construction, in social overhead capital projects such as schools, hospitals, roads, parks, museums, and prisons, will also be somewhat dependent on the growth of the economy, not only in terms of output but also in terms of population. However, it will also be influenced by the government's social policy, which may seek to mirror or lead social attitudes. Again, some categories of this form of investment may be dependent on the *level* of income. If income (and tax revenues) are high, central and provincial governments may feel that these projects can be 'afforded' whereas if they are low, such projects cannot be considered. Nevertheless, growth, whether actual or expected, has a distinct influence here.

Certain types of investment, in contrast, may not need any growth in sales to justify them. They will seem worthwhile whether output grows or not, and may well involve scrapping of existing equipment before it is worn out. Innovations and inventions, leading to new products to supplant old or yielding better methods of producing existing products, form the basis of this investment which is required to get these new products produced or these lower-cost methods into operation. For example, the adoption of containers for ocean freight caused traditional dock methods and equipment to be changed by new investment; again, developments in road transport led to the demise of branch-line trains. Changed methods in agriculture have led to farm investment in agricultural machinery without necessarily requiring any growth in sales to justify it.

If the price of capital services were to fall relative to the cost of labour services, this might lead entrepreneurs to use more capital and less labour in their productive processes provided there was any scope for substituting these inputs. Generally, this is not possible with established equipment which frequently has fixed capital–labour requirements, but with new projects or replacement investment it may well be possible to adopt more capital-intensive ways of producing a particular amount of output, so that a fall in the price of capital services (either through lower interest rates or technical progress cheapening the cost of machines) relative to wages could cause a rise in investment.

Table 5.1   **Project _H_ capital cost £2,600**

Year	Annual expected earnings at end of year
	£
1	1,000
2	2,000
3	500
4	0

Investment appraisal

These, then, are some of the important factors which can cause desired capital stock to exceed actual capital stock and lead to the formulation of investment plans.[1] They will form the background for a firm (or government department) contemplating a particular investment project, which will have (i) _an estimated expected stream of earnings_ (gross sales receipts _minus_ costs of co-operating factors such as fuel, labour, raw materials) or _estimated social benefits_ stretching

1. We are assuming that we can include in desired capital stock innovating and cost-saving projects.

into the future, and (ii) *a supply price* (or construction cost) now. Assuming that firms seek to maximise profits (or the government seeks to choose the most worthwhile project), the question confronting the firm is whether it will be more profitable to devote finance to this new project or to use the finance in another way (e.g. holding interest-earning securities) if its own finance were to be used to effect the project; or not to borrow if someone else's finance were to be used. How then can such a project be appraised?

Project H. Let us consider project *H* set out in Table 5.1, which has a stream of expected earnings in the future as indicated and whose capital cost or supply price is £2,600 payable now. What must NOT be done is to add the yields together to get £3,500 and compare this with £2,600 plus interest charges of £780 (three years at 10 per cent, say) to find that the project yields a surplus of £120. *This is a totally incorrect way of appraisal.* For whereas the cost of the machine is payable *now*, the expected earnings are receivable one, two, and three years in the future. The basic point is that £500 receivable in three years' time is not the same as £500 receivable today; it will be less desirable, for one has to wait for its receipt and waiting has a distinct cost, namely loss of interest.

Present value and discounting

If I had £1,000 now, I could purchase, say, a risk-free 8 per cent government bond for one year with this sum and, during the coming year, earn £80 interest, so that in one year's time my £1,000 has become £1,080. In other words, if the rate of interest is 8 per cent, the present value of £1,080 receivable in one year's time is £1,000, for £1,000 now amounts to £1,080 in one year's time at 8 per cent risk-free. I would be able to sell the guaranteed receipt of £1,080 in one year's time for £1,000 now: ready cash has its price.

What, then, is the present value of £1,000 receivable in one year's time if the rate of interest is 8 per cent; or what sum will amount to £1,000 in one year at 8 per cent? If we let the sum be x, then this will earn interest of $\frac{8x}{100}$ in the year and x must be such that

$$x + \frac{8x}{100} = 1,000$$

whence $x = 1,000 \times \frac{100}{108} = \frac{1,000}{(1 \cdot 08)} = £926$ (approx)

Hence £926 is the present value of £1,000 receivable in one year's time if the rate of interest is 8 per cent. In more general terms, if the rate of interest is R (expressed as a fraction of 100, so that 8 per cent would correspond to $R = 0.08$), £1,000 now would amount to £1,000 + 1,000R = £1,000(1 + R) in one year's time. The present value of £1,000 receivable in one year's time would be £$\frac{1,000}{1 + R}$, for this sum would amount to £1,000 in one year's time at R interest rate. (Interest would be £$\frac{1,000R}{(1 + R)}$ and principal £$\frac{1,000}{1 + R}$, which when added together make £$\frac{1,000 + 1,000R}{(1 + R)}$ = £1,000). Note that the higher is the interest rate R, the smaller will be the present value of the £1,000 receivable in one year's time, for one is dividing the same number (1,000) by a larger number (1 + R).

Again, if I had £1,000 now available for two years, I could purchase a similar 8 per cent bond for one year and receive £1,080 at the end of the year. I could then use this sum to buy another 8 per cent bond and receive back at the end of the second year principal of £1,080 and interest of £86.4, making a total of £1,166.4 as a result of the operation of compound interest. Hence the present value of £1,166.4 receivable in two years' time is £1,000.

In more general terms, if the rate of interest is R:

In the first year £1,000 earns £1,000R interest and amounts to £1,000(1 + R) at the end of the year. In the second year £1,000(1 + R) earns £1,000(1 + R)R interest and amounts to

£1,000(1 + R) + 1,000(1 + R)R
= £1,000 + 1,000R + 1,000R + 1,000R^2
= £1,000 (1 + 2R + R^2)
= £1,000 (1 + R)^2 at the end of the second year

The present value of £1,000 (1 + R)^2 receivable in two years' time is £1,000, and it follows that the present value of £1,000 receivable in two years' time is £$\frac{1,000}{(1 + R)^2}$.

This operation of obtaining the present value of sums receivable in the future is known as *discounting*, and is really compound interest in reverse. The general rule is that if the interest rate is R (the percentage figure is expressed as a fraction of 100 so that 8 per cent corresponds to a value of R of 0.08), the present value of £A

receivable in 'n' years' time is given by present value $= \dfrac{A}{(1 + R)^n}$.
In other words, at 8 per cent, the present value of £1,000 receivable
in five years' time is $£\dfrac{1,000}{(1 + 0.08)^5} = \dfrac{£1,000}{1.469} = £681$. Because the
£1,000 is receivable at the end of five years, the discounting factor of
1·08 has to be applied five times.

Table 5.2   **Project H capital cost £2,600 now**

		(a)	(b)	(c)
Year	Annual earnings at end of year	Present value at 5 per cent	P.v. at 10 per cent	P.v. at 20 per cent
	£	£	£	£
1	1,000	$1,000 \div 1 \cdot 05 \quad = \quad 952 \cdot 4$	909·1	833·3
2	2,000	$2,000 \div (1 \cdot 05)^2 = 1,814 \cdot 1$	1,652·9	1,388·9
3	500	$500 \div (1 \cdot 05)^3 = \quad 431 \cdot 9$	375·7	289·4
4	0		0	0
Total present value of earnings stream		3,198·4	2,937·7	2,511·6

Appraisal of Project H

The future earnings of a project have to be discounted appropriately
at the ruling interest rate to get their individual present values, which
may then be legitimately added together to get the present value of
the total stream of expected earnings stretching into the future. This
can then be compared with the cost of the project in an appraisal
of it. Table 5.2 recalls project H and provides present values of the
expected earnings stream (a) when the rate of interest of 5 per cent
(i.e. $R = 0.05$), and (b) when it is 10 per cent ($R = 0.1$), and (c)
when it is 20 per cent ($R = 0.2$). From this Table it will be seen that,
as the interest rate employed for discounting rises, so the present
value falls. In this method of appraisal, therefore, it is vitally important to choose the interest rate correctly.

The investment appraisal consists of comparing the present value
of the stream of expected earnings with the supply price (or capital
cost) of the project. If at the ruling rate of interest the present value
of this stream of earnings exceeds the cost of the project, the project
is worth undertaking, because this stream of expected earnings can

be purchased for less than its present value by investing in the project. Alternatively, the excess of present value over cost implies that the employment of a sum equivalent to the cost in fixed interest-bearing securities (yielding the same return as the interest rate used in the discounting operations) will be incapable of producing the

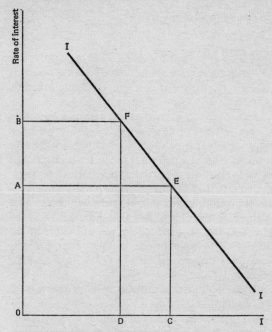

Figure 5.2 The investment schedule

stream of earnings.[2] If, however, the present value of the stream of earnings is less than the supply price or the cost of the project, then it is not worthwhile (that is, not profitable) for the firm to adopt the project. For example, project *H* is worth undertaking at interest rates of 5 per cent and 10 per cent; but at 20 per cent it is clearly not worthwhile, as the present value of the expected earnings is less than £2,600. In this way the firm can judge whether or not the project

2. For example, if project *H* is considered with an interest rate of 10 per cent, £2,600 at 10 per cent in bonds amounts to £2,860 at the end of the first year, from which £1,000 is taken, leaving £1,860 to be re-employed in the second year. This amounts to £2,046 at the end of the year from which £2,000 is taken leaving £46 to be re-employed in the third year. This amounts to £50·6 by the end of the year which is clearly less than the £500 expected earnings of the project in year 3.

looks worthwhile in terms of *expected* values. For it to be worthwhile when completed, the expectations about earnings must be at least fulfilled in realised values. The importance of soundly based expectations and their fulfilment cannot be overemphasised, and the role of uncertainty and miscalculation must not be ignored.

Planned investment in the aggregate

Private

So much for the appraisal of a given project. Let us apply this appraisal approach to an economy as a whole with a wide range of possible investment projects, to see if we can derive a schedule relating planned investment to the rate of interest.

At any particular interest rate (OA), with given earnings estimates of firms and given supply prices of equipment, we can draw up a list of projects whose present value of expected earnings are greater than their cost, and finish with the marginal project whose present value just equals its cost. We can add the supply prices of these various projects together, so that at interest rate (OA) planned investment in aggregate at given prices or in real terms will be OC and E will be a point on the investment schedule (see Figure 5.2). If the rate of interest rises to OB, this will reduce the present value of the projects without altering the supply prices so that fewer projects are worthwhile, and planned investment falls to OD with F another point on the investment schedule.

In this way II (which relates planned investment to the rate of interest) is drawn up under the assumptions of profit-maximising firms, who push planned investment up to the point at which present values of expected earnings of a project just equal its cost. It is clear that as the interest falls so planned investment rises, and *vice versa*.

One problem must be faced when aggregating investment projects. Undertaking one project may enhance or detract from the worthwhileness of another project, depending on their degree of complementarity or competitiveness. It is assumed here for simplicity that we can neglect this problem, or that we can estimate its influence and take care of it when aggregating.

Public

The same kind of analysis can be applied to those public investment projects which it is thought fit to evaluate on a commercial basis —for example, nationalised industry investment—and the results incorporated in the *II* schedule. Other public projects whose feasibility depends on a cost-benefit study can likewise be incorporated, if their estimated net social benefits in the future are discounted at the same interest rate to yield their present value, which can then be compared with their cost or supply price.

Those public projects to which it is not thought fit to apply such analysis, but which are deemed necessary on political or social grounds, will provide a given amount of investment spending in any time period, depending on current social and political policies. Yet even this category might be marginally reduced when interest rates are high, and expanded a little when they fall. Hence the introduction of public sector capital formation does not alter the previous findings applicable to private investment that, with given earnings expectations and supply prices, planned investment spending can be related to the ruling rate of interest in a downward sloping schedule. (It is assumed that all the investment goods required can be supplied as required.)

Table 5.3 **Project *H* cost £2,600**

Year	Expected earning at year end	Present value of earnings at discount rate of 17·6 per cent
	£	£
1	1,000	850
2	2,000	1,444
3	500	306
4	0	0
	Total present value £2,600	

The marginal efficiency of investment approach

An alternative approach to investment appraisal which Keynes employed is to compare the profit rate, or marginal efficiency of investment, or internal rate of return of a project with the ruling interest rate. The marginal efficiency of investment is defined as that rate of discount which makes the present value of a stream of expected earnings from a proposed investment project just equal to its supply price.

For project *H* (see Table 5.1), if we let *d* be the discount rate (the percentage value expressed as a fraction of 100), then *d* can be computed from the equation:

$$\frac{2,600}{\text{(supply price)}} = \frac{1,000}{(1 + d)} + \frac{2,000}{(1 + d)^2} + \frac{500}{(1 + d)^3}$$

present value of stream of expected earnings
discounted at the rate of d

Generally these equations are awkward to solve, which makes this approach less attractive in practice than the earlier approach, which is far simpler to evaluate. For project H the rate of profit or marginal efficiency of investment works out at 17·6 per cent which is applied in Table 5.3 and which makes the present value of the expected earnings just equal to the supply price of £2,600.

For investment appraisal, it is worthwhile to undertake the project, provided that the marginal efficiency of investment (thus defined) is greater than, or just equal to, the ruling rate of interest or cost of borrowing. If we consider a range of projects, an increase in the rate of interest will reduce the number of worthwhile projects and reduce planned investment spending, while a fall in rates will expand investment. Given a range of projects, expected earnings and supply prices of equipment, we can draw up a list of worthwhile projects at each interest rate (whose marginal efficiencies are greater than, or just equal to, that interest rate) and evaluate planned investment spending to derive a similar downward investment schedule to that depicted in Figure 5.2 above.

The influence of the rate of interest

Both approaches have made planned investment in a given economic climate dependent on the rate of interest, so that one could say that if the rate of interest was OA, then investment spending would be OC in aggregate. Care is needed, for this casually assumes that each firm can acquire as much finance or credit as it requires for the project, or that finance is freely available at each interest rate.

This may not be the case in practice, so that lack of availability of finance could reduce planned investment below the level OA, which the ruling interest rate would dictate. This is particularly likely in economies where the rate of interest tends to be set as an administered price by institutional and customary forces, rather than by market forces. In such circumstances an alteration in the stock of money could have a direct impact on planned investment by its effects on the availability of finance. These considerations have distinct relevance for the efficacy of monetary policy, which seeks to regulate the flow of spending by altering the availability and cost of finance, as do the slope or steepness of the investment schedule and its stability.

Various empirical studies have supported the belief that investment (in Britain, at least) is not very sensitive to variations in the rate of interest altering the cost of borrowing, so that the slope of the investment schedule might be expected to be steep. However, it does seem that longer-range investment with more predictable future earnings such as on housing, shops, and office blocks is more keenly affected by the cost effects of interest rate changes than short-period investment.

Frequently, investment decisions in practice are not so precisely balanced that a rise in interest rates from 6 to 9 per cent, a major rise for the financial markets, will affect matters. Interest costs can be set against profits tax payable, thus blunting the effects of the rise in interest rates. Again, a firm may have a range of future earnings estimates of a project stretching from extreme pessimism to extreme optimism within which the change in the rate of interest may be of slight importance, as compared with the firm's final decision about future earnings.

Because of uncertainty and risk, firms may prefer a distinct margin to exist between the present value of expected future earnings and the supply price of the project, or between the marginal efficiency of investment and the rate of interest; and they may well be prepared to absorb a rise in interest costs within this margin. If all other factors were known for sure and constant, the rate of interest would be of extreme importance in investment decisions. However, in practice they are not constant, and this increase in uncertainty detracts from the importance of changes in interest rates in influencing planned investment spending.

Stability of expectations

In Britain there has grown up a certain economic folk-lore that a rise in the Bank Rate of the Bank of England portends bad economic weather ahead, a fall in Bank Rate a better economic climate in the near future, or in traffic-light symbology the former is the red light, and the latter the green light for economic advance. Hence if the Bank Rate is changed and the other interest rates follow suit, these alterations could cause firms to change their earnings estimates, a rise in interest rates causing a downward revision of earnings and *vice versa*, so that the whole position of the investment schedule is altered as the psychological mood of businessmen is varied by Bank

Rate changes. A small change might have no effect, but a large change might have a disproportionate effect as expectations were revised.

This consideration introduces the whole problem of the stability of the investment schedule over the time period. While the supply price of equipment is likely to be predictably steady, the same cannot be said for expectations concerning future earnings of an unconstructed factory or commercial venture. Expected earnings are in any case the difference between expected future receipts and direct

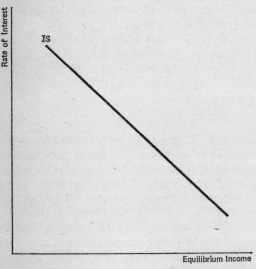

Figure 5.3 The rate of interest and equilibrium income

costs of production (roughly), so that their variability is greater than that of their individual components. Expected earnings estimates may be highly coloured by recent performance and profit records of the firms, by current enthusiasms and fashions; and the present and immediate past may well be poor guides to the future, so that excessive reactions may set in as hopes are dashed or shown to be too modest.

This fickleness of expectations and uncertainty overlays the other important forces, such as beliefs about future growth of the economy (so essential to justify some forms of investment) and future market prospects of new products. Keynes, indeed, suggested that the moods of businessmen and their expectations would shift in a particular pattern from optimism to rashness which would be replaced by excessive pessimism and slowly reviving optimism. These changing moods give rise to shifts in the investment schedule such as could bring about 'trade cycle' fluctuations. If the government can convince firms that it is committed to a high employment policy, it may help to stabilise their expectations and to induce them to take a longer view so that the schedule shifts about much less. Further stability may be added if public investment remains on a steady course.

The *IS* curve

If, at the beginning of a time period, we have a given schedule relating planned investment to the rate of interest and a given consumption function or savings function, we can relate rates of interest to equilibrium income positions. To any given interest rate will correspond a certain value of planned investment spending which with the given consumption or savings functions, will produce a particular determinate equilibrium income level. If the rate of interest rises, investment will be lower. Hence equilibrium income will be lower. If the rate of interest is lower, investment will be higher and equilibrium income will be greater. Hence a downward sloping schedule could be built up relating equilibrium income and output to the rate of interest, working through the income generation process. Such a schedule is known as the *IS* curve and is depicted in Figure 5.3. It will be derived more formally in Chapter 11.

The acceleration principle

Earlier in the chapter the role of economic growth in influencing planned investment in certain sectors of the economy and in stocks, and in the shaping of expected earnings estimates, was mentioned briefly. It can now be presented more formally in terms of a 'capital-stock adjustment' or 'accelerator' approach. This, it will be suggested, can be linked to the marginal efficiency of investment schedule approach which has occupied the main part of this chapter. In addition it will fit in conveniently with Chapter 12 where an economic growth theory is presented.

The viewpoint of a firm

Let us suppose a firm is producing 400,000 articles a year using 200 machines to their (normal) full capacity. Each machine produces

2,000 articles a year as its full capacity output, and lasts 10 years. The stock of machines is so distributed in time that 20 wear out each year. Provided that sales are maintained at 400,000 a year, desired capital stock will be 200 machines, just equal to the actual capital stock of 200. Additions to capital stock (that is, net investment) will be zero, but replacement orders to maintain capital stock at 200 will be 20. Gross investment is 20, depreciation is 20, and net investment is zero. Furthermore, let us assume the firm can obtain as much labour as it requires. Consider the following cases.

Table 5·4

Year	(1) Sales a year	(2) Desired capital stock (machines)	(3) Actual capital stock	(4) Replacement orders (machines)	(5) Net invest- ment (machines)
1	400,000	200	200	20	0
2	400,000	200	200	20	0
3	440,000	220	200	20	20
4	440,000	220	220	20	0
5	420,000	210	220	10	−10
6	420,000	210	210	20	0

Note: Actual capital stock of column (3) is at beginning of year.

(a) If sales rise to 440,000 a year, then existing machines are inadequate to produce this increased output permanently, although by over-running, overtime, and even reprieves of worn-out equipment, it may be possible to produce the extra output at extra cost. If the rise in sales is believed to be permanent, then desired capital stock will rise to 220 machines, which can be attained by net investment of 20 machines. For this will bring actual capital stock of 200 up to desired capital stock of 220. Orders to the investment good industry will rise from 20 for replacement to 40 (20 replacement plus 20 net investment) in this year, and thus constitute a doubling in demand for machines although sales have risen by only 10 per cent. If sales steady themselves at 440,000 a year, then net investment will drop to zero, and replacement demand for machines will persist.

(b) If sales fell from 400,000 a year to 380,000, then the capital stock of 200 machines would be under-utilised. If the fall in sales is believed to be permanent, then desired capital stock will fall to 190 machines. Disinvestment of 10 machines (a negative net investment) is thus required to bring actual capital stock of 200 down to desired capital of 190 machines. This can be achieved by failing to replace 10 of the 20 machines currently wearing out. Only 10 machines instead of 20 will be ordered in this current year from the investment good industry so that gross investment will be 10 machines, depreciation 20 machines, and net investment *minus* 10 machines. Hence capital stock will drop to 190.

From these two cases a basic principle emerges. *A change in sales or output*, which is believed permanent, is required to bring about net investment, either positive or negative. This is illustrated in Table 5.4 with some sales figures and the associated desired capital stock. Note that this relationship has been deduced under very restrictive conditions—full capacity operation already; no scope for working equipment more intensively as a permanent feature; fixed proportions between machines and output with no room for technical progress; extra labour available; no financial problems about paying for the extra machines; no worries about the profit rate as compared with the rate of interest. Nevertheless, there is a basic truth here. Growth in sales is a highly important factor motivating (in a loose way) net investment by making existing capital stock inadequate.

The macroeconomic view (This section may be omitted at a first reading. Recommence with **A joint view**, p. 96.)

Planned investment in any time period ($*I_t$) is equivalent to the excess of desired capital stock ($*K_t$) over actual capital stock at the beginning of the period (K_{at}). One major reason why this has occurred is provided by economic growth (actual or expected) which is making previous capital stock inadequate in businessmen's eyes. For the time being, we shall assume that this is the sole reason for the need to adjust capital stock, but later we shall relax this. The rate of interest is assumed constant with a perfectly elastic supply of finance or, alternatively, investment can be assumed insensitive to the price and availability of finance.

Let us suppose that businessmen desire to keep their capital stock in a fixed ratio to output per period, or that they have a desired ratio of capital stock to output $\left(v = \dfrac{K}{Y} \right)$. At the level of the individual firm, this would correspond to the ratio of capital-stock to output at full capacity operation.

If firms, last period, were operating at this desired ratio, and if sales should rise in this period, over-capacity working results and, if believed permanent, leads to pressure to increase capital stock in a definite ratio to increased output, in order to restore the desired ratio. This is conveniently illustrated arithmetically.

Suppose (i) desired capital stock in $t = 2 \cdot 5 \times$ planned output in t

$$\text{or } {}^*K_t = 2 \cdot 5 \, {}^*Y_t \left(\text{here } v = \frac{{}^*K}{{}^*Y} = 2 \cdot 5 \right)$$

(ii) in time period 1 planned output $({}^*Y_1)$ is 1,000 and desired capital stock of 2,500 $({}^*K_1)$ is achieved by the end of the period, so that the desired capital to output ratio is attained. Furthermore, actual capital stock on the first day of the period 2 (K_{a2} is 2,500), which was actual capital stock at the end of period 1 (K_1)

We have $2,500 = {}^*K_1 = K_1 = K_{a2}$

$\qquad 1,000 = {}^*Y_1 = Y_1$ (production plans realised)

(iii) In time period 2 sales are confidently expected to rise to 1,100 and at least to remain at that level in the future. Firms then plan to produce 1,100 $({}^*Y_2)$ in time period 2. Desired capital stock in period 2 $({}^*K_2)$ will be $2 \cdot 5 \times {}^*Y_2 = 2 \cdot 5 \times 1,100 = 2,750$. As actual capital stock at the beginning of 2 is 2,500, investment $({}^*I_2)$ of 250 will be planned to bring actual capital stock up to desired capital stock.

Table 5.5

	(1)	(2)	(3)	(4)	(5)
Time period	Planned output $^*Y_t$	Desired capital stock $^*K_t$	Actual capital stock at beginning of period K_{at}	Planned investment $^*I_t$	Actual capital stock at end of period K_t
1	1,000	2,500	2,500	0	2,500
2	1,100	2,750	2,500	250	2,750
3	1,100	2,750	2,750	0	2,750
4	1,200	3,000	2,750	250	3,000
5	1,400	3,500	3,000	500	3,500

Note: Desired capital stock $= 2 \cdot 5 \times$ planned output.

We have $*Y_2 = 1,100$

$\therefore *K_2 = 2 \cdot 5 * Y_2 = 2,750$

$*I_2 = *K_2 - K_{a2} = 2,750 - 2,500 = 250$

It will be noted that planned output rose by 100 and that planned investment is $2 \cdot 5 \times$ the planned rise in output ($\triangle Y$).

(iv) If in time period 3, planned output is kept at 1,100, then desired capital stock will remain 2,750, which is the same as actual capital stock at the end of period 2 if planned investment of 250 has been carried out. Desired capital stock equals actual capital stock, so that planned investment is zero. Output has not grown, so no extra capital stock and hence no investment have been needed.

These relationships between Y, K and I are essentially based on the technical requirements of production, and are used purely to illustrate the acceleration principle or the capital stock—adjustment theory of investment decisions. They take no account of the analysis of the previous chapters, in which an equilibrium position between spending and producing was derived. Clearly, then, a change in planned investment from 250 in period 2 to zero in period 3 would have considerable effects on spending with a given propensity to consume schedule. (Later, in Chapter 12, growth in planned output will be blended with growth in planned spending to produce an equilibrium expansion path.)

Table 5.5 illustrates these accelerator relationships with an uneven expansion in planned output. It will be noted how stagnation in output between periods 2 and 3 causes planned investment to fall to zero. Also note how the 16·6 per cent expansion in planned output between periods 4 and 5 would lead to a 100 per cent increase in planned investment. Hence the accelerator.

In more general terms (with production plans realised):

Suppose (i) $*K_t = v*Y_t$ where $v =$ accelerator

(ii) $K_1 = vY_1$

the desired ratio has been achieved by the end of time period 1 and actual capital stock at the beginning of period 2 (K_{a2}) is $K_1 = vY_1$.

(iii) Expected sales, and hence planned production, rise in period 2 to $*Y_2$ so that actual capital stock is inadequate since desired capital stock has risen:

$*K_2 = v*Y_2$

Hence $*I_2 = *K_2 - K_{a2} = *K_2 - K_1 = v*Y_2 - vY_1$

$= v(*Y_2 - Y_1) = v\triangle *Y$

i.e. $*I_t = v(*Y_t - Y_{t-1}) = v\triangle *Y$

Here $\triangle * Y$ refers to the planned increase in output between the two time periods (either between periods 2 and 1, or between t and $t - 1$). The rise in planned output has induced planned net investment, which is determined as follows:

Planned induced investment
$$= \text{accelerator} \times \text{planned change in output}$$
$$*I = v\triangle * Y$$

A joint view

Note that the *level* of net investment is related to the (expected) *change* in sales and output. If output is expected to rise, net investment should take place; if output is expected to remain constant, net investment will be zero but worn-out equipment will be replaced; if output is expected to fall, firms will disinvest by not replacing some or all of their worn-out equipment to reduce their capital stock.

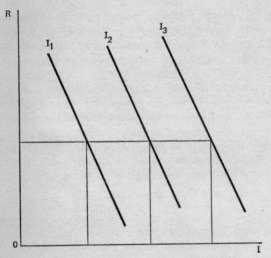

Figure 5.4 Shifts in the investment schedule

In practice firms will not always react to a change in output in exactly this rigid way, since they may have excess capacity from which to meet extra demand, or they may not believe the increase permanent, or new methods may be adopted with different capital–output ratios. Nevertheless, this approach does stress rightly the importance of economic growth as a key factor in bringing about planned net investment. However, attempts to test the accelerator have yielded unsatisfactory results. Reference to the economic history of Britain since 1945 shows that when output growth has slackened, or has been expected to slacken because of restrictive governmental economic policy (the stop phase of stop–go), industrial investment has tended to respond by falling or ceasing to grow.

Not all investment can be explained by this capital–stock adjustment principle; some categories depend on the level of income, while other categories are more autonomous depending on discoveries, inventions, wars, governmental policies, changes in taste. At any one time a compound of these factors will cause desired capital stock to exceed actual capital stock. The expectations regarding economic growth, the enthusiasm with which innovations are taken up, the strength of desire of a government to pursue its social and political policies and their investment requirements will shape the expected earnings estimates on new private or public projects, or the social-benefits estimates on public projects, and hence influence very considerably indeed the *position* of the investment schedule relating planned investment to the rate of interest.

If growth in sales of industrial products is expected to be slight, this would cause induced investment to be low or, in another way of looking at things, it would imply that expected earnings on new industrial projects would tend to be low and the marginal efficiency of investment schedule would occupy such a position as I_1 in Figure 5.4. If more rapid growth was expected, induced investment would be higher, or expected earnings estimates would be higher, so that the schedule would move to I_2 for the time period in question. Furthermore, ready adoption of a new process or innovation, or a massive housing construction policy could yet further shift the schedule out to I_3.

Given the expectation of a particular growth in sales and output, the accelerator would indicate a particular amount of planned investment at some particular interest rate. Higher rates of interest would erode some induced investment plans while lower rates might encourage other plans. In this way the various approaches outlined here reinforce and complement each other, and should not be seen as competitors in explaining planned investment spending in an economy.

Summary

This chapter has argued that planned investment will take place when desired capital stock exceeds actual capital stock. It further presented a method of appraising the worthwhileness of an investment project by comparing the present value of expected earnings (computed by discounting the earnings estimates by an appropriate interest rate) with the cost of the project. If the former exceeded the latter, then the project should be undertaken.

From this approach an investment schedule for the whole economy was derived, in which planned investment was related to the rate of interest, such that a higher interest rate brought a lower amount of investment. It was suggested that planned investment might not be very sensitive to variations in the cost of finance alone.

By using this investment schedule with a given propensity to consume schedule the equilibrium level of Y corresponding to each rate of interest could be derived to yield the IS curve.

Another approach to investment decisions was provided by the acceleration principle, which relates the *level* of planned investment to the (planned) *change* in output under specific circumstances. This approach could then be combined with the earlier approach, for the size of expected growth in sales and output would be one important feature influencing the size of expected earnings and the position of the investment schedule.

Chapter 6

Money and Interest

The stock of money

This chapter seeks to show how the interaction of the demand to hold money and the available stock (or supply) of money determines the rate of interest, and how monetary forces impinge on economic activity. How, then, can we define the supply of money, or the stock of money in existence at a given date? This is a vexed question among economists, who have argued that appropriate definitions of money can vary depending on the context; and it is certainly true that any definition will be arbitrary. One essential characteristic of money, or the money substance, is that it must be *generally acceptable* in exchange for goods or in settlement of debts, and this may help us along in our quest for a reasonable definition.[1]

A modern monetarily developed economy possesses a wide range of financial assets which are claimants to be considered as 'money', or at least 'near-money'. They include coin and bank notes ('legal tender'), bank deposits subject to cheque, post office and trustee savings bank deposits, deposits with discount houses, certificates of deposit, building society deposits, national saving certificates, and cover also treasury bills, commercial bills of exchange, and even short-dated government bonds. Of this wide range of assets some holders will differ from others as to where they draw the line between what they consider 'money' and 'near-money'; some assets will be acceptable to some users or creditors in settlement of debt but not to others, who may insist on payment in 'cash'.

In this sense any definition of the money supply may be felt to be subjective (I may consider a building society deposit as generally acceptable, whereas you may not) and clearly will depend on the attitudes of holders, users, and recipients and their intentions, as well as the degree of their financial sophistication. Wherever the line is drawn between 'money' and 'near-money', 'near-money' is a close substitute for 'money' and is shown to be inferior only when the

1. Monetary affairs are dealt with in more detail in G. H. Peters, *Private and Public Finance*, in this series.

actual time for payment arrives. To compensate for this, 'near-money' may earn a higher rate of interest over and above risk considerations. 'Near-money' has to be turned into 'money' before it can be spent, whereas 'money' can be spent straight away in its existing form.

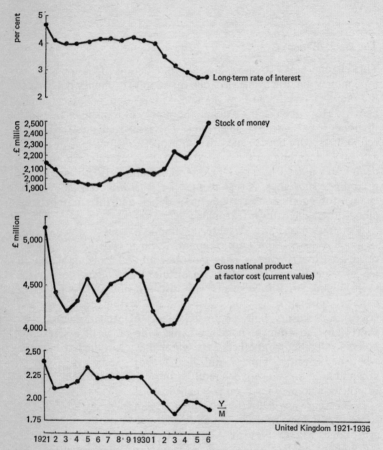

Figure 6.1 United Kingdom 1921–36. Interest rates, money, and incomes

Earlier we have been concerned with expenditure of various kinds, and hence we are now essentially interested in the spending aspects of 'money' in framing any definition. This leads to the proposition that the most acceptable definition of the supply of money would be notes and coin in circulation in the general public's hands, plus bank deposits subject to cheque (including in the British context both current and deposit accounts). For these financial assets can be used immediately for spending purposes since they command in general very wide acceptability. Money, indeed, is what you can spend.

As such, the supply of money will be dependent on both central and commercial banking regulations and policies, as well as the public's preferences for notes rather than bank deposits. Further, it may be influenced by the state of the government's accounts, for, with a budget surplus, balances will be transferred from the private sector to the government, and *vice versa* for a deficit. Again, a balance of payments deficit may mean the transfer of balances to foreign ownership as payments abroad exceed receipts with the result that the money stock falls—whereas a balance of payments surplus could bring an increase in the money stock. At any one time, nevertheless, the supply of money may be taken as given, determined by banking structure and policy, this reflecting indeed governmental policy.

To avoid confusion, it must be emphasised that whenever the terms 'quantity of money', or 'supply of money', are used, we mean the actual quantity of money in existence at a given date (a *stock* concept). By the demand for money we mean the actual quantity of money demanded to hold at a given date (another *stock* concept). Within the context of a developed financial system we are seeking the mechanism which brings into equality the demand to hold money with the available stock of money at a given date.

Some U.K. experience

In Figure 6.1 is shown the behaviour of some of the important monetary magnitudes for the United Kingdom for the period 1921–36. The long-term rate of interest (the actual percentage yield on British government securities) is reasonably steady from 1922 to 1930 at around 4·0 to 4·5 per cent after which it falls sharply to under 3 per cent. The stock of money, defined as notes and coin in circulation, plus deposits of clearing banks, falls to 1926 and grows thereafter. Money value of gross national product fluctuates over the period in accordance with the trade cycle as prices and output moved up in booms and down in slumps.

Last of all is presented the ratio of gross national product divided by the stock of money. This gives an impression of how many times a unit of money was used in financing transactions which were involved in gross national product, and is sometimes known as the *income-velocity of circulation*. After displaying reasonably steady behaviour from 1922 to 1931 it plunges downwards in the early 1930s. The analysis in this chapter will try to explain these behaviour patterns.

The demand for money

Why do individual asset-holders, who can be households or firms, prefer to hold money and forego the yields they could obtain by purchasing assets such as bonds, ordinary shares, property? Why do they demand money? What are their motives for liquidity preference (i.e. their desire to hold money)? Following Keynes, we shall divide these into:

  (i) The transactions demand to hold money
 (ii) The precautionary demand to hold money
(iii) The speculative demand to hold money

The transactions demand

This motive is based essentially on the proposition that the *convenience* of holding money (up to a certain figure) outweighs the monetary yield foregone. Money is required for making day-to-day payments—we all know the inconvenience, embarrassment, and difficulties experienced if we forget our wallet or purse, or have no small change—and thus it is necessary to hold some of our wealth in monetary form. Furthermore, even if (temporarily) we have surplus money holdings before a payment falls due in a week's time, it may very well be that it is not worth the trouble incurred to lend money out for a very short period, since the costs and bother of the loan transaction can easily outweigh the interest yield. (Short-period loans can be worthwhile if the size of the transaction is large enough—for example, money at call and short notice lent by banks to discount houses.) We do not usually bother to lend out half of our monthly salary for the first half of any month.

Both people and companies find that the patterns over time of their receipts of money and their spending of it do not coincide: receipts may be at fixed intervals (weekly or monthly pay-days), or over irregular periods, while expenditures may be more evenly spread out. There is no likelihood at all that one will receive money just at the moment one needs to make an expenditure. People and companies can forecast their expected expenditures in the near future and can regulate their monetary holdings accordingly. In short, it will be necessary to hold certain sums of money to bridge such expected gaps as may occur between receipts and payments.

What factors will determine the demand for money for transaction purposes? First and foremost, the size of money holdings desired for transactions purposes will be related to the size of expenditures to be incurred. In boom periods with rising activity, turnover, receipts, and payments, it will be felt necessary by each economic unit to increase the amount of money held for transactions purposes, while, in slump periods with low activity, the amount held will be reduced. In so far as expenditures are linked directly to money incomes, we can say that this demand for money depends on the level of money incomes.

Secondly, the time interval patterns between receipts and payments will influence the size of these holdings, with less needing to be held if receipts and payments occur regularly at frequent intervals than if they occur irregularly and less frequently. For example, the average money holdings of an income recipient will be lower if he is paid weekly than if he is paid monthly or quarterly. Again, the nature of the monetary system can be important. How readily are cheques accepted, how speedily can they be transmitted and payments cleared? Is there a Giro system in operation?

Furthermore, if interest rates change, the yields foregone (which are weighed against the convenience of money) alter, and this might influence cash holdings for transactions purposes, causing economies to be made in cash holdings as interest yields rise, and *vice versa*. For the time being we shall assume interest costs as unimportant, but will return to this point later in the chapter.

Once again, important simplifying assumptions can be made as some forces seem slow-moving and others unimportant. Monetary habits, the receipt-payments patterns and the nature of the monetary system can be taken as relatively settled in the short run so that we can assert that in an economy with fairly stable monetary habits and environment the transactions demand to hold money depends simply on the level of money national income.

The precautionary demand

We have already discussed how people hold money to meet *expected* transactions involving expenditure, but many would agree in this uncertain world that this holding alone may prove insufficient. When we are planning an expedition or holiday, we may budget carefully for expected expenditure and then add on a further sum to take care of *unexpected* needs for money, a form of contingency allowance or insurance, if we are prudent. It is uncertainty in general and the need to cope with the unexpected which give point to the precautionary demand to hold money. Here, the holding of money is desired in order to provide for contingencies requiring sudden expenditure (for example, illness, accidents, death, loss of employment) and for sudden unforeseen opportunities of advantageous purchases and dealings. Holding cash, besides yielding convenience, also conveys a sense of security in a world in which too often expectations are falsified.

Broadly speaking the precautionary motive for holding money can be lumped together with the transactions motive in a settled environment as dependent on money income levels.[2] If the combined transactions demand for money is denoted by M_1 and money incomes by pY where p is the price level and Y is real income and output, a rise in pY (which could come about either by a rise in Y or a rise in p or both) would cause M_1 to rise, while a fall in pY would cause a fall in M_1. In simplest form we could write the demand schedule as

$$M_1 = kpY$$

where k is a constant. For example, if $M_1 = 0.4\,pY$; then £400 million of money would be demanded for M_1 purposes if money incomes were £1,000 million, and a rise in money incomes of £20 million would increase the demand for money for M_1 purposes by £8 million. If prices remained constant, as we had earlier assumed, then p would remain constant, so that M_1 would be affected only by variations in real output (Y), and we could write $M_1 = l_1 Y$ where $l_1 = kp$. Although we have conducted much analysis in terms of fixed prices, it is important to remember that the transactions and precautionary demand to hold money depends on money incomes which can vary because of price as well as output changes.

If this was the sole demand for money, and if there was a given stock of money, then equilibrium in the money market would require that the demand for money equalled this given supply, so that no one was holding more money than desired, and no one was holding less money than desired. So long as k could be assumed constant,

2. Once again it is assumed that interest rate changes have no influence on this demand for money. This will be relaxed later.

money incomes or the price level and output would have to adjust to the given stock of money to bring equilibrium.

The speculative demand

Economists before Keynes published his *General Theory* would have largely agreed with our formulation of the demand for money for M_1 purposes and they would have considered the equation we derived as one version of the so-called Quantity Theory of Money which held that changes in the stock of money would influence prices and output. However, Keynes introduced a fresh motive for holding money, and one which requires a developed financial or capital market in the economy, with the result that the direct link between money, prices, and output was severed.

As already discussed, the wealth-owner, or asset-owner, has the choice of keeping his assets in liquid form (money) or in the form of earning assets such as bonds, shares, land, property, or in some combination. We have seen some reasons why people and firms prefer to hold money and forego interest yields, and it would seem reasonable to think that once these motives have been satisfied the asset-holder would deploy the rest of his wealth in earning assets to maximise his income from rent, dividends, and interest.

Most small and institutional asset-holders might be expected to behave like this, but some others may be much more interested in the possibilities of making capital gains or of avoiding capital losses by judicious purchases or sales of earning-assets as their prices vary. These possibilities will be all the more attractive if capital gains are less severely taxed than equivalent marginal increases in incomes. In certain circumstances, then, they might be expected to hold additional sums of money, over and above their transactionary and precautionary needs, for speculative purposes.

In order to simplify the exposition it will be assumed that there are only two assets available to the wealth-holder, money (which earns no interest) and fixed-interest-bearing bonds, free from default, which can be bought and sold freely in the capital market and whose prices are free to vary. The wealth-holder can substitute these two assets one for the other in accordance with his preferences. In practice there is in any monetarily developed economy a vast range of alternative earning-assets available, but the essential points can be made in terms of this simple situation, while in an undeveloped economy it could make sense to substitute land for bonds.

If a wealth-holder who is interested in the possibility of making capital gains (known hereafter as a 'speculator') *believes* that the present market price of bonds, determined by market forces, is *unduly low* (i.e. he believes their prices will rise in the future), he will hold bonds instead of money (his demand for money for speculative purposes will be zero) and will be in a position to make a capital gain, *if his belief proves correct*. On the other hand, if he believes that the present price of bonds is unduly high (i.e. he believes their prices will fall in the future) he will hold money rather than bonds (he will demand money for speculative motives) and forego any interest yields, so that he can avoid making any capital loss if his belief proves correct. His demand for money for speculative purposes will thus depend on his expectations as to the future course of bond prices, and it is the uncertainty about the future price of bonds which gives point to this motive.

The present market price of bonds indeed reflects the predominant market opinion as to its likely future course, and it is this opinion which the speculator is trying to beat. This theory pre-supposes divisions of opinion on the future course of bond prices, for such speculative opinions cannot be universal. If everyone in the market thought the price of bonds unduly high, they would all try to sell bonds to hold money, and so precipitate a collapse in bond prices as has happened in various historic stock market panics. The theory, then, requires a split in opinion in the market between those who think prices unduly high and hold money (Bears) and those who think prices unduly low and hold bonds (Bulls). As a result of their activities, the market price is determined. Hence, our speculator will be in a position to profit, if he believes he knows better than the market and if he is proved right. Thus, as Keynes said, under the speculative motive, money is held with 'the object of securing profit from knowing better than the market what the future will bring'.

At this stage the rate of interest can be introduced. Although in practice a whole complex of interest rates exists, corresponding to the range of earning assets, we shall talk of the long-term rate of interest —the *actual* rate of yield earned on our bonds which bear a fixed nominal rate of interest. For example, our bond may have taken a form similar to $2\frac{1}{2}$ per cent Consols, under which the issuer or debtor (the British Government) undertakes to pay £2·50 annually to the holder of £100 nominal unit of this stock, and it is to this yield that the purchaser of such stock or such a bond acquires the right. But the actual market price of such a £100 nominal unit is not necessarily £100—far from it, historically, in the case of $2\frac{1}{2}$ per cent Consols.

Suppose it was £50. The £2·50 annually could be acquired for a purchase of a £100 nominal unit, and this would provide an *actual* yield of 5 per cent. At the time of writing (January 1971) the price of such a unit is £25½, and this provides an actual yield of 9·8 per cent annually. Thus, the lower the price of a fixed-interest-bearing bond, the higher the actual rate of interest or yield. In the case of irredeemable fixed-interest bonds of nominal denomination of £100 units the actual percentage yield or rate of interest can be calculated from the formula

$$\frac{£100}{\text{Price of bond}} \times \text{the fixed percentage interest payment}$$

This is a logical connection, not a casual statement. Hence, if a speculator thinks the price of bonds unduly high, he is likewise

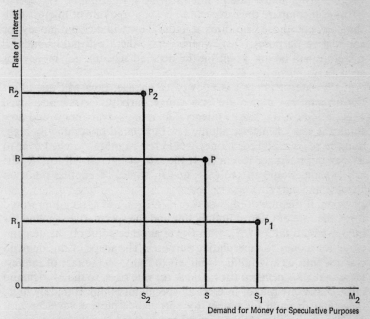

Figure 6.2 Demand for money for speculative purposes

thinking the rate of interest unduly low and is expecting it to rise in the future. He will prefer to hold money for speculative purposes if he thinks the actual current rate of interest is unduly low, and to hold bonds if he thinks the actual current rate is unduly high (he is expecting bond prices to rise).

The speculative demand schedule

How, then, can a demand curve for money to hold for speculative purposes be constructed?

Suppose there is a given stock of bonds and there are in the bond market given expectations on the part of individual speculators, each with given total assets, as to what each thinks is a safe long-term rate of interest, or what each thinks is the likely rate of interest at the end of time period over which each is prepared to carry out speculative activities. These expectations are assumed given, but it must be pointed out that in practice they can be subject to rapid revision as varying economic and political forces alter beliefs and expectations.

Further suppose that there is a given market price of bonds and hence a given actual rate of interest (OR in Figure 6.2). The speculators will compare their expectations about the rate of interest with this rate, and those who think it unduly low will demand money for speculative purposes (OS), whereas the others will hold bonds. P therefore will be one point on the demand schedule for money for speculative purposes (M_2).

If the rate of interest is allowed to change, how will this affect the demand for money for speculative purposes? Assuming given expectations, if the rate of interest fell, more speculators would now think the rate of interest unduly low (and bond prices unduly high) and the M_2 demand for money would rise as more switched over to money in preference to bonds. If the rate of interest fell to OR_1 the M_2 demand would rise to OS_1, and P_1 would be another point on the demand curve.

Again, if the rate of interest rose to OR_2, fewer speculators would think the rate of interest unduly low and the speculative demand for money would fall to OS_2, with P_2 yet another point on the demand curve for money for speculative purposes. The shape of this demand curve is thus clearly falling from left to right; as the rate of interest falls, so the M_2 demand rises; and as the rate rises, so the M_2 demand falls. If at some rate of interest all speculators think it unduly high, then their demand for money for speculative purposes will be zero and the curve will meet the vertical axis at this point. Furthermore, if everyone believes that the current rate of interest is unduly low, and that bond prices will not rise any more, then the curve will stop at this point and level out. Here the interest yield is no longer sufficient to induce anyone to hold bonds and assume the risk that their prices will fall so that it is no sacrifice to hold money in increasing amounts. It must be emphasised that this demand curve for money depends on expectations which can be highly volatile. Consequently this curve is likely to move about in an unstable fashion. The reader should not be misled by the apparent stability of the figures.

Determination of the rate of interest

Let us suppose that the supply of money is given. Then all of it at any one time must be held by people and companies, willingly or unwillingly. It is only when the actual holdings of money by people

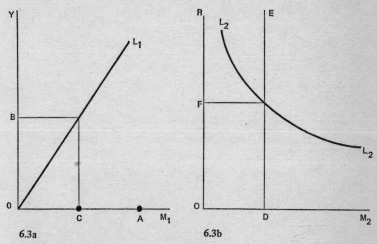

Figure 6.3 The demand and supply of money

and firms equal their desired holdings that equilibrium will exist in the money market, and the factor bringing about the equality between the supply and demand for money will be shown to be the rate of interest.

Now if the demand for money for transaction and precautionary purposes depends on the level of money income, and if income is given, then the M_1 demand for money is determined. The difference between the total stock of money and the M_1 demand is thus available for speculative purposes. If at the current rate of interest the sum demanded for speculative purposes exceeds the supply of money available, disequilibrium exists as the total demands for money exceed the stock. Dissatisfied asset-holders will sell bonds to acquire money and prolonged attempts to do this will bring a fall in bond prices and a rise in the rate of interest. This will tempt some speculators to acquiesce in bond-holding and cut their demand for money. Rising interest rates will cut the excess demand for cash to hold, and the process will continue until equilibrium in the money market is established: i.e. when the interest rate has risen sufficiently to eliminate the excess demand for cash.

Again, if at the current interest rate the M_2 demand for money falls short of the available supply, people will be holding too much money and will seek to move out of money and buy bonds. Persistent

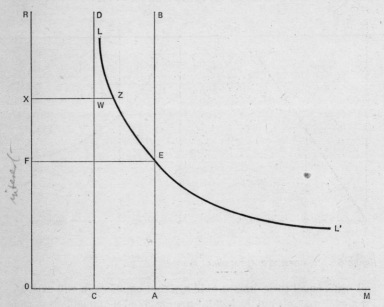

Figure 6.4 Total demand for money with constant money income

pressure to buy bonds will bring rising bond prices and a falling rate of interest, which will cause the M_2 demand to hold money to increase and thereby cut the excess supply of money. The process will continue until the excess supply of money (or the excess demand for bonds) has been eliminated by a sufficient fall in the rate of interest, or a sufficient rise in bond prices.

In this way interaction between the demand and supply of money determines the rate of interest, or alternatively the rate of interest equilibrates the demand to hold money with the available supply. It is very important to note the assumptions made to arrive at this conclusion: that the demand schedules for money remain fixed; that the level of money income is constant; that people with excess money holdings buy bonds rather than currently produced goods with it; and that people with inadequate money holdings seek to replenish these by selling bonds rather than by cutting their expenditure on goods.

The argument may now be illustrated diagrammatically. In Figure 6.3a is depicted the demand curve to hold money for M_1 purposes (L_1) in which M_1 depends on the level of income Y (the price level has been assumed constant) and in part (b) the L_2 schedule relating the M_2 demand to hold money to the rate of interest R. The total stock of money is fixed at OA. Money income is given at OB, thus yielding an M_1 demand of OC and releasing for speculative purposes CA. In Figure 6.3b OD is marked off equal to CA and either of these amounts denotes the available supply of money for speculative purposes, with DE drawn vertically upwards. OF is clearly the equilibrium rate of interest which will match exactly the demands for money with the available supply. If the rate of interest was currently above OF, excess supply of money would exist; while if it lay below OF excess demand for money would exist. Market forces would work to eliminate these positions in the manner described above to reach equilibrium at OF. In this way the rate of interest, or the level of bond prices, finds its equilibrium value.

This argument may be illustrated also in an alternative diagrammatic way. In Figure 6.4 the vertical axis measures the rate of interest and the horizontal the demand for money and the supply of money. The supply of money is given as before at OA, and with a given money income the M_1 demand is read off and marked off at OC. CD is then drawn vertically to indicate the transactions and precautionary demand for money which we have assumed to be unaffected by changes in the interest rate.

The speculative demand is then added by placing O of Figure 6.3b on C and letting the axes fall along CM and CD. The L_2 curve is then rechristened L'. Alternatively, at each interest rate the M_2 demand for money is read off the L_2 schedule, and added horizontally to CD at the appropriate place. For example, at interest rate OX, WZ is demanded for speculative purposes and this is added to $XW (= OC)$ to give XZ as total demand for money at interest rate OX. All points such as Z can then be linked up to give L', which is the total demand curve for money under the assumption of a given money income, and given M_1 and M_2 demand curves for money. Draw AB vertically (the supply of money line) and the equilibrium rate of interest is *OF*, with the demand for money equalling the stock of money.

This diagram is useful in that it depicts the interaction of the demand for money with the available supply on one set of axes, and does not have the split treatment of Figure 6.3, which, however, is useful in its turn because it brings out clearly the importance of the assumption of a given money income. This is apt to be forgotten in the single *L'* curve treatment as *Y* does not appear explicitly.

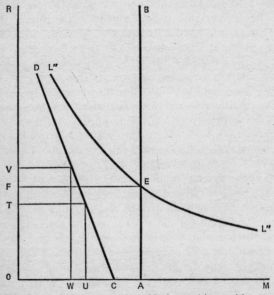

Figure 6.5 The demand for money when M_1 demand is sensitive to the rate of interest

The method of forming the *L'* curve has another advantage, since it could allow us to cope with the situation in which the M_1 demand for money is affected by variations in the rate of interest (something previously assumed away). Let us suppose, again, a given money income and that as the rate of interest rises, holders of money for M_1 purposes reduce their desired cash holdings. If the rate of interest was *OT* in Figure 6.5, then *OU* would be demanded for M_1 purposes; if it rose to *OV*, then *OW* would be demanded for M_1 purposes. In this way a new M_1 demand curve *CD* would be traced out, which showed some sensitivity to the rate of interest.

To this is added the speculative demand curve to form L'', so that the horizontal distance between CD and L'' at any rate of interest corresponds to the M_2 demand for money. This new demand schedule will be more sensitive to changes in the rate of interest than the one of Figure 6.4 for any given speculative demand curve. Once again, adding the supply of money line AB will yield the equilibrium

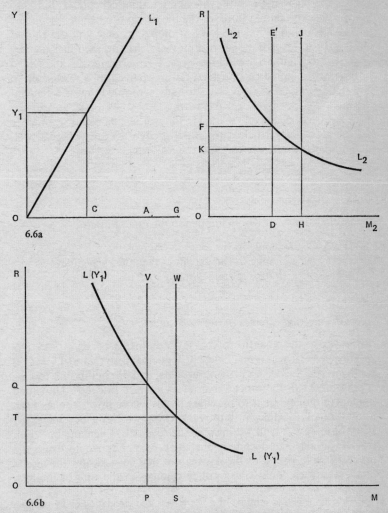

Figure 6.6 The influence of an increase in the stock of money

interest rate of OF. In each case the supply of money and the demand for money (liquidity preference) determine the rate of interest, and the rate of interest is thus very much a monetary affair, it would seem.

This approach suggests that it may be better not to subdivide the demand for money so precisely into parts: M_1 dependent only on money incomes and M_2 dependent only on the rate of interest. For it is reasonable to think of the rate of interest influencing M_1 holdings too. Rather one should think of the the demand schedule for money as dependent jointly on the level of money income and the rate of interest. If the level of money income was constant, then such a curve as shown in Figure 6.5 would emerge. Furthermore, this undivided form is better suited to statistical testing. Indeed, it is reassuring to find that empirical research has strongly confirmed that the demand for money is positively related to the level of incomes and to the price level, and negatively related to the rate of interest as our theory has suggested. Nevertheless, the subdivided forms will be used as well as the joint form in working out the following exercises.

Exercises with this analysis

Let us consider what would happen to the rate of interest if

  (i) there was a change in the stock of money
 (ii) there was a change in the demand for money schedules
(iii) there was a change in money income

Interest rates and changes in the stock of money

(ia) Suppose the quantity of money was increased by AG to OG (Figure 6.6a).[3] There is no change in M_1 demand so that OH ($= CG$) is now available for speculative purposes, and disequilibrium (excess supply) exists in the money market at interest rate OF. Unwilling holders of money use it to purchase bonds whose prices rise, and the interest rate falls sufficiently to reach OK at which the new increased stock of money is held willingly as the speculative demand has risen to OH. Similarly, a decline in the stock of money would cause the interest rate to rise. This theory, then, would suggest how the monetary authorities could cause policy changes in the rate of interest,

3. This could be the printing of notes to put into circulation or by banking operations. See G. H. Peters, *Private and Public Finance* in this series.

always providing that the L_2 schedule was not horizontal at some minimum rate of interest.

(ib) Consider in Figure 6.6b an increase in the stock of money from OP to OS. This causes the rate of interest to fall from OQ to OT to equilibrate the demand to hold money with the available supply. The demand curve for money is unchanged at $L(Y_1)$ on the assumption that money income remains unchanged at Y_1.

Interest rates and changes in schedules

(ii) If, because of a sharp rise in Bank Rate, for example, speculators all revised upwards their views about the long-term rate of interest, this would mean that at any interest rate more of them would think it unduly low, and hence the amount of money demanded for speculative purposes would be greater. In other words, the whole L_2 schedule (and the $L(Y_1)$ schedule in Figure 6.6b) would shift outwards and, with a given money supply, this would cause the rate of interest to rise. Likewise a downward revision of views would bring a fall in interest rates. If people and firms demanding money for transactions purposes found that reorganisation of monetary affairs meant that they could economise in money holdings, this would cause an upward (anti-clockwise) twist to the L_1 schedule. Hence at a given income level, the M_1 demand would be lower, so that more money would be available from a given stock for speculative purposes, and the rate of interest would fall. Such shifts in schedule can be shown very clearly on the 'split' diagram and the reader is recommended as an exercise to represent the above analysis in diagram form.

Interest rates and incomes: the LM curve

(iii) Suppose that the quantity of money remains fixed and the demand schedules for money are unchanged, but that money income changes. A rise in money income increases the M_1 demand, reduces the available supply for speculative purposes, and forces the rate of interest up. Some wealth-holders sell bonds in order to acquire increased money holdings for M_1 purposes, but speculative holders are unwilling to relinquish any of their money holdings until the rate of interest rises sufficiently to tempt them to part with liquidity and acquire bonds at lower prices. A fall in money income would reduce M_1 demands and increase the supply available for speculative holdings, thus causing the rate of interest to fall. Under the above assumptions and that of equilibrium between the demand and supply of money, a direct relationship can be traced between income and the rate of interest—as income rises so does the equilibrium rate of interest, and *vice versa*. This relationship will be discussed fully in Chapter 11 and is known as the *LM* curve.

Real and money income

In the analysis in this chapter we have made the demand for money (or liquidity preference) dependent on the rate of interest and money incomes. If we continue our earlier assumption of fixed prices, then

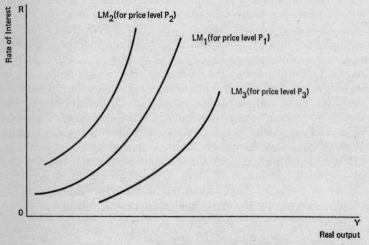

Figure 6.7 The price level and *LM* curves

for money incomes we could substitute incomes and output at constant prices or real income and output—the *Y* of Chapters 2 and 3. The *LM* curve would then relate rates of interest to real output or output at constant prices, so that a rise in real output would cause the rate of interest to rise. It would then provide another relationship between real output and rates of interest to link with the *IS* schedule. (This was discussed in Chapter 5 where the equilibrium income level was related to each interest rate when the investment schedule and the propensity to consume schedule were given. See pp. 90–1.) The *LM* curve is shown in Figure 6.7 as LM_1 for price level P_1.

However, we must remember that with output unchanged in

volume, a rise in the price level, to P_2 say, would increase the money value of incomes and outputs. If the stock of money was given, and the liquidity preference schedules were unchanged, this would bring an increase in the demand for money for transactions purposes, and a fall in the available supply for speculative purposes, so that the rate of interest would rise. This rise would be true for every level of real output along LM_1. Hence the new LM curve for the rise in the price level to P_2 would lie above LM_1 and is shown as LM_2 (for price level P_2). Similarly if the price level fell to P_3, LM_3 (for price level P_3) would lie below LM_1. These are also shown in Figure 6.7.

To repeat, in a price flexible economy the demand for money will depend on the rate of interest, the price level, and real output. If we plot LM curves relating the rate of interest and real output, there will be a separate LM curve for each price level.

Implications of this analysis

Clearly, then, the rate of interest is more than a monetary phenomenon, for its level depends on the behaviour of output (and prices, when the fixed-price assumption is dropped). Furthermore, qualifications have to be added to our earlier analysis. Suppose businessmen become more optimistic about the future and at the ruling interest rate increase investment spending. This causes output and income to rise through the multiplier process, but the rising incomes will cause the interest rate to rise—unless the quantity of money is increased—and this increase in the cost of finance may well choke off some of the increased investment spending so that the multiplier process is checked. This feed-back effect should make us wary of concentrating on 'real' aspects and production, and of forgetting the money market mechanism.

Likewise, having concentrated on monetary processes here, the mention of spending should make us reflect on one vitally important point. We have argued that if a wealth-holder has excess money holdings, he will use them to purchase bonds; if he has inadequate money holdings, he would augment them by selling bonds. It is quite possible that some wealth-holders might use excess money holdings to buy goods, and that others might seek to replenish money holdings by cutting spending from a given income, so that more direct influences on incomes might be discerned than our theory would suggest in its strict form. Such behaviour reactions may be very important when economic policy is formulated.

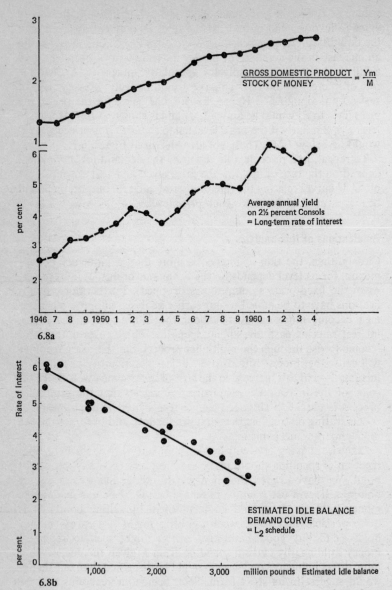

3

2

1
6

per cent

GROSS DOMESTIC PRODUCT / STOCK OF MONEY = $\frac{Y_m}{M}$

Average annual yield
on 2½ percent Consols
= Long-term rate of interest

1946 7 8 9 1950 1 2 3 4 5 6 7 8 9 1960 1 2 3 4

6.8a

Rate of Interest

per cent

ESTIMATED IDLE BALANCE
DEMAND CURVE
= L₂ schedule

1,000   2,000   3,000   million pounds   Estimated idle balance

6.8b

Figure 6.8 United Kingdom 1946–64. Money, interest rates, and incomes

Some empirical findings

This theory of interest-rate determination would suggest that, if M_1 was related to money income in the manner shown, and M_2 to the rate of interest, then if money income (Y_m) rose more quickly than the supply of money, the rate of interest would rise.[4] Hence we could compare the actual behaviour of $\frac{Y_m}{M}$ with the interest rate over time. If they both moved together in the same direction, this would provide some support for the theory. In Figure 6.8a they are plotted for Britain for the years 1946 to 1964 and both exhibit similar broad movements.

Further it is possible to make some *crude* estimates of idle or speculative balances by assuming that at the highest value found of $\frac{Y_m}{M}$ the size of speculative balances is zero. All the stock of money is then held for transactions purposes and k in $M_1 = k Y_m$ can then be found. It will be the reciprocal of this highest value, or $\frac{M}{Y_m}$. This can be applied to values of Y_m for other years to find M_1, which can be subtracted from the supply of money to yield estimates of speculative or idle money holdings. These are then plotted against the average long-term rate of interest for the relevant years in Figure 6.8b. It is reassuring to find that they fall closely about a downward sloping line, as we suggested earlier in this chapter.

Summary

In this chapter definitional problems regarding the supply of money were encountered, which we settled in an arbitrary fashion by defining money as notes and coin in circulation, plus bank deposits subject to cheque. The motives of people and firms for demanding money to hold (for future use) were analysed into (i) transactionary, (ii) precautionary, and (iii) speculative purposes, the latter being the crucial element for introducing the rate of interest. The first two were held to be dependent on money income in a settled monetary environment, while the speculative demand was dependent on the rate of interest and was to be regarded as essentially unstable because

4. If the supply of money rose more quickly than money income, we would expect the rate of interest to fall. Look back at Figure 6.1 to see this expectation confirmed as $\frac{Y_m}{M}$ falls after 1930.

of volatile expectations. More generally the demand for money was taken to be jointly dependent on money incomes and the rate of interest without separation, or as dependent on real incomes, the price level, and the rate of interest.

Given the level of money income, the stability of the demand-for-money-to-hold schedules and the stock of money, the rate of interest was determined at that level which equated the demand for money with the available supply. The rate of interest in this analysis is seen as the price of money (the price paid to tempt money-holders to part with liquid control over money) with much emphasis on holding money, albeit for future *use*. It would seem at first sight to be a monetary phenomenon balancing the supply of money with liquidity preference. Yet, if the assumption of a given money income is removed, the rate of interest is no longer determined, although it is related in a definite way to money incomes (the *LM* curve).

It must be remembered always that what goes on in the market for money affects, and is affected by, the forces of spending and producing in the product market. *The rate of interest is not a purely monetary phenomenon.*

Chapter 7

Output, Demand and Prices

Up to this point the analysis has been conducted in terms of fixed prices of goods and services, with a passive reaction of the supply of output to variations in planned aggregate demand until full employment output was reached. Although in practice this is not a bad working assumption in the short run, it is time now to relax the assumption of fixed prices and to account for variations in the price level, as well as investigating the possible influences of variations in prices on equilibrium output and employment positions.

Figure 7.1 which presents British experience from 1954 to 1969, indicates that such an assumption of fixed prices must be relaxed. Per head income from employment rises steadily in monetary terms, as does income from employment per unit of output but at a slower rate. The latter provides a measure of the behaviour of labour costs per unit of output, and the retail price index rises in line with these costs. At the same time we find that, besides rising prices, labour costs and pay, both real output and real output per head also grew over the period. Between 1954 and 1968 real product grew by some 45 per cent, real product per head by 38 per cent. However, income from employment per head increased by 134 per cent, unit labour costs by 68 per cent, and retail prices showed an overall rise of 58 per cent. The analysis in this chapter will suggest some possible explanations both for this and for the behaviour of prices over the broader sweep from 1900 (see Figure 1.1, p. 10).

The quantity theory of money

A first approach to the behaviour of prices on average, or the price level, has been provided by the much-maligned 'quantity theory of money' approach. This is presented here both as a useful lead-in to the problem and because economists have been showing revived interest in a more sophisticated version of it as a weapon for managing the economy.

Let us consider a simple economy where the various components of final goods and services are produced by integrated firms and are

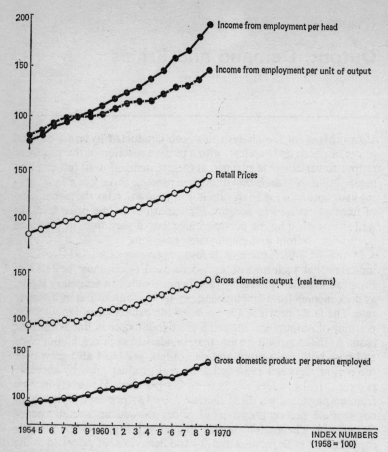

Figure 7.1 United Kingdom, 1954–69

INDEX NUMBERS
(1958 = 100)

sold to households or to firms. In any year total national expenditure can be looked at in two aspects:

(i) as equivalent to the average prices × volume of goods sold = PQ
(ii) as equivalent to the stock of money × the number of times each unit of money has been used on average in the year = MV

For example, if total national spending (PQ) was £10,000 million in the year and the stock of money (M) was £5,000 million, then on average each £1 unit of money has been used 2 times in the year, so that

V, known as the income velocity of circulation, has taken on the value of 2. Hence arises the truism or identity that in any year:

$$MV \equiv PQ$$

because each side is an alternative way of looking at national expenditure and is equal to the other by definition.

The concept is further widened to take account of the varied transactions in a more complex economy with inter-firm purchases of intermediate products, second-hand goods sales, purchases of property and financial assets. The volume of such transactions was indicated by T and the average of prices by P so that in this version we have:

$$MV \equiv PT \equiv \text{total value of all transactions}$$

where the definition of V is no longer income velocity but just velocity of circulation of money with respect to all transactions.

There is clearly nothing wrong with this approach in indicating ways of looking at the total value of transactions of total national expenditure that have been recorded for any year, and in incorporating important economic variables such as the stock of money or the price level or the volume of output. The danger comes when we are tempted to take this identity and *uncritically* use it to explain economic events, to predict future events, and to form the basis of policy.

Suppose it is proposed to increase the stock of money from £5,000 million last year to £6,000 million for this year. Economists of years ago, and politicians of more recent vintage, were tempted to say— and usually succumbed—that prices must also rise by 20 per cent on the *supposition* that V (depending on monetary habits) and Q (assuming full employment and no possible expansion in output) could be taken as fixed. From the identity $MV \equiv PQ$ they had made the transition to the equation or economic function $P = \alpha M$ where α was a constant equivalent to $\dfrac{V}{Q}$, so that the identity was transformed into a theory explaining variations in the price-level by variations in the stock of money.

It is important for us to ask how far it is reasonable to suppose that V and Q can be taken as constant, and enquire *by what process* changes in the stock of money influence prices, and under what conditions. This enquiry will help us to see part of the role of money in an economy as well as leading us to a better understanding of price-level variations.

Effects of an increase in the stock of money

Let us consider what may happen when a greater stock of money is made available to an economy. At any one time all of this must be held, willingly or unwillingly, by households and firms. If the stock of money has increased without any other economic change taking place, it seems reasonable to suppose that there will be some economic units holding more cash than they want to hold or, in other words, who have excess cash holdings. What action they then take is vital. Let us list possible actions:

(i) They may just acquiesce in increased holdings of cash and turn over their money stock less frequently, or in other words a fall in V takes place and there is no change in P or Q.

(ii) They may seek to spend more on currently produced goods and services and thus increase planned aggregate demand. This could also be interpreted as increased availability of finance increasing planned consumption or investment spending.

(iii) As a variant of (ii), they may seek to lend their excess cash to other units who then spend more on currently produced goods and services.

(iv) They may seek to increase their stock of earning assets by purchasing property, land, bonds, or shares (the sellers of which use the proceeds in a similar way). The analysis in Chapter 6 is relevant here and for (v).

(v) As a variant of (iv), they may seek to lend their excess cash to other units who seek to increase their holdings of earning assets.

[(iii) and (v) could well represent the behaviour of banks and other financial institutions with surplus 'cash'.]

Effects on income

Clearly the lines of actions (ii) and (iii) directly increase planned spending. If there was plenty of idle capacity in the economy or if there was substantial unemployment of men and machines, so that supply schedules were perfectly elastic, this would increase output and (after multiplier processes) a fresh equilibrium could be reached with no changes in prices. In terms of our earlier analysis this could be interpreted as an upward shift in the consumption function and/or an outward shift in the marginal efficiency of investment schedule. Further, although as one economic unit got rid of its excess cash holdings by spending it, another's cash position would move into excess so that a further stimulus to spending could result, the general rise in activity in the economy would tend to increase the need for money holdings. Eventually, then, these additional stimuli would die away as no unit had surplus cash holdings, and the economy would settle to a higher equilibrium output position. Q, then, would have risen as a result of the increase in M.

On the other hand, if the increased planned spending was confronted with no spare capacity and with full employment of men and machines, so that Q was fixed (suppose that previously full employment output and equilibrium output had coincided), then planned effective demand (and new equilibrium output) would exceed maximum output in real terms. A situation of excess demand for goods and services would exist and in a price-flexible economy prices would rise. P then would have risen as a result of the rise in M. (In an open economy the excess demand could be met at the cost of a balance of payments deficit and no rise in prices. This is a subsidiary complication.)

Effects on asset prices

Lines of action (iv) and (v) would increase the demand for a given stock of earning-assets so that their prices would rise. If the sellers held the proceeds in cash passively, this would be equivalent to (i), but if they used the proceeds to buy alternative earning assets the rise in the price of bonds, or property, or land, or ordinary shares, could continue.

In so far as such rising prices brought a more optimistic business outlook the marginal efficiency of investment schedule would shift to the right, thereby increasing investment and effective demand so that some effects would be felt in the product markets as well as in stock markets or property markets. Furthermore, rising bond prices would imply falling actual rates of interest, so that there might be a further stimulus to increased spending. Nevertheless the main weight of (iv) and (v) would be felt initially on the level of security and share prices, and property and land prices.

Further analysis

In terms of the analysis of the previous chapter, a rise in the stock of money would in these circumstances tend to bring a fall in the rate of interest as wealth-holders sought to reduce excessive holdings of cash by buying bonds. Pressure to buy bonds would force up bond prices and the actual interest yield would fall. This process would continue until the fall in the rate of interest had increased the demand for money sufficiently to match the increased supply.

The fall in the rate of interest would tend to stimulate planned investment and, via the multiplier, to increase incomes and output. Nevertheless, the direct impact on the flow of spending would be less than under (ii) and (iii) above. The lower the rise in spending, the greater would be the fall in the velocity of circulation (here thought of as the stock of money divided into the level of income). This, indeed, provides an important reason why the velocity of circulation should not be treated as a constant. Its size may well be linked to the rate of interest, when changes in the stock of money have their primary impact on the price of bonds.

It is obvious that much depends on the reactions of economic units to changes in the stock of money and to their money holdings, and again it may be important which economic units are the initial recipients of increased money holdings. For example, if a million £5 notes were dropped from the air on a suburban housing estate, we might expect (ii) to predominate, while if they were dropped in the City of London, effect (iv) might perhaps be more important. Hence, it is dangerous and unsound to predict uncritically that a rise in the stock of money will bring a rise in the price level. Likewise it is a mistake to think that a rise in the stock of money affects bond prices and the rate of interest alone. Varying circumstances alter cases, and processes need to be specified.

For example, in the sixteenth century the influx of gold and silver from the New World to Europe helped to bring rising prices, as it was treated as an increase in money stock and used by its recipients to increase their planned spending on goods and services as well as property and land. These were in virtually fixed supply so that the price level was forced up by excess demand. On the other hand, in slumps the stock of money may be increased as a remedial measure and banks may then be holding excess amounts of cash and liquid assets because no one who is credit-worthy wants to borrow. This would be a simple case of a fall in V. Hence, an uncritical quantity theory ($MV \equiv PQ$) approach is inadequate because it hides all this and merely predicts one particular response with V and Q assumed constant. Furthermore, not a word has been said about costs and supply conditions.

It has already been suggested that where rises in the price level of goods and services have occurred, they have come about because the increase in the stock of money had caused planned aggregate demand to rise in a situation where the supply of output was fixed. However, changes in planned aggregate demand can come about from a variety of causes, of which a change in the stock of money is merely one, so that the behaviour of the price level must be considered in the general context of changes in aggregate demand and supply, and supply conditions must be studied explicitly.

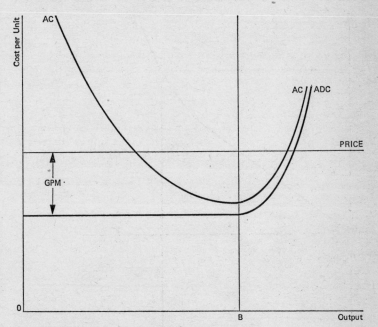

Figure 7.2 Average cost curves and pricing for a firm

Total supply schedule

By the concept of a total supply schedule is meant the various total real outputs of final goods which profit-maximising businessmen are willing to supply at each price level, when their equipment and plant is given, but they can vary their inputs of labour, raw materials, and semi-finished goods. It is based on the behaviour of the costs of production of firms and their actual pricing policies under these short-run conditions of a given-sized plant and given prices of inputs.

Total costs are divided into (i) direct costs which vary with output (for example, raw-material costs and wages of production workers) and (ii) fixed costs which are unchanged for a given-sized plant. We can then divide these various cost figures by output figures to obtain average costs per unit of output, average direct costs, and average fixed costs; and it is the behaviour of these that we shall consider, for they underlie our total supply schedule.

From industrial investigations it emerges that average direct

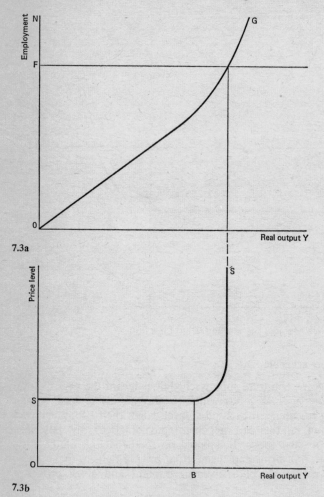

7.3a

7.3b

Figure 7.3 Employment, the supply of output, and the price level

costs are constant over a wide range of output and only turn up significantly beyond the point of normal full capacity (*OB* in Figure 7.2). Average costs, obtained by adding average fixed costs to average direct costs, also exhibit this flatness over a considerable range of output. Costs turn up sharply with over-capacity working as more strain is thrust on plant and management, more inefficient workers and methods may have to be used—in short, diminishing returns to labour set in sharply. Furthermore, the industrial practice of price fixing by adding a gross profit margin to 'normal' average direct costs will mean that businessmen will be willing to supply a wide range of output up to *OB* at given prices. They will be most reluctant to meet a recession in demand by price cuts which they believe will be copied by competitors, so that a decline in the price line with no significant expansion in sales results. They will be fearful of choking off an expansion of sales by price increases until full capacity operation is reached by themselves and most of their competitors.[1]

This stickiness of prices in practice, which is reinforced by the costs, nuisance, and bother of frequent industrial price revision, is the basis for our earlier assumptions of fixed prices and must be seen within the context of fixed input prices for firms. Should these change, they will affect each firm's direct costs to much the same extent in any given industry, and will lead through the price-fixing routine to equivalent changes in quoted prices. Once over-capacity operation is reached there will be strong pressure for temporary price increases to cover rising costs in the short run, and, if the increased volume of output is believed permanent, for expansion of the plant in the longer run.

If the various outputs which firms are willing to supply at each price level are aggregated (volumes being valued at some given set of prices and added to yield real output), a total supply schedule of real output for the economy can be obtained as depicted in Figure 7.3b in which price level is plotted against real output. After remaining flat over the range *OB* it commences to rise more gently than the cost curve analysis would suggest and then becomes progressively steeper. For less efficient plant has to be brought into operation to supply extra output, and for this to be done on a profit-making basis

1. It should be pointed out that this process is known as 'full-cost' or 'normal cost' or 'mark-up' pricing and corresponds to industrial practice. It is distinct from textbook perfect or imperfect competition in that it seeks to explain price formation in an uncertain and risky world which does not possess enough information to use such marginal analysis.

higher prices are required, while higher prices will also induce the more efficient to move up the rising part of their cost curves and supply extra output by overcapacity operation.

This total supply schedule can be linked to employment through the notion of a short-run production function for the economy as a whole, relating total output to inputs of labour (with a constant working week) as demonstrated in Figure 7.3a. Labour is the variable factor, while the stock of capital is given. Over a considerable range

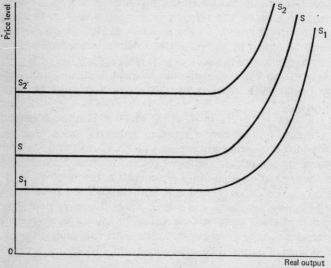

Figure 7.4 Total supply schedules with varying factor prices

of output we could expect a constant link between the two of the form 'x more labour required to produce one more unit of real output'. This would correspond to the flat portion of the average direct cost curve with given money wages and prices of other inputs. Then, as output expanded further, diminishing returns would make their presence felt so that increasing amounts of labour would be required to produce one more unit of output.

This is indicated by the steepening slope of *OG* in Figure 7.3a. The limit to output, where *SS* is vertical, could come from the full employment of a given labour force *OF*, or because *OG* becomes vertical before the labour force is fully employed. We shall concentrate on the former aspect, while the latter is more a problem for underdeveloped economies, with a shortage of land and capital relative to population.

Shifts in the total supply schedule

Let us consider what could cause the total supply schedule to shift up or down. It was calculated on the basis of given prices of inputs and a given profit margin. Hence general cuts in money wages (unmatched by productivity cuts), or cuts in raw-material input prices, or general price-cutting by frenzied businessmen in a severe depression would displace the whole total supply schedule in Figure 7.4 bodily downwards to S_1S_1. On the other hand, should there be general rises in money wages (unmatched by increases in output per man), or rises in material input prices, the total supply schedule would be displaced upwards to S_2S_2. Again, if there were given money wages and rises in output per man so that average direct costs fell, the whole schedule would be displaced downwards unless producers were in league to maintain prices and so expand profits.

The determination of the general price level

Our earlier analysis under fixed prices has shown how planned aggregate demand in real terms determined output; and how, with a given consumption function, a given marginal efficiency of investment schedule, and a given rate of interest, equilibrium output was reached. Our concern here is how planned aggregate demand will interact with a given total supply schedule to determine the price level, and the extent to which planned aggregate demand in real terms is sensitive to price-level changes.

Suppose it is the case that planned spending at fixed prices, or spending plans in real terms, are unaffected directly or indirectly by variations in prices. In other words, we are supposing that, whether the price index is 105, 125 or 85, the position of the propensity to consume schedule, which relates planned real consumption to real income and output, is unaltered and that planned real investment is unchanged. In these circumstances, real income and output (or output at constant prices) will be determined as in Chapter 3. Then from the total supply schedule we can read off the price level at which businessmen are prepared (with given input prices) to supply this equilibrium output. To repeat, this is asserting that planned spending in real terms is unaffected by price-level variations.

How reasonable is this assertion? One may initially argue by analogy with microeconomic theory that if the price level is higher, the quantity of output demanded will be lower, as in the case of the demand for apples or butter. And this would be true if given money incomes were confronted with rising prices. But we are dealing with the economy as a whole in which, if a given output is sold at a 10 per cent higher price level, then the money value of sales receipts will be 10 per cent higher and money incomes in aggregate will be 10 per

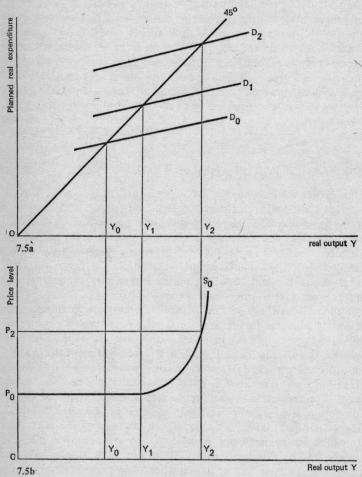

Figure 7.5 Effective demand and the price level

cent higher, although their distribution may have altered. Alternatively, if a given output is produced at a 10 per cent higher price level, money incomes derived from production will be 10 per cent higher so that real income and real consumption are unchanged. If firms are concerned with 'real' conditions, they will not alter their real investment plans, and in the economy as a whole the determinate output position will be unchanged.

This process of the determination of the price level is illustrated in Figure 7.5. In part (a), the initial equilibrium position is Y_0 where planned investment and the propensity to consume schedule yield the planned spending line of D_0. This output is supplied at a price level of P_0 as read off the total supply schedule S_0 in part (b). The planned spending line can rise up to D_1 in real terms and equilibrium output reach Y_1 before there is any need for the price level to rise. If the planned spending line in real terms is D_2, equilibrium output is Y_2, which producers will only supply at a price level of P_2. The increase in planned effective demand from D_1 to D_2 has brought about a rise in the price level from P_0 to P_2.

In this analysis we have not allowed for any influence of changes in the price level on planned aggregate demand in real terms. If, regardless of price-level changes, businessmen still intend to invest to the same real extent, and the consumption function which relates

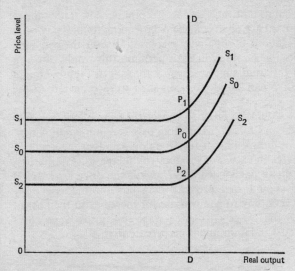

Figure 7.6 Price-level changes and effective demand

real consumption to real income (= output) remains unchanged, then planned aggregate demand in real terms is unchanged and un-influenced by variations in the price level. The aggregate demand schedule based on D_2 and equilibrium real income would be drawn with respect to price as a vertical line up from Y_2 in Figure 7.5b.

Policy implications

These conclusions carry important policy implications. If general cuts in money wages were undertaken in the hope of alleviating unemployment by making labour and products cheaper, so that more would be bought and more employed, the above analysis would suggest that this was futile. For all that would happen would be a downwards movement in the total supply schedule from S_0S_0 to S_2S_2 in Figure 7.6, where DD indicates that planned real aggregate demand would be unaffected by price-level alterations, and equi-librium output would remain at OD with no change in employment. The price level would fall with no benefit to employment, and with great social cost in the process of forcing down money wages. Such reasoning formed the basis of Keynes's objections to orthodox economic prescriptions (cut money wages to reduce unemployment) of the inter-war period for remedying the mass unemployment in Britain at that time.

On the other hand, if at times of low unemployment, trade unions were able by militant action in collective bargaining to raise pay rates in excess of any labour productivity increases all over the economy so that there was a general rise in costs per unit, this would cause an upward shift in the total supply schedule to S_1S_1 in Figure 7.6 and a general rise in prices, unless businessmen were prepared to see profits squeezed.

Once again it would be futile to expect that rising prices would choke off the demand for goods, leading to a rise in unemployment and a consequent dampening of future union aggressiveness and of likely pay increases in excess of productivity increases. Equilibrium output would remain unchanged at OD, while the price level would rise to P_1. This could well provoke demands for increased pay throughout the economy to compensate for increases in the cost of living, and thus the 'wage–cost–price–wage' or 'price–wage–cost–price' spiral of cost inflation might perpetuate itself.

Monetary factors

The above analysis has ignored monetary factors with which we started this chapter and which were analysed earlier in Chapter 6. This must now be remedied. With a given money supply and given demand schedules for money, an increase in money incomes, it will be recalled, will lead to a rise in interest rates. This rise in money incomes could have resulted from a rise in real output, or from a rise in the price level. Hence a rise in the price level will bring a rise in the rate of interest, unless the stock of money is expanded. Likewise a fall in the price level will bring a fall in the interest rate.

Hence we could expect a rise in the price level to be accompanied by a rise in the interest rate, a fall in planned real investment, and a fall in the determinate level of real income. A fall in the price level would bring a fall in the interest rate, a rise in planned real investment, and a rise in the level of real output. The schedule relating the price level and real output on the spending side would now no longer be vertical as DD in Figure 7.6, but downward sloping. The degree to which it slopes will depend on the sensitivity of the interest rate to alterations in the price level, and the sensitivity of planned investment to changes in the interest rate. The vertical position amounts to saying that these sensitivities are negligible.

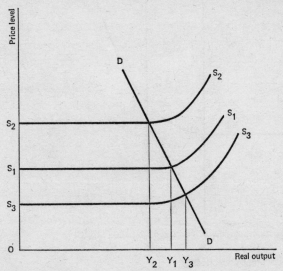

Figure 7.7 Sensitivity of equilibrium output to the price level

What, then, are the implications of this? If there is a general
increase in money wages (which shifts up the total supply schedule)
and a consequential rise in prices, interest rates will rise, check
investment, and lead to a fall in output and employment. This may
well curb future increases in money wages as the bargaining position
of labour is less strong. On the other hand, if there is a general cut
in money wages (which shifts down the total supply schedule) and
a fall in prices, interest rates will tend to fall, expanding planned
investment, and bringing a rise in output and employment. If there
was substantial unemployment, some relief could be provided in this
fashion by cuts in money wages.

These conclusions are demonstrated in Figure 7.7. Initially the
economy is at Y_1 and operating with total supply schedule S_1S_1.
If the rise in money wage shifts the schedule to S_2S_2, output sags
to Y_2, while if the cut in money wages shifts the schedule to S_3S_3,
output expands to Y_3. Other possible effects of alterations in the
price level on planned real spending are discussed in the appendix
to this chapter. However, for the remainder of this chapter we shall
assume that planned real spending is insensitive to variations in the
price level.

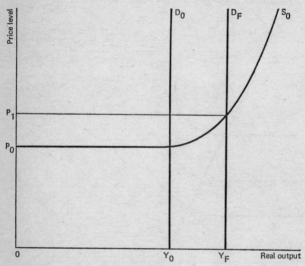

Figure 7.8 Full employment and prices

Stability

Suppose that the economy had its real output equilibrium position at Y_0 with the price level at P_0 as shown in Figure 7.8, but that on social and political (as well as economic) grounds it was felt that there was excessive unemployment associated with this level of real output. A greater output and effective demand of OY_F was needed to eliminate the undesired unemployment, and it is clear that if by policy measures this level of output was achieved, the price level would rise to P_1. From the earlier analysis it would seem highly likely that this rise in prices could touch off an inflationary spiral with labour in a stronger bargaining position as unemployment was reduced. A policy trade-off would face the government between higher unemployment and price stability, and lower unemployment and rising prices.

Reversibility

Another interesting question arises. If planned aggregate demand rises from D_0 to D_F causing a rise in the price level from P_0 to P_1 in Figure 7.8, will a subsequent fall in aggregate demand back from D_F to D_0 bring a fall in the price level? It may well be that if the economy has time to settle with price level OP_1 a subsequent fall in effective demand may reduce output *alone* and leave prices unchanged at OP_1. It is hard to be dogmatic *a priori*; the economic system in question needs close study. The answers could be vital for a policy's success, if the policy seeks to reduce prices in order to make the economy more competitive internationally by checking aggregate demand.

Stability again in depression

By incorporating the analytical device of a total supply function it has been possible to show how variations in planned aggregate demand are likely to bring variations in output with unchanged prices over a considerable range of output. However, this is short-run treatment. For if, with low aggregate demand, considerable under-capacity operation of plant and unemployment of labour persists, pressures are likely to develop leading to price-cutting by desperate businessmen and to efforts to depress money wage rates. In this deflationary condition of the economy, sagging prices and money wages are the most probable result, with the considerable under-capacity and unemployment persisting, for downward sliding prices are unlikely to improve the aggregate demand positions as gloomy expectations offset any favourable effects. These depressive conditions come about as the result of a fall in planned aggregate demand, one reason for which—but only one among many—could be a fall in the stock of money and the availability of finance. This needs to be kept in mind in order to keep the quantity theory of money in its place.

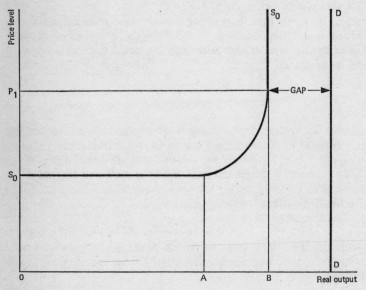

Figure 7.9 Excess demand for products

Excess demand inflation

On the other hand, the approach also shows that as planned aggregate demand rises and overshoots *normal* full capacity output, pressure is put on prices as costs of production rise, once position *A* has been passed in Figure 7.9. The curve S_0S_0 then becomes vertical at output *B*, which may be thought of as the maximum possible output, given the stock of capital and the labour force. The reader should think whether *A* or *B* will make the better definition of full employment and full-capacity operation of the economy, since this is often taken as an important goal of national economic policy.

As far as production is concerned, it is impossible to go beyond position B in the short run. But it is obviously possible for planned aggregate demand to exceed maximum output in real terms, as depicted in Figure 7.9. Here at a given price level P_1, planned aggregate demand exceeds maximum output in real terms by BD. Once again, there are many reasons why planned aggregate demand should be so high, of which a rise in the stock of money is only one. How the economy will respond to this situation of excess demand will be discussed later.

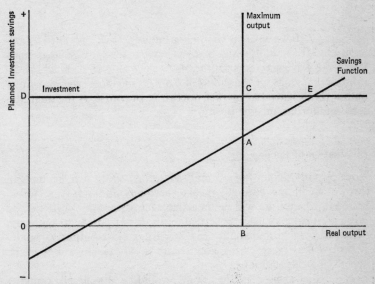

Figure 7.10 The inflationary gap

This, indeed, is *excess demand inflation* where planned aggregate demand in real terms exceeds maximum real output. At any given price level, spending on goods and services exceeds maximum available supply valued at that price level, the excess of planned spending over output being known as an inflationary gap. Together with this excess demand for goods and services will *almost* certainly go excess demand for factors of production—labour and capital will be in excess demand.

Using the earlier notation we have in a simple economy (no government, no trade):

Planned investment + planned consumption exceed
$$\text{maximum output at current market prices}$$

$$*I + *C > Y_{max}$$

If expected real income, on the basis of which savings and consumption decisions are made, is the same as maximum real output we can write

$$*I > Y_{max} - *C$$
$$*I > *S$$

In Figure 7.10 we have maximum output as OB with planned investment of OD ($= BC$), while planned savings from the savings function are BA at maximum output. AC is the excess of planned investment over savings, or the excess of planned spending over maximum output (both valued at market prices). E, of course, is the unattainable equilibrium income position.

Elimination of the gap

However, in accounting or realised terms, there will be no gap thrown up in the national income accounts and statistics. Gross national expenditure will be the same as gross national income and gross national product in recorded terms, for *ex post* total aggregate demand in real terms cannot exceed total aggregate output, except by *undesired* falls in stocks of goods, and this is taken care of in the accounting calculations.[2]

The basic answer is that some would-be purchasers (making their plans on the basis of current prices, expected incomes, availability of finance and goods) are disappointed, as not all planned demands can be satisfied. Precisely how they are disappointed. whether it is forcibly by rationing or by unexpected price increases, will depend on the type of economic system and its institutions.

---

2. For although realised spending could exceed output by running down stocks of goods, when the investment component is calculated it will be total realised fixed investment plus rises in stocks of goods, or minus falls in stocks of goods, so that national expenditure (allowing for changes in stocks) must be the same as national product in realised terms.

Controls case

In a price controlled economy (for example, a siege economy in wartime or a centrally planned and organised state) the excess demand will show itself in physical shortages of goods, falling stocks, lengthening queues at shops with those at the rear getting nothing, and lengthening order books. Would-be spenders will be unable to purchase on the scale they desire, so that their savings are forced to rise and they accumulate over time financial assets on a greater scale than they had planned, which in the future they may well seek to spend on goods. In such circumstances, measures of quantitative rationing will frequently be adopted to allocate goods 'fairly', and unofficial, illegal price-flexible markets may develop. The excess demand in real terms is forcibly eliminated for the year in question, but will reappear in the next time period unless there are changes in planned injections, leakages, and maximum output.

Free market case

Rather similar initial symptoms may be found in a 'price-sticky' economy where firms set prices for a period of time, with lengthening order books and mounting pressure on prices and wages as shortages persist. The labour market may be the first to react to excess demand, with employers competing hotly to get more men by paying more than negotiated rates, and unions exploiting the sellers' market for labour services, so that prices are adjusted upwards as industrial costs rise.

If planned aggregate demand at current prices (expected to prevail throughout the time-period) is £1,200 million, while maximum output at the same prices is £1,000 million, spenders can succeed in spending £1,200 million on the output if prices rise by 20 per cent, but they will not obtain the *volume* of goods they had hoped for. The excess demand has been eliminated for the time period in question by *unexpected* price increases, but if nothing more fundamental has occurred to disturb the position of the planned injections and leakages and maximum output *in real terms*, excess demand will reappear in the next period.

In a price-flexible economy the reactions of the prices of goods will be more speedy than the previous case and will probably beat the response of the labour market. Effects on excess demand will be similar to the preceding case with similar conclusions about its reappearance in the next period. If we take account of international transactions, the increase in prices may be mitigated if excess demand for goods is met by cutting exports and expanding imports, thereby worsening the current account balance of payments unless there is world-wide excess demand.

Essentially, excess demand inflation reflects a *disequilibrium* situation between plans to spend and ability to produce, which 'force' or 'fraud' temporarily suppresses, and in an economy with no price controls manifests itself in *rising* prices (rather than a rise in prices). There may, however, be forces working to lessen the disequilibrium in the planned sense. If prices rise relative to money wages the share of profits in national income will rise, so that, if profit recipients have a higher propensity to save than wage recipients, there will be an upward shift in the savings function, thereby lessening the size of the excess demand gap.

Further, if the availability of finance is unchanged while rising prices increase the need for finance, the interest rate may rise and lessen planned investment, although businessmen may have such high hopes of success that they ignore the rising cost of finance.

Cost inflation and its persistence

Furthermore, these increases in prices, which serve to reduce the ability to buy in real terms, will depress real wages (money wages remaining unchanged); and it would be very short-sighted to think that no further wage adjustments would occur.

Two sorts of pressure can develop on money wages: first, excess demand for labour tends to increase pay rates as employers are willing to pay more to get more men, and as trade unions are in strong bargaining positions. Secondly, as prices rise there will be strong pressure to seek cost-of-living adjustments in money wages to restore real wages, as a matter of social equity apart from anything else. Hence rising prices will be accelerated by increases in pay and costs in a spiral form of (i) rising prices → rising pay → rising costs → rising prices, or (ii) rising pay → rising costs → rising prices → rising pay which may well persist and not damp themselves down.

Which of the two spirals is to be emphasised will depend on where the excess demand has made itself felt initially, and perhaps on the political persuasion of the economic commentator. This spiral process has been called 'cost inflation' to distinguish it from 'excess demand inflation', but it is very frequently so closely entangled with excess demand inflation as to make it hard to separate out the various elements in practice. Diagrammatically, cost inflation can be thought of as an upward drift of the total supply schedule.

Nevertheless, in the modern world cost inflation seems to have developed a life of its own without the presence or persistence of excess demand inflation, so that a steady slow rise in prices continues. This process of paying ourselves 8 per cent more to produce 3 per cent more in real terms with a resultant price increase of 5 per cent has become known in continental circles as the 'British disease'.

Let us suppose that planned investment is given and there is a given savings function, so that an equilibrium real output and income position is attained at a high, but not excessive, level of employment, and that there is no change in output per head over time. However, if the labour force expects an annual rise in pay as a result of social habit built up over recent times or seeks the 'easy road' to the affluent society, quite regardless of economic circumstances, then a general rise in money-wage rates will result, even with collective bargaining for individual industries.

Suppose one organised group of workers seeks and achieves an increase in pay. Matters will not end here. Other groups, motivated by *social* as well as *economic* forces, will seek pay increases to preserve differentials and to maintain comparability of pay rates. 'Wage–wage' inflationary spirals among groups of workers transform themselves into general increases in pay, and remind economists that the sub-markets of the labour markets are *not independent* but *interdependent* when pay is changed in one.

Industrial costs per unit rise, and this could be the end of the matter, if businessmen and profit recipients are willing to be squeezed, absorbing higher direct costs in given absolute profit margins and thus keeping prices constant, since they might be fearful of losing markets if prices were increased. In these circumstances they might be expected to show tougher resistance to the next pay claim, as their share in national income is diminished. Such willingness to be squeezed is not to be expected, particularly in an economic climate where governments are committed to full employment, so that businessmen and profit recipients will seek to maintain their previous share by raising prices without having to worry overmuch about loss of orders—unless they sell predominantly abroad.

The 'average direct costs plus given percentage gross profit margin' style of pricing will naturally lead to general increases in prices as input prices rise, and as individual businessmen follow the same behaviour pattern without there necessarily being any collusion. Labour's share in real income declines as profits' share rises, and action can confidently be expected to restore labour's share by seeking cost-of-living increases in pay rates to compensate for (unexpected) price rises occasioned by earlier pay awards.[3] This can be illustrated by successive upward shifts in the total supply schedule, and the process can be expected to continue so long as each group refuses to be squeezed, except temporarily.

In this process the total of the real incomes claimed by each economic interest exceeds the total real output available, or the sum of the desired (fractional) shares of real output exceeds unity. Each economic interest seeks to protect itself from being squeezed by putting up the price it charges for its product or the productive service it supplies. No interest willingly acquiesces in being squeezed, the disequilibrium process continues, and so does the rise in the price level and in pay rates.

How quickly each element responds to protect itself will help to determine the pace of cost inflation. If battles over pay and the collective bargaining procedures are long drawn out, and if firms stick for lengthy periods to administered prices, the pace of rising prices will be slow. On the other hand, if there has been a long history of price inflation (as in parts of Latin America), and if prices are more flexible and collective bargaining more rapid, then the pace will be faster. The process may indeed be less rapid the higher the level of unemployment and of spare capacity, so that, if planned effective demand is sensitive to price increases, rising prices may cut planned effective demand, reduce employment, and mitigate the pace of cost inflation.

However, if rising prices bring balance of payments strain and a devaluation in the rate of exchange, this will tend to accelerate the price rise as domestic prices of imports and exportables increase. A depreciating exchange-rate can, indeed, be an important force accelerating the pace of cost inflation to as much as 50 to 100 per cent price rises within a year, and even into those terrifying large price increases which characterise hyperinflation where money virtually loses all value.

Recent U.K. experience

Our analysis has suggested that we could expect any rise in pay or the price level to be greater the greater the pressure of demand on available resources. In any one year, the greater the demand for labour, the greater would be the annual change in pay. Furthermore, the cost-inflation approach would suggest that the greater the annual

3. Pay rises are now sought (1970–71) to compensate for *anticipated* price rises.

change in pay the greater the annual change in prices, unless productivity changes offset this.

In the British system such a rise in the demand for labour by firms would cause those registered as unemployed to fall and unfilled vacancies notified to labour exchanges to rise. The behaviour of these magnitudes would give us a measure of the pressure of demand in the economy as reflected in labour market statistics. These series are

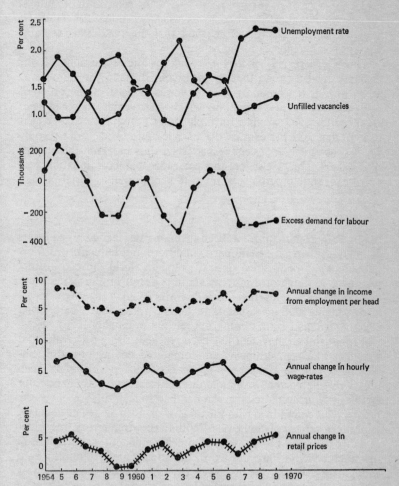

Figure 7.11 United Kingdom 1954–69. Excess demand for labour, pay-rates, and prices

plotted in Figure 7.11, from which it will be seen that 1955, 1961, and 1965–66 were peak years for the pressure of excess demand.

We can then compare with these curves the behaviour of annual changes in pay. Annual changes in income from employment per head seem to be higher in years of high pressure of demand for labour, and lower in years of weak demand. This pattern is more pronounced in annual changes in hourly wage-rates, with distinct peaks in 1955–56, 1961, and 1965–66. The behaviour of annual changes in retail prices also shows roughly similar behaviour to hourly wage-rate changes with peaks in 1956, 1962, 1965–66, and perhaps some tendency to lag behind.

British experience up to 1969 confirms the suggestions of our analysis. It also shows that when 'excess' demand for labour was at its lowest, the annual rise in pay was at least of the order of 3 per cent. This rise is something which we have not explained here. Again, after 1969 we find unemployment averaging 2·51 per cent in 1970 and 3·32 per cent in 1971, while hourly wage rates rose by 9 per cent and 13 per cent respectively, thus breaking the pattern of 1954–69. Our views on the persistence of cost inflation (see pp. 143–4) should perhaps be invoked here as well as social factors.

Summary

In this chapter more time has been spent on price increases and forms of inflation than on deflationary conditions and falling prices. This imbalance can be justified since the modern world shows a distinct resistance to downward movements in prices of products and more especially of pay rates. It is a world in which falling effective demand brings falling output rather than falling prices, and where rising effective demand brings rising output and eventually rising prices, and (once full employment has been reached) rising prices alone; a world in which governments are committed politically to full employment, and in which one major economic problem has been inflation. The current economic environment has thus shaped our emphasis. Furthermore, the chapter has sought to show how the price level is determined with the tools of planned aggregate demand, and the total supply schedule. Within this framework the older quantity theory of money, with its timely reminder that variations in the stock of money are still worth the attention of economists even though their effects are likely to be more varied than once was thought, can be fitted as a particular and special case.

From this general approach the analysis of inflation follows naturally, for we have emphasised both the 'excess demand' and the 'cost inflation spiral' aspects, as well as suggested that cost inflation may develop a life of its own. The theoretical foundations for the short-period policy management of the economy have now been laid.

APPENDIX TO CHAPTER 7
(This should be omitted at a first reading.)

In this chapter, planned aggregate demand has been treated as unaffected in real terms by variations in the price level except for the monetary influence. However, can it really be assumed that planned aggregate demand will remain unchanged in real terms as the price level varies? One can list a few possible effects of such variation, some of which may work in opposite directions to others, and some whose effects may vary depending on the reasons for variations in price.

(i) *Influence on income distribution.* Here it may be important to distinguish why prices have changed. Let us consider a fall in prices which has occurred because of a decline in equilibrium output and a move down a given total supply curve.

In this case, money wages per worker are unchanged, so that real wages per worker employed have risen; but output and hence employment are lower. It is not possible to conclude that labour's share in real income is higher, unless one discovers that the percentage fall in employment is less than the percentage rise in real wages. One can conclude that the share of those living on fixed money incomes will have risen, and it would thus seem likely that the share of profit recipients would have fallen.

In so far as the profit recipients tend to save more than the other two groups, the likely redistribution would cause a small upward shift in the consumption function, so that here planned aggregate demand in real terms *might* rise as prices fell, and *vice versa* for a rise in prices. However, if prices rose because of an upward displacement of the total supply schedule, with equilibrium output unchanged initially, various effects are possible.

First, if the shift came from a rise in money wages passed on in an equal percentage rise in prices then, with unchanged output and employment, the share of workers in real income would be the same, while the share of profit recipients would rise at the expense of fixed money income recipients. The consumption function might shift downwards.

If, secondly, the shift came from increased prices of raw-materials inputs with money wages unchanged, then labour's share would fall, as would the share of fixed money income recipients, while the share of profits of owners and producers of raw materials would rise. A more pronounced fall in the consumption function might be expected, which might be reversed by cost-of-living pay awards.

(ii) *Money illusion.* Will wage earners feel worse off if they experience a cut in money wages, even though it is matched by an equivalent fall in prices so that real wages are unchanged? If they look at money wages alone, they may conclude they can no longer afford the luxury of saving on their previous scale, and thus increase the fraction of income spent on consumption. Hence, there is an upward shift in the function relating real consumption to real income, and *vice versa* for a rise in money wages and prices.

(iii) *Real asset effect.* A fall in prices of goods will increase the real value in terms of goods of certain financial assets, such as money balances and government bonds, so that the holders of these will have a greater stock of real assets. Therefore, the marginal utility of adding to these by saving in the current period will fall while the marginal utility of consumption will remain unchanged.

Such asset-holders may well increase their real consumption out of a given real income. In other words, there will be an upward shift in the consumption function as prices fall, and a downward shift as prices rise. These are the effects for creditors. They are reversed for debtors, so that some influences net out except for cash holdings and government bond and bill holdings (assuming that the government does not alter its budgetary policy), which may be presumed to have this real asset effect.

(iv) *International trade effect.* A decline in prices would increase the volume of export sales and of purchases of import-substitutes, and thus have a stimulating effect on planned effective demand, while an increase in prices would have a depressive effect. If, however, the price levels of other countries behaved similarly, the trade effect would be substantially reduced in size.

(v) *Expectations.* If businessmen and households expect that a change in price level will be unrepeated they will go ahead in the manner suggested, tending to increase real planned expenditure with a fall in prices and tending to check real planned expenditure with a rise.

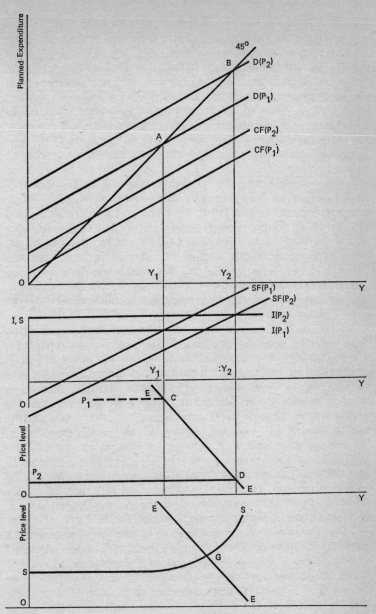

Figure 7.12 Equilibrium when effective demand is sensitive to the price level

However, if they expect that a change in the price level is the fore-runner of another similar change in the price level in the near future, they may act in the opposite manner.

Thus if a fall in prices leads to the expectation of further falls in prices, households and businessmen will tend to postpone all but the most essential purchases, thereby checking planned spending, while a rise in prices will accelerate planned spending. Again, falling prices may make businessmen pessimistic about the future and cause the marginal efficiency of investment schedule to move to the left; but rising prices may make them optimistic and shift the schedule to the right.

It would seem in summary that if expectations are of the once-and-for-all category, a rise in the price level could be expected to reduce planned real spending, a fall in the price level to increase planned real spending. Empirical work, however, suggests that these price effects are likely to be weak, and hence could be swamped by adverse expectation effects. Bearing this caution in mind, one can proceed in two ways to illustrate the equilibrium situation when consumer spending in real terms depends not only on real income but also on the price level, and when investment spending depends on the rate of interest and the price level.

(a) For each price level there will be a particular consumption function and a particular marginal efficiency of investment schedule. If for simplicity an unchanged rate of interest is assumed, the equilibrium real income and output position can be worked out for that particular price level. Figure 7.12 illustrates how equilibrium is reached when effective demand is sensitive to the price level. In Figure 7.12 at the price level P_1 the consumption function is $CF(P_1)$ and investment $I(P_1)$ so that planned demand equals output at A. At a lower price level P_2 a different equilibrium income of Y_2 is obtained, and these points are plotted in part (c) of the diagram to give EE, which shows the equilibrium income position corresponding to each price level. This can then be combined with the total supply schedule to yield the equilibrium income *and* price combination, once production conditions are taken into account for the supply of output at each price level. If there should be an upward displacement of SS as prices of inputs rise, EE will remain unchanged and a fresh equilibrium position result with lower output and higher prices.

(b) The second approach operates on the same assumptions as before: (i) that real consumption depends on the level of real income and the price level, (ii) that real investment depends on the rate of interest and the price level, and (iii) that the rate of interest is given.

In Figure 7.13 for each pair of real output and price-level combinations on a given total supply curve ($S_0 S_0$) it is possible to work out planned real aggregate demand (D) inserting them into the consumption and investment functions and reading off planned consumption and planned investment. This value of D can then be plotted against

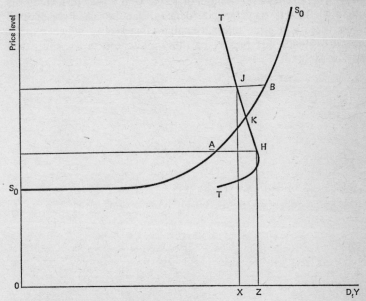

Figure 7.13 Equilibrium output and price level

the appropriate price level as in Figure 7.13, where D is measured along the horizontal axis. For example, corresponding to combination A is planned aggregate demand of OZ which is plotted as H, and corresponding to B is OX which is plotted as J. Points such as J and H are joined up to yield TT which shows planned aggregate demand at each price-output position on the total supply schedule. At position A there is excess demand of AH and at B excess supply of JB, so that the price level would tend to alter to reach K where the two curves cut and yield the equilibrium combination of prices, aggregate demand and output. With the same schedules as in method (a) the same equilibrium position would be arrived at—EE would in fact cut $S_0 S_0$ at K but would have a flatter slope. In this approach TT has to be recalculated for each shift in $S_0 S_0$, which is troublesome, but excess demand positions are clearly shown as the horizontal gap between *SS* and *TT*, whereas the gap between *EE* and *SS* has *no* such meaning. (See Figure 7.12.)

In these ways variations in the price level can be incorporated into the analysis of equilibrium real output and income, but it should be pointed out that for the purpose of analysing behaviour in an economy, where price-level changes of 10 per cent a year or less are the rule, their effects on aggregate demand can be usually neglected unless there is a large international trading sector, which is price sensitive. Hence our neglect of these influences in the main text may be excused.

Chapter 8

Managing the Economy

Introduction

As the macroeconomic analysis presented in this book became accepted, governments were not slow to realise that it offered them useful guidelines for managing their economies in the short run at least. For they could now devise economic policies to help them achieve such diverse objectives or targets as reduction of excessive unemployment, control of inflation and the avoidance of price increases, the elimination of gold losses by balance of payments adjustment, and the mitigation or elimination of economic instability. However, they have come to realise that certain objectives may conflict and that they may have to compromise by 'trading off' the level of unemployment against price increases.

This chapter will discuss various forms of economic policy to achieve these objectives which the analysis would suggest. We shall touch on matters which have not been covered in preceding chapters apart from Chapter 1. It is hoped that enough guidance on these matters is given in this chapter to make the economic analysis and policy intelligible to the reader who has worked through the previous seven chapters of Part One. Also in certain places it is assumed that readers have some general knowledge of the economic world around them other than is provided by these chapters. Furthermore, certain points will be appreciated more once the reader has tackled Chapters 9 and 10 and it is suggested that this reader will profit by turning back and re-reading Chapter 8.

In particular, it is necessary to say a few words about governmental transactions and international transactions, which are dealt with in more detail in Chapters 9 and 10. Export sales of goods and services (X) and governmental spending on goods and services (G) form categories of planned spending and are treated as 'injections' in just the same way as planned investment spending. A change in export sales or governmental spending will produce multiplier effects on output in just the same way as changes in investment, for example. Imports of goods and services (F) and taxation receipts (T) are treated as planned leakages from the flow of spending in just the same way as planned saving. Further, they can be taken as dependent on output or income such that a rise in output brings a rise in import purchases and a rise in taxation receipts. Also they will serve to damp down the size of the multiplier. (See Chapters 9 and 10.)

We shall be considering how an economy may be managed. It is important to realise that we must have targets or objectives (for example, price stability or full employment) which may well be chosen for economists by the national government, reflecting the electorate's preferences. We need economic policies to achieve these targets and we must operate on the economy with instrument variables. 'Policy' is here used in the sense of the instrument or means whereby an objective can be achieved rather than in the sense of the objective itself.

Among the various macroeconomic policies two major ones stand out:

(i) *Monetary policy* which has the rate of interest and the stock of money as its instrument variables, and which operates on such inter-mediate variables as investment spending or consumption spending to achieve the desired targets.

(ii) *Fiscal policy* which uses tax-rates and public spending as its instrument variables to achieve the desired objectives.

Unemployment

Unemployment on a tragic scale in the inter-war period provided the stimulus to the Keynesian development of this income analysis and it is only right that we should first consider unemployment and policies designed to remedy it. Various types of unemployment may be distinguished, and as each is discussed it will become clear that no one policy will remedy all.

Employment varies with the season of the year, particularly in agriculture and building because of climatic conditions, and in other areas such as the holiday and tourist trade as demand varies with the time of year. Little can be done to alleviate this unless it is possible to link in the same area occupations with opposite seasonal patterns of employment.

Secondly, 'frictional' unemployment may arise as men and women are temporarily idle when they are changing from one job to another and have to spend time seeking a new job, more especially if they have not left their previous jobs voluntarily. This kind of unemployment is inevitable in an economy subject to technical change and to changing patterns of demand, but policy should seek to minimise it by providing as much information as possible about employment opportunities to people seeking work, and by encouraging employers to notify vacancies widely. The British labour exchange system seeks to do this by making the labour market more 'informed' as well as by providing machinery for bringing hirers and employees together more regularly.

Employment has also varied severely with the varying tempo of business activity as economies have boomed or slumped. This cyclical category will be the subject of later analysis, as will the long-run stagnation type which seems to persist in a permanently depressed economy. Both of these types are spread somewhat evenly over the economy and manifest themselves as mass unemployment.

Persistent and heavy unemployment may also materialise on a more localised or concentrated form amidst a high average employment situation for the economy as a whole. Certain localities and trades may experience much higher unemployment than the national average in a depression as, for example, the North East of England, Wales, and Scotland experienced in the period 1920–1939. Such unemployment may be dubbed 'structural' or 'technological'.

The term 'structural' applies when there has been a permanent shift in demand away from an area's main product and few alternative employment opportunities exist in that area, or when a market has been lost for a highly localised trade, and for various economic and social reasons the geographical mobility of labour is low so that localised pools of heavy unemployment persist.

'Technological' is a more appropriate title when as a result of technological progress changes in techniques render some labour permanently redundant in a particular industry and when it is difficult to retrain these workers for alternative employment which may not even be available in the area. Industrial immobility and lack of retraining facilities underlie this type, which is closely allied to structural unemployment.

If the labour market was perfect and composed of highly mobile individuals, structural and technological unemployment would not exist, let alone persist, but because it is not, we must devise a conscious policy, bearing in mind that employment is not a purely economic affair. Social factors are important and should not be ignored. Furthermore, in framing any policy it is important to recall that such categories of unemployment are particularly associated with technical change and demand change, which underlie much of the economic growth and development in both rich and poor countries. We all seek the fruits of growth: surely we should compensate the victims on a generous scale.

The essentials of a policy are to maintain a high overall level of employment, and to pursue a conscious location-of-industry policy, encouraging by various measures the development of new industry in a depressed area. Yet this should not be pursued too mechanically as it may be better economically to abandon certain areas and concentrate on growth points, where economic gains outweigh social costs and losses. Hence, on occasion, measures designed to increase the mobility of labour geographically can form an important part of policy, while generous retraining facilities and allowances to increase industrial mobility always form an integral part of the fight against this type of unemployment.

Last, unemployment may occur because of the lack of co-operating factors of production, such as land or machines or even spades. This is more associated with poor underdeveloped economies which are overpopulated in relation to their natural resources and accumulated capital. It may even be 'disguised' in the sense that because of the social system three men 'share out' the work of two or that a fifth of the work-force in peasant agriculture could be withdrawn with no loss in output, yet all are apparently employed. Remedies for this type of unemployment must be sought in the process of economic development, and the provision of wider employment opportunities through industrialisation since the historic remedy of emigration is apparently unacceptable nowadays.

In mature industrial economies especially, the quantitatively most important type of unemployment has been 'cyclical', which in persistent depressions merges into the 'stagnation' type. In Britain in the fifty years before 1914 unemployment in booms was of the order of 2 per cent of the labour force, while in slumps it rose to 8–10 per cent of the labour force. Between 1920 and 1939 'boom' years indicated 10 per cent unemployed, and slump years up to 22 per cent unemployed. Cyclical variations in activity clearly must explain the bulk of the unemployment, only a small portion of which can be attributed to seasonal and frictional factors (say 2 per cent).

Why unemployment?

Our analysis indicates that the basic reason for periods of heavy unemployment is provided by *inadequate spending*. Planned spending (in real terms or at given prices) is insufficient to purchase full employment output (in real terms or at given prices) so that the equilibrium output position is one at which there are unemployed resources of labour and capital. In symbolic terms:

Planned consumption + investment + exports + governmental spending (all valued at market prices) < full employment output valued at market prices and including normal import content

Secondly, it indicates that in the current social, economic, and institutional environment of most economies, the market mechanism is incapable of remedying this deficiency of expenditure so as to promote full employment, and that we must not assume full employment to be the normal state of affairs to which the economy naturally tends.

Hence, if the diagnosis of the mass unemployment is inadequate spending, the policy prescription naturally follows 'increase spending' by various governmental actions. However, we must pause. We are assuming that we want to do something about lessening the unemployment under the 'value' or 'ethical' judgment that it is a desirable thing to lessen unemployment until a point 'full employment' is reached. Most people would agree to this, but if our attempts to increase employment increase prices, what of people living on fixed money incomes? They will be worse off since their real incomes will have fallen and they may oppose such measures. Similarly, other people may disagree if they believe that unemployment is needed to make organised labour 'behave' and not indulge in inconvenient strikes—a sort of disciplinary need for unemployment! Differences in ethical judgments among other things give rise to differences about the desirability of a particular economic policy, but there is more general agreement about the desirability of eliminating excessive unemployment than about most other economic measures.

Policies to remedy unemployment

Policies to stimulate spending can conveniently be classified into (i) monetary policy and (ii) fiscal policy headings, and should be thought of as complementary to each other rather than as rivals. They will only be discussed in outline here as they are the subjects of detailed treatment in another volume in this series.[1]

(i) The essence of monetary policy in a slump is provided by the phrase 'cheaper credit, more readily available', and it is the task of the government and central monetary authority to bring about lower interest rates and a greater willingness on the part of banks and other financial intermediaries to make loans. The latter measure runs

1. See G. H. Peters, *Private and Public Finance.*

contrary to an assumption made in the investment chapter (Chapter 5) that there is a perfectly elastic supply of finance at any interest rate, but a restricted source of finance is a feature of the real world, to which we must pay regard in policy, as is the linkage of short-term interest rates to the central bank's rediscount rate (Bank Rate in Britain). Certain interest rates within the structure of rates are administered prices, and by arbitrage they tend to influence somewhat other (longer) rates. Furthermore, the theory of the rate of interest discussed in Chapter 6 suggests that an increase in the stock of money should lower the rate of interest, unless one is already on the horizontal (liquidity trap) part of the L_2 schedule.

Hence for an easy or cheap money policy, the authorities should cut Bank Rate and increase the availability of credit by expanding the stock of money and perhaps relaxing the reserve ratios required for commercial banks. Such governmental regulations as exist on hire-purchase transactions may also be relaxed, and will be followed by the finance companies, provided that they do not exceed the bounds of financial prudence. Downward pressure will be exerted on interest rates, and loans will be more readily available to *credit-worthy* borrowers.

In evaluating the efficacy of these measures to increase planned spending, we must ask 'who is credit-worthy in a slump?' We must consider the sensitivity of spending decisions (investment and consumption) to falls in the rate of interest, about which we came to gloomy conclusions in Chapter 5. Again, in slump conditions with idle machinery and excess capital stock, entrepreneurs must be far-sighted creatures to increase their planned investment and demand for loans on any scale. We must conclude that monetary policy on its own is unlikely to stimulate spending on a sufficient scale in a slump *unless* businessmen are firmly convinced that full employment is the normal state of affairs which the government is politically committed to achieve by resolute economic policy, and that it is capable of achieving it. Even then, monetary policy will work better if fiscal policy is also employed, and cheap money can be very important in facilitating public borrowing to meet any budget deficit which fiscal policy may bring.

(ii) Fiscal policy may be thought of as government actions via its revenue-raising and spending powers to influence the planned aggregate spending of an economy. It should be noted that without any changes in policy there may well be stabilising effects from governmental transactions. While other categories of spending are falling in real terms, many elements of governmental spending may be unchanged, and some (unemployment relief) may actually rise. Again, a fall in incomes will not be passed on in full as many tax yields are related positively to incomes in such a way that a fall in incomes of 100 may bring a fall in consumption of only 50 as savings fall by 20 and taxation by 30. These features of the existing budgetary policy of a government can clearly help in mitigating depressive forces and in stabilising the economy at a floor, with a higher level of employment than otherwise. What must not happen here, and with discretionary policy (discussed below), is for the government to lose its nerve and worry over the old shibboleth of 'balancing the budget'.

Discretionary policy involves a combination, in whatever blend seems appropriate to the government, of increased governmental spending and of decreased tax rates, which will clearly cause tax receipts to fall relatively to spending and perhaps increase the need for public borrowing. Extra spending may take the form of increased public works, more public (social) investment, or the form of *increased* unemployment allowances, which one can assume will be spent by their recipients in entirety. Problems may arise with increased public investment. Are schemes available and ready for speedy execution? Will there be the usual planning permission delays or public enquiry delays, or can the 'rights of the individual' be swept aside in the interests of the speedier elimination of unemployment? Delays seem inevitable in implementing plans to increase public spending.

Cuts in direct tax rates, such as income tax rates, national insurance contributions, or profits tax rates will have the effect of allowing a greater disposable income to accrue to households from a given national income, so that (if they behave in accordance with their consumption function) consumer spending will increase. However, it is always possible in slump conditions that people receiving tax rebates may save such remissions 'for a rainy day', thus undoing the efficacy of these measures from the point of view of generating employment. Alternatively, the government may seek to stimulate investment spending by firms by allowing them to set more than the cost of the project against tax liabilities, or by making an outright grant to subsidise an investment project

Cuts in indirect taxation (such as lower excise duties on beer, petrol, spirits, tobacco, and lower purchase taxes or sales taxes) will lower the prices of these products, and thus increase the real purchasing power of a given disposable income in monetary terms so that, in aggregate, consumption expenditure may increase in real terms. Again the crucial behaviour question remains. Will people in slump conditions increase their real consumption expenditure as their real disposable income is increased in this way? Lower prices may prove a strong temptation.

In some political systems it is easier than in others to achieve these fiscal changes with speed, and within a given system it may be possible to achieve tax rate cuts more quickly than expenditure increases, so that the former measures may influence spending before the latter. Yet because of administrative problems it may only be possible to change certain (direct) tax rates once a year. Furthermore, a tax cut of 100 and an increase in public spending of 100 each have a primary effect of worsening the budgetary position by 100; but the latter increases spending by 100 and the multiplier is applied to this, whereas the former increases disposable income by 100 and spending by some fraction of this—for example, 65 if the marginal propensity to consume out of disposable income was 0·65—so that the 'multiplied' effects would be lower. Hence, for a given worsening of the budget an increase in public spending will increase employment by more than a comparable tax cut, but the latter may be speedier although incapable of frequent revision. Flexibility of fiscal policy may be yet further impaired if political pledges and vested interests prevent the alteration of certain categories of taxation and spending.

We have implied that these discretionary fiscal measures, and the automatic stabilising effects of a public finance system, will worsen the budgetary position and therefore will increase the exchequer's borrowing requirements to finance the emergent deficit. If this is financed by soliciting extra loans from the general public, the lenders may cut consumer spending in order to buy new bonds with extra savings; if banks subscribe, it may mean they have smaller resources for lending to firms and households who would spend on products. To minimise these effects the government should borrow from the central bank, or even print paper money for the purpose.

In these ways, then, expenditure can be stimulated and unemployment eradicated. The diagnosis and the cure have a deceptive air of simplicity about them and one is tempted to wonder why they were not thought of and accepted earlier. In practice difficulties and complications arise.

Full employment

First, what is our objective? Full employment, surely! But what do we mean by that? It cannot be taken literally to mean that every member of the labour force is in employment. Some residual seasonal and frictional unemployment is inevitable in any modern progressive economy in which labour can move freely, although one aim should be to minimise this. However, it is impossible to say *a priori* what this minimum is. Much depends on the type of economy, its labour market and institutions, its rate of technical progress and change. Nevertheless, the economist might think 1 per cent unemployment on the low side for flexibility and 4 per cent excessive. Certainly, in post-1945 Britain, any rise in the overall unemployment rate above 2 per cent has caused concern in governmental circles, let alone among the public, half a million of whom are then registered as unemployed. On economic grounds alone it would be impossible to give an administrator a precise figure, although on political and social grounds it is easy enough to fix a figure.

Economists have turned to other approaches to full employment and away from '*x* per cent of labour force unemployed'. Prominent among these approaches has been to compare the figures provided by the labour exchanges of 'people seeking work' with 'vacancies notified to labour exchanges' and trust that these reflect accurately the balance between demand and supply in the labour market at the going money wage rates. Some economists have argued on social grounds that full employment can only exist when vacancies exceed people seeking work, while others have pointed out that this is a perfect recipe for inflation by making the labour market a seller's market so that money wages rise, prices rise, and excess demand prevails. They have suggested that a rough balance between vacancies and numbers unemployed should be aimed at. If unemployment exceeds vacancies, then spending needs to be increased to cause output and the demand for labour to rise. These concepts, like the earlier percentage figure, are aggregates and can mask uneven geographical distributions of unemployment, which need to be cared for on the lines suggested earlier.

Alternatively, it has been suggested that full employment is (i) the highest level of employment compatible with a steady price level, or (ii) the highest level of employment compatible with balance of payments equilibrium. However, what is being said here is that stable prices or external balance is the main objective to which employment aims must be subordinated. Many would disagree with these views, especially if they felt their jobs were in particular danger. The economist has to point out the 'trade-offs' of lower unemployment against lower flexibility, against higher prices, against a poorer balance of payments position, and the danger of devaluation.

The final mix of these has to be chosen on political and social grounds with (optimistically) people making their preferences felt through the political system and the economist suggesting the alternative combinations. If a government believes it can have 0·5 per cent unemployment, free collective bargaining, and stable prices, the economist has a duty to dispel this belief if past behaviour of the economy and of similar ones indicates that this is an impossible combination.

Policy difficulties

Once an objective in terms of minimum unemployment percentage or numbers unemployed has been set by the government, or by public opinion, or by the electorate, further practical problems arise. Although we know which way to alter monetary and fiscal variables to stimulate spending and achieve our target, we usually do not know precisely what this implies in interest rate cuts, in tax-rate changes, and in changes in governmental spending. Econometrics is striving to increase our *quantitative* knowledge of how our economy reacts and behaves, and it will yield very useful guide lines for policy. Hence policy at present has to be almost on a trial and error basis. If there has not been enough stimulus, more measures will be needed, while if the target has been overshot, checking measures must be introduced. Furthermore, statistics become available well after the event so that our policies (allowing also for the time of reaction to the statistics) may even lag 6 to 12 months behind the complex of events and may be overtaken by fresh events. Our progress towards full employment may well be jerky, and we may find that we can mitigate slumps but not eliminate them. The price of avoiding major instability may well be minor instability caused by jerky policy reactions to belated statistical knowledge.

How long will such measures be needed? Are they to be conceived of as purely pump-priming to get industry going again and to bring a revival of confidence, so that they can be tapered off as private investment revives? Or are they likely to be required for a long spell to revive a stagnant economy? Can we be sure that the business reactions to governmental 'interference' will be favourable, especially among those who believe firmly in a *laissez-faire* approach? Certainly, there is a danger that some public investment may supplant private schemes, particularly in the construction of houses and factories. These and other similar issues must be judged by the policy-makers with reference to their particular economic environment.

As suggested earlier, timing provides problems. Given that a minimum level of unemployment has been set as a full employment target, and that actual unemployment begins to increase above this level, just when do the government and the monetary authorities switch on these various measures? How big an 'undesired unemployment gap' must exist before action starts, for one would not want to be misled by an unusually large seasonal or freak variation. Once action is required, how speedily can measures be taken? Monetary action would seem more flexible, whereas fiscal measures are bound up with the annual ritual of budget-making, the so-called political stigma of having to bring in such extra measures as mini-budgets, and administrative constraints. They smack of inflexibility in the short run. A blend of these policies must depend on the individual environment of each economy.

As deliberate monetary and fiscal policies to increase spending, production, and employment get under way and raise spending, in an open economy we can expect that import purchases will rise without export sales being stimulated at all. Furthermore, lower interest rates may provoke a capital outflow as it is now less remunerative to keep balances in this economy than previously, and other monetary centres are rendered more attractive. The balance of payments position will 'worsen' in the sense that payments rise relative to receipts, but this may be no bad thing for international monetary good neighbourliness if previously the economy had been running a large surplus (low activity having depressed imports) and accumulating gold.

On the other hand, if previously the economy was in rough balance with no gold movements, and if it adhered to a fixed exchange-rate, then as the unemployment problem is cured it acquires a balance of payments deficit and loss of gold. Some cherished ideal must be abandoned—(i) full employment, (ii) fixed exchange-rate, and (iii) freedom from trade and payment restrictions, or at least from an intensification of such restrictions—unless it is possible to use the *theoretical* combination of dear money to hold the balance of payments by encouraging a capital influx and an easy fiscal policy to encourage spending, a combination which would only work in the short run, if at all, in practice.

If much of the increase in unemployment in an economy is centred in the industries which export a large fraction of their output and has communicated depression to the rest of the economy by the multiplier, an increase in domestic spending may do little directly to alleviate their plight, as also would be the case with structural unemployment. For policy measures it matters why export sales are depressed. If the country's price-cost structure is uncompetitively high as compared with the rest of the world, so that world demand has switched away from its exports, devaluation of the exchange-rate by lowering export prices in world markets will help to create extra sales and extra employment in the 'export' industries. However, if the depression is world-wide, so that each country's export sales are depressed, devaluation by one to gain a competitive advantage and export unemployment would be speedily followed by others with weak effects on total output. In these circumstances international co-operation among affected countries to increase their domestic spending simultaneously would increase each's demand for imports and hence another's export sales. *Concerted* mutual policies would pull everyone's export sales and employment up.

Inflation

While unemployment was a principal economic and social evil in the period 1920–39, the onset of the Second World War replaced this with the dangers of inflation, which have persisted at varying strengths right up to the present. Employment has remained high—economists have even talked of 'overfull' employment—and prices in every economy have risen consistently upwards at varying rates. It is within this context that much post-1939 management of economies has concentrated on the control of inflation.

In Chapter 7 our analysis of inflation emphasised that it essentially reflected disequilibrium in the economy, and we made the distinction between 'excess demand' inflation and 'cost' inflation when looking at inflationary processes, although it was pointed out that often they were linked very closely together. 'Cost' inflation was thought of as a mutually interacting and progressing spiral of 'rising prices → rising money wages → rising unit costs → rising prices', while excess demand inflation was held to be the situation in which planned spending on goods and services at current market prices exceeded the maximum output of the economy valued at current prices (including normal import content), or where the total of planned claims on output in real terms exceeded the amount the economy could produce. In inequality form:

Planned consumption + investment + governmental spending + exports at current market prices > maximum output (including normal import content) valued at current market prices

$$*C + *I + *G + *X > Y_{max} + *F + *T_e$$

However, in realised terms it is impossible for all spending plans at current market prices to be achieved: some are disappointed so that the 'inflationary gap' is eliminated in 'realised' terms, but it will re-appear in the next time period unless some basic changes in the economy have altered plans. It is highly likely that, in a situation where the demand for output exceeds maximum possible production, individual businessmen will all be seeking to recruit extra employees to help increase output. Vacancies notified to labour exchanges will soar, the total of unemployed people seeking work will drop, un-employment will fall to negligible levels, and excess demand will characterise the labour market also.

How are such gaps between planned claims on output and maxi-mum output eliminated within the time period? In a wartime or siege economy (or in a 'planned' economy in which prices are controlled) some would-be spenders are unable to find anything to buy so that they are forcibly disappointed. In the early stages they may be satisfied by the running down of stocks of goods, but there is a limit to this. Symptomatic of this repressed inflation are shortages, queues, and rationing, formal and informal. In a price-flexible economy the excess demand for goods forces up their prices, so that more has to be spent in monetary terms to buy a given real output. In this way the excess purchasing power is absorbed and would-be spenders are disappointed by unexpected price increases. (In the same way excess demand for labour will force up pay-rates.) The pressure of excess demand can be alleviated if extra goods are imported or fewer goods are exported, so that the gap is eliminated (partially) by an unexpected worsening in the current account balance of payments.

Why control inflation?

Why do governments seek to control inflation? Why have so many pursued disflationary policies on various occasions in the past twenty-five years? Inflation is certainly a period of high activity, high profits, apparent prosperity, and some groups are benefited much more obviously and numerously by inflation than other groups under deflation. Certainly the issue is less clear cut than with large-scale unemployment, and it is more likely that opinions will be split less unevenly between 'inflation good or bad' than 'unemployment good or bad'.

Economists suggest that the economic system will work better if inflation is controlled so that bottlenecks and shortages, which could impair production and even create temporary idleness (through fuel or raw material hold-ups, for example), are eliminated and greater flexibility obtains. If prices rise at different rates in different sectors, resources will be attracted to the most price flexible areas and the pattern of production could be seriously distorted. Night-clubs, casinos, and bars would form more attractive constructional projects than new factories, hospitals, and schools, while commercial investment would be more directed to increased holdings of stocks of goods to be unloaded later at higher prices and to real estate than to directly productive investment.

Furthermore, inflationary pressure and rising prices could destroy the incentive to save, as rising prices cut the real value of certain accumulated financial assets; and the falling propensity to save would aggravate the excess demand, besides lessening the availability of real resources for capital formation and the creation of new productive capacity. Some economists have argued that gently rising prices provide a stimulus to businessmen to invest, and that rising prices shift the distribution of income towards profits, more of which will be saved and directed towards new investment, thereby accelerating the growth in capacity to produce. However, rising money wages would ensure that this increase in the share of profits would be only temporary.

If inflationary pressure is controlled, this will help to avoid balance of payments deficits and crises which otherwise would have occurred. This will enable a fixed exchange-rate between domestic currency and foreign currencies (and gold) to be preserved, and this is an end of economic policy in many countries.

Inflationary pressure must be controlled in order to preserve a stable price level, which is often stated as a major aim of any government's economic and social policy. However, it should be noted that rising prices can alter the distribution of income between various groups. Those living on fixed incomes, such as rentiers and pensioners, and those whose money incomes are infrequently adjusted upwards, experience declines in real incomes and living standards, while those whose money incomes rise faster than prices, such as profit recipients and members of effectively militant trade unions, gain by higher real incomes. Furthermore, rising prices cut the real value of any debt expressed in monetary terms so that creditors lose and debtors gain. Again, a distributional point appears, whose desirability or otherwise will depend on whether one is a creditor or debtor. Social and ethical points enter inevitably into the control of inflation so that a government whose support comes from rentiers will tackle inflation more resolutely to the point of excessive unemployment, while a government of debtors will be relatively unconcerned.

Modest price inflation, it has been argued, should be checked to prevent it accelerating into rapid price inflation and ultimately into hyper-inflation, in which inordinately large price increases take place, money loses its value, and particular economic groups find their financial asset positions wiped out. The fabric of society may be subjected to strain from social unrest and the unfairness will be clear to all.

In general, governments have felt that inflation should be checked, but from very mixed motives both economic and otherwise. This provides a useful example of the way in which both economic and non-economic elements enter into policy-making, and helps to explain why disagreements about policies occur. Does a critic think a policy is bad (i) because he does not agree with its aims or ends (which is very much a matter of differing social, political, and ethical beliefs) or (ii) because he does not agree with its methods (which is much more a difference of opinion about the operation of the economic system and is very much an economic matter)?

Policies to control inflation

Assuming that a government is faced with a situation of excess demand inflation which it wishes to eliminate, the basic aim of its economic policies must be to try to eliminate the excess demand by cutting spending plans in the short run and by encouraging increased output in the future by higher productivity and increased efficiency of factors of production, which is more of a long-run concern. Usually the need to control is so urgent that cutting spending plans bears the full weight of policy.

Monetary policy in inflationary circumstances is simply described as 'dearer credit, less readily available' together with more stringent hire-purchase regulations, or the reverse of the monetary policy set out earlier to handle excessive unemployment. The monetary authorities should increase the rate of rediscount (Bank Rate) which will move up the short-term interest rate structure *pari passu* and have more limited effects on longer-term rates. Further, the stock of money must be contracted to lessen the availability of finance, while reserve requirements for banks may be increased thereby diminishing their ability to lend. However, the intensity of the credit squeeze on the supply of finance may be diminished if increased interest rates attract foreign funds into the domestic monetary system. Once again the impression is that domestic spending in an inflationary period is unlikely to be sensitive to monetary stringency unless industrial investment is heavily dependent on bank finance (as in Japan), and that it would be ill-advised to rely on monetary policy alone to control inflation.

As planned spending rises in an inflationary situation, governmental transactions may lessen the impact, for some categories of public spending fall as activity rises (for example, unemployment pay), while rising tax yields will damp down the transmission of increased spending through increased incomes to further spending increases. These stabilising effects will be enhanced if, as money incomes rise, the income tax system levies higher marginal rates (i.e. it is progressive). Discretionary fiscal policy to check inflationary pressure comprises a blend of reduced public spending and of increased tax rates to cause planned spending to fall in real terms.

On the face of it nothing would seem easier than to cut governmental spending until one realises how much is inevitable, given current social, defence, and educational policies, and hence the acute political difficulties involved in any cuts. If cuts are made, it may take time before they become effective as existing commitments have to be honoured. It may seem an easy short-run solution to delay or cut back a road-construction programme or an educational programme, but in the long run growth may well be impaired as transport bottlenecks build up or as shortages of skilled labour mount. Often, indeed, governmental spending appears sacrosanct so that in an inflationary situation although it does its best to prevent it rising in real terms, it has to turn to increased taxation as the main fiscal weapon to check planned spending.

The primary effects of tax rate increases appear straightforward enough as the opposite of tax rate cuts discussed earlier, but before discussing them it is important to note the possibility of certain secondary effects which seem to weigh more heavily in an inflationary situation. Increased taxation may lessen the incentive to take risks and to work hard by lessening the real rewards so that output might well decline. Certainly higher taxation on expenditure will increase prices in order to depress planned spending in real terms, but this may well provoke demands for higher pay, thereby perhaps accelerating the cost-inflation spiral. If extra taxation bears predominantly on the richer households, the distribution of disposable income will become more equal, and this should increase the propensity to consume, which would be inflationary. In so far as increased taxation cuts undistributed profits (company savings) this may well check productive investment and impair longer-run growth.

Increases in direct tax rates such as income tax, national insurance contributions, or profits tax, will lower the size of disposable income accruing to households from a given national income, so that consumption expenditure will fall in real terms unless increased taxes are paid at the expense of saving. Such increases will be more efficacious if they are levied on those with high marginal propensities to consume (the poor) rather than those with low marginal propensities to consume (the rich) even though the social aspect of such measures may be abhorrent to many. Higher profits tax, besides affecting the distribution of dividends, may cause undistributed profits to be lower and hence investment of firms to decline. Some countries (e.g. Sweden) have at times gone so far as to tax investment projects in an effort to postpone planned investment spending.

Higher tax rates on expenditure will increase the prices of products, and thus lower the real purchasing power of a given disposable income in monetary terms, so that aggregate consumption spending will be decreased in real terms. In this way excess demand will be reduced so that these tax increases can be viewed as disinflationary even though they raise prices and may provoke pay claims.

Fiscal policy clearly works on the flow of planned spending more directly than monetary policy but, as pointed out in remedying unemployment, may lack flexibility and speed because of political systems or administrative difficulties, and again cuts in governmental spending of the same size as increases in taxation will reduce the inflationary gap to a greater extent, but are harder to achieve.

Policy problems

Once again it must be asked what is the objective of disinflationary policy. Surely the elimination of excess demand both for products and labour. But how big is the inflationary gap? It is the difference between planned spending and maximum output at current prices; it is the residual gap between two estimates. Hence its size is virtually a matter of guesswork, or 'guestimating' if we wish to be polite, and as it is eliminated in realised terms we never know if we are right. It is thus very difficult to say precisely how much policy intervention is needed: rather a government has to proceed in steps. Because of lags in the presentation of statistics in the formation of policy, and in the response of the economy to policy measures, restrictive policies may well be kept in force for longer than strictly necessary so that the economy may be pushed into less than full employment by public economic policies.

Given the discretionary fiscal policy outlined above it is reasonable to expect the government's budget to move into surplus so that it is in a position to repay some of its previous borrowings (the National Debt). If privately held debt is repurchased, there is a real danger that the recipients will use the proceeds to buy more goods rather than other financial assets so that planned spending would rise. If bank-held debt is repurchased, the banks could find they now have resources to lend to would-be spenders. Hence it would be best to retire central-bank-held debt if at all possible. As a budget surplus materialises, and before it is used to reduce the national debt, money balances will move from private sector ownership to public sector ownership at the central bank, so that the stock of money in private hands declines and the credit squeeze is reinforced. Repurchase of private or commercial-bank-held debt would reverse this, as the balances would move back to the private sector in exchange for government bills or bonds. It is important to bear in mind the inter-linked aspects of fiscal policy, debt management, and their monetary effects, a subject which is discussed at length in another volume in this series.[2]

Cost inflation

The above disinflationary policy suggestions have been designed to tackle excess demand inflation with the hope that, once excess demand has been eliminated, the price level would cease to rise. However, a characteristic of the modern world has been the persistent rise in prices and pay despite the elimination of excess demand and the maintenance of an unemployment rate which some have felt to be on the high side. The essential elements in the cost-inflationary spiral have been analysed elsewhere (Chapter 7), where it was felt that the essence of the process was the refusal of each economic interest to accept a cut in what it believed to be its just reward, a refusal to be squeezed. General money wage increases (from individual wage–wage inflation) in excess of productivity increases bring rising average costs which squeeze profit margins until firms raise prices. Real wages are then squeezed by the rise in the cost of living, and fresh pay claims are then submitted, and so on.

Control of this process would seem to be very difficult unless a government is prepared to risk electoral suicide and create consider-able unemployment to damp down labour's bargaining strength and the ease with which businessmen can pass on higher costs to price increases. There does seem to be evidence that the annual increase in

2. G. H. Peters, *Private and Public Finance*.

pay is lower the higher is the unemployment percentage, but the underlying economic mechanisms are still open to dispute.

On the assumption that this requisite degree of unemployment (perhaps of the order of 4–5 per cent) is undesirable, other lines of attack must be selected. The social habit of expecting increases in pay regardless of particular and general economic circumstances, to which most of us are addicts, must be broken. If I get a pay rise of 10 per cent and no one else does, that's in order; but everyone thinks like this, so that general pay rises of 10 per cent materialise when output per man has risen 3 per cent, and everyone is then surprised that prices rise by some 7 per cent. A group may realise this process, and the apparent silliness of seeking 10 per cent to gain 3 per cent in real terms. But can it afford not to seek 10 per cent, when others will, in a system of free collective bargaining?

Hopes that the wider spread of economic education would help to break this habit have proved vain, as have the hopes placed on a voluntary incomes policy. Individual and national interests clearly clash in these matters, as well as the feeling that one cannot trust the other chap not to get a jump ahead if you voluntarily exercise restraint. Compulsory incomes policy and a national board to decide pay claims (and adjudicate on price increases) would seem the only way out of the impasse—if you want to eliminate cost inflation. Yet in a democracy it will be well-nigh impossible to impose such a board with effective sanctions unless it commands wide acceptance; otherwise right-wing supporters of *laissez-faire* can be expected to join hands with trade unions in condemning this as 'economic fascism'.

Perhaps we must realise that in current societies as we know them the simultaneous achievement of various objectives may well be impossible. Attainment of desired levels of employment may be incompatible with a stable price level and free collective bargaining, or with the maintenance of a fixed exchange rate for international transactions. We have to sort out priorities and trade off one set of objectives against another.

International uses

For example, another use of the macroeconomic analysis developed in this book is the correction of balance of payments deficits which are causing an undesired loss of foreign exchange reserves and threatening the stability of the exchange rate. Dear money and restrictive fiscal policies are then imposed to cause payments abroad to fall relative to receipts from abroad.

First, higher interest rates may attract fresh short-term capital funds from abroad or check the outflow of such funds, thereby temporarily strengthening the balance of payments. Secondly, monetary stringency and deflationary fiscal policy will check planned domestic spending so that, if exports remain unchanged, output and import purchases will fall and the balance of payments will improve at the cost of a check to home output and an increase in unemployment. A government committed to full employment and a fixed exchange-rate faces a dilemma which may be postponed somewhat if other countries and the International Monetary Fund lend it foreign exchange for a temporary period. A government's position may be eased if manufacturers whose home sales have fallen react by tackling export markets more vigorously and sell more abroad. This will cause output and employment to be higher than otherwise, and the expansion in exports will more than offset the increased imports associated with this higher output. Some economies have responded strongly like this (for example, West Germany, Italy, Japan) whereas others (for example, Britain) have not.

For the economies whose reactions bring this awkward choice between full employment and the balance of payments, priorities must be sorted out. Further it would suggest that where we have *two* objectives—full employment and external equilibrium in the balance of payments—it will not always be possible to achieve them both with a one-policy weapon (monetary and fiscal being regarded as one weapon). Two-policy weapons will usually be needed: (i) monetary and fiscal policy working on planned spending for full employment, and (ii) a policy of variations in the exchange rate for equilibrium in the balance of payments or a policy of variations in trade and payments restrictions for the same end.

Summary

This chapter has indicated the ways in which the macroeconomic analysis developed earlier in this book can be used to try to manage the economy. Knowing which way to kick the economy is straightforward, but how hard and when are more difficult. Nevertheless, we do have the ability to eradicate mass unemployment and to curb excessive demand, and to lessen major instabilities which have so plagued economies in the past; but to claim that instability can be avoided completely is vain and extravagant. Similarly, to list various objectives and to believe they can all be met simultaneously may prove a dangerous delusion. The economy can be managed with some success, but as with management of a company it is a mixture of both science and art, or flair.

PART TWO

Chapter 9

International Trade and the Multiplier

Introduction

No treatment of macroeconomics can neglect international economic transactions and, in particular, the ways in which these impinge on income and production. In Britain everyone is aware of its dependence on imported raw materials and foodstuffs, of growing imports of manufactures and of sales of British goods and services to other countries to pay for our imports.

In Figure 9.1 are presented two portions of British historical experience. In the top portion, we have plotted exports of goods and services (including income from abroad) and gross national product at current prices for the period 1950 to 1968. Imports have been omitted as they roughly coincide with the export curve. In this period, U.K. gross national product at current prices expanded by 213 per cent, whereas exports rose by 180 per cent and imports by 206 per cent. Exports of goods and services as a share of gross national product fell from 32 per cent in 1950 to 29 per cent in 1968, while imports of goods and services sagged from 30 per cent in 1950 to 29 per cent in 1968.

Secondly, in the lower portion of Figure 9.1 we have plotted net national income, exports of goods and net services and net income from abroad, and merchandise imports for the period 1890–1913—all at current prices. The gap between the export and the import curves represents the current account balance of payments surplus. In 1890 exports as a share of net national income were 33 per cent, falling to 29 per cent in 1900 and then soaring to 39 per cent in 1913. The behaviour of imports was less volatile as a share of net national income they amounted to 26 per cent in 1890 and 1900, rising thereafter to 29 per cent in 1913.

International economic transactions, such as these, are (and have

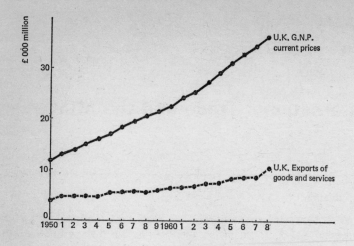

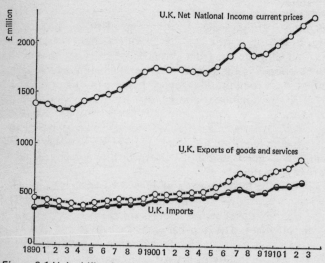

Figure 9.1 United Kingdom income and trade

been) vital to the economic life of the British economy and any macroeconomics text must pay attention to them.

How, then, should we incorporate these current international economic transactions into our analysis? What difference will they make to equilibrium income? What will happen to the multiplier? These are some of the questions which this chapter aims to answer.

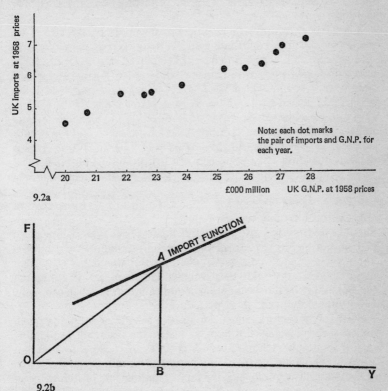

Note: each dot marks
the pair of imports and G.N.P. for
each year.

9.2a

9.2b

Figure 9.2 (*a*) Imports and output, United Kingdom 1958–69; (*b*) The import function

Foreign trade and income

Exports of goods and services X form another category of spending on a country's output, as well as consumption and investment spending. They represent the rest of the world's purchases of the country's output and for the purposes of this analysis will be taken as determined autonomously as far as the supplying country is concerned.[1]

Imports of goods and services F are the country's purchases of the other countries' output and are one category of spending which does not go on to generate incomes in the purchasing country. They form a *leakage* from the flow of spending in the importing country and contribute to the flow of spending in other countries as their exports.

What forces will determine the size of import purchases? If we assume constant prices at home and abroad, then as output rises or falls so we would expect purchases of imported raw materials, fuels, and semi-finished goods to rise and fall likewise. Again, higher real output and income will mean higher purchases of imported food-stuffs and finished goods and services. Hence a close direct relationship can be expected between the level of output and the level of import purchases at constant prices, which we could call the import function or the propensity to import schedule. In Figure 9.2a is depicted the close association between British import purchases and gross national product at constant (1958) prices or real national product.

Another factor influencing import purchases is the prices of imported goods and services as compared with domestic prices. Should import prices rise relative to home prices then with a given real output we would expect that expenditure would switch from imported goods to home goods wherever this was possible, so that import purchases would fall in volume. However, we are ruling out this possibility by our assumption of constant prices, which can really be justified only in the short period.

Many other factors influencing import purchases should be mentioned such as changes in popular tastes, the changing availability of raw materials at home, new discoveries of cheap raw materials abroad, the changing pace and nature of economic advance and development. They influence the input requirements of industry and the availability and demand for goods. Attention must also be directed to changes in the intensity of import restrictions and protective duties and of the development of customs unions. They are listed to show that the economist must be very careful when he proceeds as we are now doing and takes import purchases at constant prices as dependent in a definite way on national income and

1. Clearly (i) the level of world real income and production, and (ii) the relationship between the prices of the exports of the country concerned and world prices will be very important determining factors.

output. It is reasonable to do this, only if we are prepared to keep in mind the various influences whose effects we are assuming unchanged.

The propensity to import

In Figure 9.2b we have the behaviour relationship between import purchases (F) and national output or income (Y) at constant prices, which is known as the *import function* or the *propensity to import schedule*. This enables us to say what the level of import purchases will be if we know the level of output. Furthermore, as incomes and output rise, so will imports, while a fall in output will bring a fall in import purchases.

At any point on the schedule the ratio of imports to output $(F \div Y)$ is known as the *average propensity to import* and in Figure 9.2b is $AB \div OB$ or the slope of the line OA. If output changes, the ratio of the change in imports $(\triangle F)$ to the change in output $(\triangle Y)$ is known as *the marginal propensity of import* $\left(= \dfrac{\triangle F}{\triangle Y} \right)$, and is represented by the slope of the schedule at the point in question. The marginal propensity to import will indicate how much of a change in our activity will be transmitted to other economies through variations in our purchases of their goods. Likewise our export sales will depend on the rest of the world's propensity to import our goods and services. The rest of the world's import function of our goods is our export function.

For our subsequent analysis we assume a straight-line import function or propensity to import schedule, which will have a constant slope and hence a constant marginal propensity to import. However, there is some evidence that in practice we might expect the marginal propensity to import to rise as real incomes rise and households exhibit a growing appetite for foreign goods and holidays abroad.

Imports and exports fit into national income accounting as we demonstrated earlier (Chapter 1):

National expenditure at factor cost $\equiv$ national income
$$X + C + I - F \equiv Y$$

where X, C, I, F are all valued at market prices and Y is measured (as usual) at factor cost. The relationship above is in realised terms and is hence an accounting identity.

From this relationship we can find the counterpart to the *current account balance of payments* which is export sales (X) minus import purchases (F).

$$X + C + I - F \equiv Y$$
$$X - F \equiv Y - C - I$$
$$X - F \equiv Y - (C + I)$$

Hence the current account is equivalent to actual national income (net of import content) minus actual domestic spending on consumption and investment (at market price), or as income minus domestic absorption. A surplus means that income exceeds absorption; a deficit that absorption exceeds income.

Table 9.1

(1)	(2)	(3)	(4)	(5)	(6)	(7) Planned spending =	(8) Planned leakages =	(9) Planned injections =
If *Y	*then* *C	*then* *S	*then* *F	*I	*X	*C+*I+*X−*F	*S+*F	*I+*X
350	330	20	70	80	90	430	90	170
400	370	30	80	80	90	460	110	170
450	410	40	90	80	90	490	130	170
500	450	50	100	80	90	520	150	170
550	490	60	110	80	90	550	170	170
600	530	70	120	80	90	580	190	170
650	570	80	130	80	90	610	210	170
700	610	90	140	80	90	640	230	170

Note: Values for *C and *S have been derived from consumption function $*C = 50 + 0.8 *Y$ and its associated savings function $*S = -50 + 0.2 *Y$, while values for *F have been derived from import function $*F = 0.2 *Y$. The same functions are in Figure 9.3.

Determination of equilibrium income

The introduction of international transactions involves exports of goods and services (X) which are treated as an autonomous spending item or injection (like investment), and imports of goods and services (F) which are handled as a leakage (like savings) and are assumed to depend on income, as discussed above. This assumption of a given import function along with a given consumption function will enable us to say what the level of income will be when investment spending and export sales are both given at particular figures, or will enable us to answer the following question: What level of income (or output) at factor cost will generate sufficient planned savings and imports to equal planned investment and exports so that total leakages from this flow of income and expenditure are just matched by injections into it?

In short, what level of $*Y$ (planned production) will satisfy the equilibrium conditions? We have:

Planned spending at factor cost = planned output at factor cost

$$*I + *C + *X - *F = *Y$$
$$*I + *X = *Y - *C + *F$$
$$*I + *X = *S + *F$$

Planned injections = planned leakages

Clearly if $*I$ and $*X$ are given, while $*C$, $*S$, $*F$ each depend in a definite way on $*Y$ (the consumption, savings, and import functions), then either of the equilibrium conditions reduces to an equation in one unknown, $*Y$. This is now demonstrated in various ways.

Tabular version

Let us assume a given amount of planned investment (80) and given export sales (90), a given consumption function and a given import function which are set out arithmetically in Table 9.1, while columns (1) and (3) represent the associated savings function. At each income level, planned or intended spending at factor cost is calculated by adding investment and exports to the appropriate amount of planned consumption expenditure and subtracting the appropriate value of planned import purchases to yield column (7). Once again, spending plans on consumption, investment, exports, and imports are realised.

Furthermore, additional columns representing planned injections and planned leakages at each level of income (or output) are added. At income of 550 consumption is 490, and planned spending at factor cost is 490 + 80 (investment) + 90 (exports) - 110 (imports) = 550. This is the determinate equilibrium income level. For planned output or expected income at factor cost is 550, and will just be matched by planned spending at factor cost, so that an equilibrium position will result. If Y was less than 550, say 500, then planned spending would exceed it at 520, thus causing Y to rise until 550 was attained: if Y was greater than 550, say 600, then planned spending would be 580, thus inducing a fall in Y until 550 was reached.

The same conclusions follow if planned injections are compared with planned leakages. At Y of 550 planned savings are 60, while planned import purchases are 110, making a total of planned leakages of 170 which just matches total planned injections of exports (90) and investment (80). Below that level of Y, planned injections exceed leakages so that the flow of income and expenditure rises to 550, while above that figure leakages exceed injections so that the flow slackens to 550.

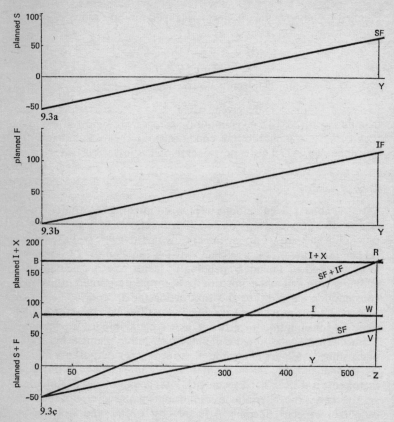

Figure 9.3 Equilibrium income with trade

At this equilibrium position, where overall planned injections equal leakages, it will be noted that, while exports are 90, imports are 110, so that there is a current account balance of payments deficit of 20, whereas planned domestic investment spending exceeds saving by 20 to match this deficit. There is no inherent necessity for the equilibrium income position to be accompanied by equality of exports and imports and a zero current account position. If exports are fixed at 90, imports would only equal exports at an income position of 450, to attain which it would be necessary for investment to be 40 to provide planned injections of 130 to match the planned leakages of 130 at this income position.

Alternatively if planned investment is fixed at 80, it would match planned savings of 80 at an income of 650, and planned exports would need to be 130 to match planned imports and provide planned injections of 210 to match planned leakages of 210 at this income position. Hence only certain pairs of values of planned investment and planned exports will yield a current account balance of zero together with equilibrium income.

Diagrammatic version

These relationships and analysis are illustrated diagrammatically in Figure 9.3 where the savings function is plotted in part (a), the import function in section (b), and the combined import and savings function in (c). The latter is obtained by adding to the savings function at each level of income the amount of imports purchased, so that at any level of income the vertical distance between the combined savings plus imports schedule (or 'leakage' function) and the savings function is the value of imports. For example, in part (c), at income OZ, RV is planned imports, ZV planned saving, and ZR total planned leakages. The given amount of planned investment (80) is represented by OA and a horizontal line AI is drawn at this level, while the given export sales (90) are indicated by AB and BR is drawn horizontally to show the combined value of (170) of exports and investment or planned injections at each level of income. The equilibrium income position is at R with income OZ and planned leakages equal to planned injections. Below OZ planned leakages fall short of planned injections so that income rises, while above OZ leakages exceed injections so that income falls. Imports are VR, while exports are $WR = AB$, so that the current account balance of payments deficit is indicated by VW, which is also the excess of investment $ZW (= OA)$ over savings ZV. This form of diagram is the more useful for indicating the equilibrium position in terms of planned leakages and injections when we move from the simple economy and incorporate trading and governmental activities. The diagram using the consumption function becomes complicated and can even be misleading when international and governmental transactions are added to it. Hence the latter is not presented here or later.

Stability

It has been shown in various ways how the assumptions of given planned investment and exports together with a given propensity to import schedule and a given propensity to consume (or save) schedule produce an equilibrium income position at which planned spending at factor cost equals planned production at factor cost, or at which planned injections equal planned leakages. In the examples given above, if the value of Y exceeded or fell short of the equilibrium, there were forces at work to cause it to converge on this level, so that it was a stable position in the sense that a disturbance from equilibrium would unleash forces leading back to the original position.

It will be recalled that in Chapter 3 a stable equilibrium resulted if the slope of the planned spending line was less than one. Stability required that a given change in $*Y$ of 100 should bring about a change in planned spending of less than 100 in the simple closed economy case. Otherwise a rise in planned output above the equilibrium level would generate a greater rise in planned spending, which would lead to a yet greater rise in output, and to a divergent process.

With the introduction of international transactions the principle remains much the same. Now the requirement is that a change in output *at factor cost* should bring about a smaller change in planned spending *at factor cost*. If investment and exports are unchanged, a given change in Y will cause planned spending at factor cost to alter by the planned change in consumption *minus* any change in imports. This amounts to requiring that the marginal propensity to consume minus the marginal propensity to import should be less than one.[2]

In a wider sense international economic transactions increase the likelihood of disturbances. Planned export sales can alter as well as planned investment, and the import function could shift as well as the consumption function. This now brings us to the multiplier in this wider environment. It will be recalled from Chapter 4 that a change in planned investment led to a multiple change in output and income between the old and the new equilibrium positions. Will this relationship still hold?

2. Suppose $\triangle Y$ of 100 brings $\triangle C$ of $100c$ and $\triangle F$ of $100f$, where c and f are the marginal propensities to consume and import respectively. Planned spending at factor cost changes by $100c - 100f = 100(c - f)$. Stability requires that $100 > 100(c - f)$ or that $(c - f) < 1$.

The foreign-trade multiplier

What will happen to the equilibrium income position if either investment or exports change? For example, suppose planned exports rise by 20 to 110 within the context of Table 9.1 (p. 178). This will cause planned injections to rise to 190, which match planned leakages of 190 at Y of 600. Alternatively, this would make planned

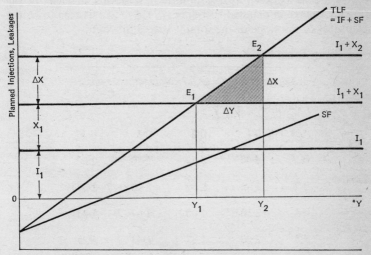

Figure 9.4 The foreign-trade multiplier

spending corresponding to Y of 600 change from 580 to 600. 600 is then the equilibrium income level as compared with 550. The multiplier effect, which is change in income between two equilibrium positions ($\triangle Y = 600 - 550 = 50$) divided by the primary change in planned spending ($\triangle A = \triangle X = 20$), is 2·5. Although the savings function has not changed, there has been added an imports leakage from the flow of spending which lessens the amount of planned spending being passed on to create new incomes. This relationship can now be investigated graphically and algebraically.

A straight-line savings function and a straight-line import function are assumed, with a constant margin propensity to save $\left(s = \dfrac{\triangle S}{\triangle Y}\right)$, and a constant marginal propensity to import $\left(f = \dfrac{\triangle F}{\triangle Y}\right)$. They are added together to yield a straight line total leakage function whose slope is the sum of these marginal propensities $(= s + f)$.[3] A given amount of planned investment (I_1) and a given value of exports (X_1) yields an equilibrium income position of Y_1, as shown in Figure 9.4. Let us suppose that export sales then rise to X_2 where $\triangle X = X_2 - X_1$, and raises the planned injections line to $I_1 + X_2$ so that a fresh equilibrium income position is established at Y_2 with $\triangle Y = Y_2 - Y_1$. The multiplier which is change in income as between two equilibrium positions divided by the primary change in planned spending $(\triangle Y \div \triangle X)$, is seen to be the reciprocal of the slope of the total leakages function.

Table 9.2

a. Values of multiplier for combinations s and f

$$\text{Multiplier} = \frac{1}{s + f}$$

$f \downarrow$ \ $s \rightarrow$	0·1	0·2	0·3	0·4
0·1	5·00	3·33	2·50	2·00
0·2	3·33	2·50	2·00	1·67
0·3	2·50	2·00	1·67	1·43
0·4	2·00	1·67	1·43	1·25

b. *Multiplier reactions for different stimuli*

	Case 1		Case 2		Case 3	
f	0·2		0·45		0·05	
s	0·3		0·05		0·20	
Multiplier	2·00		2·00		4·00	
	(a)	(b)	(a)	(b)	(a)	(b)
$\triangle X$	100	0	100	0	100	0
$\triangle I$	0	100	0	100	0	100
$\triangle Y$	200	200	200	200	400	400
$\triangle C$	140	140	190	190	320	320
$\triangle S$	60	60	10	10	80	80
$\triangle F$	40	40	90	90	20	20
$\triangle B$ of P	+60	−40	+10	−90	+80	−20

3. For its slope is $\dfrac{\text{change in total leakages}}{\text{change in income}} = \dfrac{\triangle S + \triangle F}{\triangle Y} = \dfrac{\triangle S}{\triangle Y} + \dfrac{\triangle F}{\triangle Y} = s + f.$

For $\dfrac{\triangle X}{\triangle Y}$ = slope of total leakages function = marginal propensity to save + marginal propensity to import = $s + f$

So that the multiplier = $\dfrac{\triangle Y}{\triangle X} = \dfrac{1}{s+f} = \dfrac{1}{1-c+f}$

(since here $MPS + MPC = 1$)

Precisely the same formula would have been derived if we had let investment change instead of exports or, indeed, any change in autonomous spending such as a shift in the propensity to consume schedule. It will be seen that the denominator is now larger by the addition of the marginal propensity to import so that the multiplier is now smaller than in the no-trade case for a given marginal propensity to save.

Let us derive the formula algebraically from the requirement that between two equilibrium positions the change in planned spending at factor cost must equal the change in planned output at factor cost, and let us assume planned investment changes but planned exports remain constant (i.e. $\triangle X = 0$).

Change in planned spending = change in planned output

$$\triangle *I + \triangle *C - \triangle *F = \triangle *Y$$
$$\text{but } \triangle *C = c\triangle *Y$$
$$\triangle *F = f\triangle *Y$$
$$\therefore \ \triangle *I + c\triangle *Y - f\triangle *Y = \triangle *Y$$
$$\triangle *I = (1-c+f)\triangle *Y$$

We have the multiplier = $\dfrac{\triangle *Y}{\triangle *I} = \dfrac{1}{1-c+f} = \dfrac{1}{s+f}$

Multiplier patterns

Table 9.2a provides values for the multiplier for different combinations of the marginal propensity to save and the marginal propensity to import while in part (b) the reactions of different economies are studied in relation to (i) rise in exports of 100 and (ii) rise in investment of 100. Case 1 might be taken as typical of a rich country with a high marginal propensity to save and an average involvement in trade. Case 2 is typical of a poor underdeveloped country, producing food and raw materials and trading them for manufactures, with a very low marginal propensity to save and a high involvement in trade. Case 3 could indicate a largely self-sufficient and inward-looking economy with fairly high standards of living.

Note particularly the different income reactions of 1 and 2 compared with 3, and the widely differing balance of payments reactions of all three. For example, on balance of payments grounds 3 can afford an investment-led boom far more easily than 2, but on the other hand if 2 and 3 have balance of payments difficulties, a given cut in imports of 90 can be achieved in 2 by a much smaller cut in investment and incomes than in 3 (100 and 200 in 2 against 450 and 1,800 in 3, respectively). The temptation for 3 to indulge in trade restrictions will be very great.

International fluctuations

This analysis indicates that changes in income and output can come about not only through fluctuations in investment but also through fluctuations in export proceeds, and that fluctuations in each will bring about fluctuations in imports. Imports, however, are some other countries' exports so that variations in activity in an economy will be transmitted thus to other countries and if the economy is a large one it may have significant influences on their activities. Furthermore, it indicates that if a country reduces its investment spending, its income and imports will fall and its current account balance of payments improve, exports remaining unchanged. If, however, imports were autonomously determined, unrelated at all to incomes, so that f was zero, the multiplier would become $\frac{1}{s}$ or $\frac{1}{1-c}$.

In the previous chapters one main source of fluctuations in income and output was to be seen in fluctuations in investment, but the introduction of trading relations has brought a fresh possibility that fluctuations in income, or instability in domestic economic life, can arise for external reasons as a country's export sales vary. This, indeed, will be more important for a given change in exports, the larger is the ratio of exports to national income, and historically it has been a major cause of instability in those countries which export a high proportion (say, above 20 per cent) of their output. For some economies the causes of their trade cycles may have to be sought in international economic forces rather than domestically.

Again, if a boom arises through rising exports bringing rising incomes, our analysis indicates that the rise in planned injections (in this case the increase in exports) will be matched by a rise in planned leakages in the new equilibrium position. This will be composed of a rise in savings and a rise in imports so that the increase in imports will fall short of the increase in exports. For the change in injections is entirely accounted for by the change in exports, while the equal

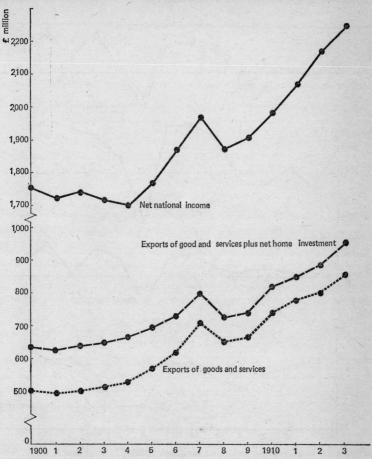

Figure 9.5 United Kingdom 1900–13. National income and exports

change in leakages is composed of changes in savings as well as imports. Hence the balance of payments on current account will improve—unless the marginal propensity to save had been zero.

Had the boom arisen for domestic reasons (rising home investment) the balance of payments situation would have worsened as exports remained unchanged and imports rose. On the other hand, if a slump arose because of a decline in exports, imports would fall less and the balance of payments would worsen. However, where declining home investment was producing the depression in income,

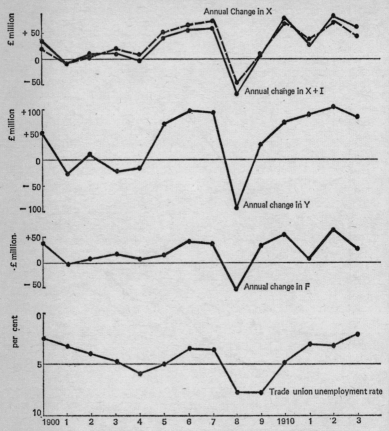

Figure 9.6 The multiplier in United Kingdom 1900–13. Note that *X, I, F,* and *Y* are all at current values

imports would fall and, with exports unchanged, the balance of payments would improve.

These differing patterns of balance of payments behaviour between export and investment induced booms and slumps can be very important for economic policy in differing types of economy.

Table 9.3

Year	(1) $\triangle X$	(2) $\triangle I$	(3) $\triangle X + \triangle I$	(4) $\triangle Y$	(5) $\triangle F$	(6) Trade union unemployment percentage
			£ million			
1900	+33	+16	+49	+50	+38	2·5
1901	−10	+1	−9	−23	−1	3·5
1902	+6	+4	+10	+13	+6	4·0
1903	+17	−5	+12	−23	+14	4·7
1904	+4	−7	−3	−13	+8	6·0
1905	+53	−11	+42	+72	+14	5·0
1906	+67	−10	+57	+98	+43	3·6
1907	+71	−13	+58	+92	+38	3·7
1908	−51	−23	−78	−91	−53	7·8
1909	+13	−2	+11	+32	+32	7·7
1910	+73	+6	+79	+77	+54	4·7
1911	+31	−3	+28	+92	+2	3·0
1912	+75	+6	+81	+105	+65	3·2
1913	+40	+21	+61	+84	+24	2·1

Notes:

(i) $\triangle X$ refers to change in value of exports as compared with previous year. Likewise for $\triangle I$, $\triangle Y$, and $\triangle F$.

(ii) Values are at actual prices, not at constant prices.

(iii) These figures are displayed in Figure 9.6.

Source: *Abstract of British Historical Statistics*, ed. B. R. Mitchell and P. Deane, Cambridge University Press.

An historical illustration

The foreign trade multiplier's operation can be suggested from the material presented in Table 9.3 and Figures 9.5 and 9.6. Figure 9.5 presents the course of net national income (at current prices) as compared with the behaviour of exports of goods and services and net domestic investment over the period 1900–13. Both curves exhibit the similar patterns which the multiplier analysis would lead us to expect. In Figure 9.6 annual changes in injections (i.e. exports *plus* investment) are compared with annual changes in net national income for the United Kingdom over the period 1900–13. It will be seen that they are closely related as the multiplier effect would predict. Further, it is clear that the major source of changes in injections is provided by changes in exports. The behaviour of changes in imports is broadly similar to changes in incomes.

Although we have used money values of variables so that price variations are included as well as quantity variations, it is worth noting how closely the trade union unemployment percentage behaves in line with changes in the money value of national income. In this way the concept of the multiplier can be used to explain the impact on the British economy in this period of changes in injections. Calculations indicate that the size of the multiplier relating changes in injections and changes in national income (as we have defined them above) was in the range of 1·3 to 1·5. Furthermore, the ratio of average annual change in income to average annual change in exports, *plus* investment, works out at 1·5.

The *IS* curve again

Under the assumptions of given planned exports and given consumption and import schedules, it is possible to derive the *IS* curve which relates interest rates and the corresponding equilibrium income and output positions. To a given interest rate there will correspond, with a given investment schedule, a particular amount of planned investment. This will be sufficient with the above assumptions to provide a determinate equilibrium output position. If the rate of interest rises, planned investment spending will fall and income will fall to a fresh equilibrium position. The foreign-trade multiplier will operate exactly as in the closed economy case examined earlier (pp. 64–76). If the rate of interest falls, planned investment spending rises and equilibrium income will rise. The *IS* curve still slopes downwards but it has been derived under more complicated conditions. A rise in export sales, for example, would cause the whole *IS* curve to shift to the right.

Summary

This chapter has discussed the introduction of international economic relationships into the income flow analysis. Exports have been regarded as an injection into this flow of spending and imports regarded as a leakage. Furthermore, imports have been assumed to be determined by the level of output under the assumption of constant prices. This procedure has enabled us to find the determinate equilibrium income position by using the equilibrium conditions of either (i) planned spending at factor cost equalling planned output at factor cost, or (ii) planned injections equalling planned leakages. This equilibrium was shown to be stable if the marginal propensity to consume *minus* the marginal propensity to import was less than one.

The foreign trade multiplier by which some primary change in spending brought a particular change in income between two equilibrium positions has been examined together with patterns of response under different circumstances. The introduction of the import leakage has lessened the size of the multiplier for any given marginal propensity to consume as compared with the no-trade case.

Chapter 10

The Government and the Multiplier

Introduction

Economic transactions of central and local governments have grown in importance relative to national product over the past century, and are of such a size that we can no longer ignore them. For example, in many economies governmental current spending on goods and services exceeds 20 per cent of gross national product—in 1968 it was 21·2 per cent for the United Kingdom. Tax receipts exceed this proportion since they are used to finance such spending and to make transfer payments such as social security benefits and national debt interest. These, it will be recalled, are essentially a redistribution of income by taxation and disbursement to those entitled to receive such benefits. This chapter and its appendix will discuss the impact of governmental transactions on our macroeconomic system.

The British experience

In Figure 10.1 are presented the behaviour of U.K. tax receipts for the period 1958–68 and the behaviour of public authorities current spending on goods and services, as well as transfers of public-debt interest payments and current transfers to the personal sector (mainly social security and pension payments) for the same period. They are expressed in terms of actual monetary receipts and payments rather than in real terms.

A better impression of their importance for the economy can be gained if they are expressed as a percentage of gross national product at factor cost. Public current spending on goods and services as a percentage of gross national product amounted to 20 per cent on average for the period 1965–68, while interest payments amounted to 5 per cent. Current grants to the personal sector came to 9 per cent of gross national product. The size of transfer payments (14 per cent of gross national product) relative to public current spending (20 per cent) should be noted.

Taxes on income (including national insurance contributions) were as an average 20 per cent of gross national product for the years 1965–68, while net taxation on expenditure (including rates paid to local authorities) amounted to 15 per cent of gross national product. Taxation was thus financing (i) current public spending on goods and services, and (ii) transfer payments from one group to another. Indeed, 40 per cent of taxation receipts were being employed to effect transfers in one form or another from one group to

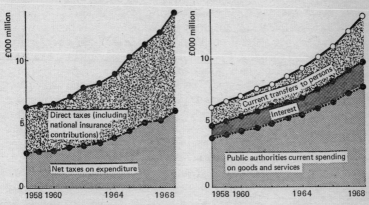

Figure 10.1 United Kingdom Public authorities 1958–68. Selected transactions at current values

another in these years. Hence the percentage of taxation to gross national product (35 per cent in 1965–68) gives a grossly exaggerated impression of the public sector's claims on real resources and goods and services.

These figures illustrate the importance of the public sector's share in the economic life of the British economy and the necessity for us to study the impact of government in macroeconomics.

The government and income

(i) Spending by the public authorities, whether for current or capital purposes, on goods and services (*G*) forms another category of spending as well as investment and consumption expenditure. It is treated as autonomously determined because it is subject to political decisions and it is independent of the level of income. (ii) Taxation is best divided into (*a*) taxation on expenditure or indirect taxation and (*b*) direct taxation on incomes.

(a) Taxation on expenditure (T_e) causes spending at market prices to exceed spending at factor cost and ensures that not all spending at market prices goes on to generate incomes. Some portion—the indirect tax payments—leaks away from the circular flow of spending and incomes. Subsidies to producers which cause the market price to be less than the factor cost of an article are treated as negative indirect taxes and T_e is net of such items.

(b) *Direct taxation* (T_d) forms a compulsory withdrawal of income from income-recipients. It causes disposable income (Y_d) which is available to recipients for spending or saving to be less than national income (Y). Once again it produces a leakage from the circular flow of incomes and spending by diminishing the size of income available for spending on consumer goods or for saving.

In most modern economies tax systems are such that with given tax rates the yields of tax revenues vary with the level of income and output at constant prices. The yields of taxation on expenditure (for example, excise duties on beer, wines, spirits, tobacco, petrol, and purchase taxes on durable consumer goods) will clearly rise as the flow of spending and output rise. Rising income will also swell the yields from direct taxation of personal incomes and company profits. It is, indeed, unusual to find much revenue being raised from taxes which are insensitive to changes in incomes. Hence it would make good economic sense, with given tax-rates, to develop two taxation functions, the first relating indirect taxation or taxation on expenditure to the level of income and the second linking direct taxation to the level of income.

(iii) *Transfer payments* made by the public authorities (B)—for example, old age pensions and sick pay or national debt interest—are payments to people, which do not correspond to the *current* production of any goods and services. However, the personal recipients of them treat them as (part of) their disposable income, and they make disposable income higher than it otherwise would have been. They are best treated in analysis as autonomously determined at some fixed level, although some portion may fall as income, output, and employment rise, such as unemployment relief payments.

Our national income and output accounting identities then become:

(i) National expenditure at factor cost $\equiv$ national income

$$I + C + G - T_e \equiv Y$$

(ii) Disposable income $\equiv$ national income $-$ direct taxation $+$ transfers

$$Y_d \equiv Y - T_d + B$$
$$whence\ Y \equiv Y_d + T_d - B$$
$$Y \equiv C + S + T_d - B \quad since\ Y_d \equiv C + S$$

(iii) Putting these together:

$$I + C + G - T_e \equiv C + S + T_d - B$$
$$I + G + B \equiv S + T_d + T_e$$

Realised injections $\equiv$ realised leakages

(iv) A balanced budget would imply for the government

$$G + B \equiv T_d + T_e$$

so that its borrowing requirement was zero

Taxation functions

(i) The indirect tax function relates receipts from indirect taxes (T_e) directly to the level of income and output (Y) at constant prices on the assumption that tax rates are unchanged. The form of the function is such that as output and income rise so do indirect tax yields, which also fall as income falls. The slope of the function which is the ratio of the change in indirect taxation to the change in output, or $\triangle T_e \div \triangle Y$, is known as the marginal propensity to pay indirect taxation.

A straight-line version of this function would be $T_e = 0.15Y$ which would imply that if national output (Y) was 1,000, then indirect tax receipts would be 150, or 15 per cent of national income and output. The marginal propensity to pay indirect taxation would be 0.15.

(ii) The direct taxation function relates receipts from direct taxation (T_d) to national income and output at constant prices (Y) with given tax rates. As income changes, so will proceeds from direct taxation change in the same direction. The slope of the schedule at any point is the ratio of the change in direct taxation to the change in national income and output, or $\triangle T_d \div \triangle Y$, and is known as the marginal propensity to pay direct taxation.

A straight slope version would be provided by $T_d = 0.2Y$, which would imply that 20 per cent of incomes was claimed by direct taxation with a marginal propensity to pay direct taxation of 0.2.

This would be an example of proportional taxation for it would mean that on average the tax rate was 20 per cent irrespective of the size of income. As the income of individuals rose, the tax rate would be unchanged. However, this is clearly not the case in many countries nowadays where a 'progressive' system of income taxation is in force. For here as an individual's income rises so the tax rate at the margin rises.

This would suggest that the direct tax function might bend upwards with an increasing slope, but for simplicity in the analysis we shall pass over this point and work with a linear form of the schedule. Indeed, we must remember that other forms of direct taxation, such as profits taxation or corporation taxation or social security taxation, are very probably proportional with given tax rates so that the influence of a progressively increasing income tax rate at the margin would be damped down in the case of direct taxation in aggregate.

Consumption and savings schedules

The national income accounting relationships have stated that national income is disposed of on direct taxes, consumer spending, and savings. We already have suggested that the level of direct taxes

Table 10.1

(1) $*Y$	(2) $*T_d$	(3) $*Y_d$	(4) $*C$	(5) $*S$
400	80	320	306	14
500	100	400	370	30
600	120	480	434	46
700	140	560	498	62
800	160	640	562	78

Notes:

Direct taxation derived from $T_d = 0.2Y$

Consumption derived from $\quad C = 50 + 0.8Y_d$ with m.p.c. $= 0.8$

Savings derived from $\quad\quad S = -50 + 0.2Y_d$ with m.p.s. $= 0.2$

Adjusted consumption schedule can be deduced as $C = 50 + 0.64Y$

Adjusted savings schedule can be deduced as $\quad\quad S = -50 + 0.16Y$

For $Y_d = Y - T_d = Y - 0.2Y = 0.8Y$

Substitute $Y_d = 0.8Y$ into the consumption function $C = 50 + 0.8Y_d$
  to yield $\quad C = 50 + (0.8)(0.8Y)$
  whence $\quad C = 50 + 0.64Y$

(The reader should derive the adjusted savings schedule)

depends on the level of national income and (in Chapter 2) we developed the propensity to consume schedule and the propensity to save schedule, under which households disposed of their incomes on consumption and savings. Planned real consumption and planned saving depended on households' real *disposable income* which was the same as real *national income*. However, with the introduction of public transactions we have seen that national disposable income is equal to national income *minus* direct taxation *plus* transfers. A consumption function or propensity to consume schedule based on households' disposable incomes is no longer the same as one based on national income, and realism dictates that we relate planned consumption and saving to disposable income in the first instance.

However, we need to be able to make the transition from consumption dependent on disposable income in this propensity to consume schedule, to consumption dependent on national income for the purpose of finding the determinate income and output position. For we need to know how much planned consumer spending will be generated by any particular level of planned national output, since our equilibrium requirement is that planned spending at factor cost should equal planned production at factor cost.

This is shown in Table 10.1 where columns (1) and (2) represent the direct tax schedule and column (3) is disposable income, obtained by subtracting direct taxes from national income. For simplicity we assume transfers are zero. Columns (3) and (4) represent the propensity to consume schedule and columns (3) and (5) the propensity to save schedule. Note that (i):

Disposable income = consumption + saving

$$Y_d = C + S$$

Divide by Y_d

$$1 = \frac{C}{Y_d} + \frac{S}{Y_d}$$

i.e. the sum of the average propensities to consume and save out of disposable income is unity.

and that (ii):

Change in disposable income = change in consumption
+ change in saving

$$\triangle Y_d = \triangle C + \triangle S$$

Divide by $\triangle Y_d$

$$1 = \frac{\triangle C}{\triangle Y_d} + \frac{\triangle S}{\triangle Y_d}$$

i.e. the sum of the marginal propensities to consume and save out of disposable income is unity.

In Table 10.1 the marginal propensity to consume out of disposable income is 0·8 and the marginal propensity to save is 0·2.

By considering columns (1) and (4) it will be seen that to each level of *national* income there corresponds a distinct value of planned consumption spending. We shall call this relationship linking columns (1) and (4) the *adjusted* propensity to consume schedule out of national income, while columns (1) and (5) provide the adjusted propensity to save schedule out of national income. If we know the direct tax schedule we can deduce these adjusted schedules from the propensity to consume and save schedules out of disposable income.

It should be noted in Table 10.1 that as national income rises by 100 (from 500 to 600, for example) so planned consumption spending rises by 64 (from 370 to 434). Hence change in consumption divided by change in national income is 0·64. We may call this the adjusted marginal propensity to consume out of national income, and it may be compared with the marginal propensity to consume out of disposable income of 0·8. Likewise as national income changes by 100, so planned saving changes in a similar direction by 16. Hence we have an adjusted marginal propensity to save out of national income of 0·16. Furthermore as national income rises by 100, so direct taxes rise by 20 so that the marginal propensity to pay direct taxation is 0·2. It will be noted that the sum of these three marginal propensities to consume, save, and pay direct taxation out of national income add up to 1. This is not accidental. We have:

Change in national income = change in consumption + change in saving + change in direct taxation

$$\triangle Y = \triangle C + \triangle S + \triangle T_d$$

divide by $\triangle Y$

$$1 = \frac{\triangle C}{\triangle Y} + \frac{\triangle S}{\triangle Y} + \frac{\triangle T_d}{\triangle Y}$$
$$1 = c' + s' + t_2$$

(We reserve c and s for the marginal propensities to consume and out of disposable income.)

We now have planned consumption in the adjusted propensity to consume schedule dependent on planned national income and output. We have been able to do this because we said that (i) direct taxation depended on national income and (ii) transfers were zero. If transfers were some positive value or if they depended on national income, we could have adopted the same procedure to get a some-what different expression relating planned consumption to national income (see appendix to this chapter).

The determination of equilibrium income

The introduction of governmental economic activities involves governmental spending on goods and services (G). This is treated as an autonomous spending item or injection just like exports or in-vestment. Taxation is treated as a leakage and has been subdivided into taxation on expenditure (T_e) and direct taxation (T_d) both of which are assumed to depend on income. The treatment of taxation on expenditure is precisely the same as our previous treatment of imports, while the treatment of direct taxation parallels the treat-ment of savings. For simplicity, we are confining our treatment in the main body of this chapter to these activities and assuming that trans-fer payments are zero.

The assumption of given tax functions along with the given propensity to consume schedule enables us to say what the equi-librium level of income will be, when planned investment and govern-mental spending are both at particular figures. It will yield answers to the following questions. (i) What level of planned output at factor cost will generate an equivalent amount of planned spending at factor cost? Or, (ii) what level of planned output and income at factor cost will generate sufficient planned saving and tax receipts to equal planned investment and governmental spending, so that total leakages from this flow of income are just matched by in-jections into it?

In short, what level of planned output or income ($*Y$) will satisfy the equilibrium conditions? We have:

Planned spending at factor cost = planned output at factor cost

Planned investment + governmental spending + consumption
   − taxes on expenditure   = planned output at factor cost

$$*I + *G + *C - *T_e = *Y$$
$$\therefore \quad *I + *G = *Y - *C + *T_e$$
But $\quad *Y = *C + *S + *T_d$
$$\therefore \quad *I + *G = *S + *T_d + T_e$$

Planned injections = planned leakages

Table 10.2

(1)	(2)	(3)	(4)	(5)	(6)	(7)	(8)	(9) Planned spending at factor cost $= *I + *C + *G - *T_e$	(10) Planned injections $= *I + *G$	(11) Planned leakages $= *S + *T_e + *T_d$
*Y	*T_d	*Y_d	*C	*S	*T_e	*I	*G			
500	100	400	400	0	50	40	230	620	270	150
600	120	480	470	10	60	40	230	680	270	190
700	140	560	540	20	70	40	230	740	270	230
800	160	640	610	30	80	40	230	800	270	270
900	180	720	680	40	90	40	230	860	270	310
1,000	200	800	750	50	100	40	230	920	270	350

Notes: Values for direct taxation   from $T_d = 0.2Y$
Values for consumption   from $C = 50 + 0.875Y_d$
Values for savings   from $S = -50 + 0.125Y_d$
Values for taxation on expenditure from $T_e = 0.1Y$
Adjusted propensity to consume schedule is $C = 50 + 0.7Y$
Adjusted propensity to save schedule   is $S = -50 + 0.1Y$

Clearly, if $*I$ and $*G$ are given, while $*C$, $*S$, $*T_d$, $*T_e$ each depend in a definite way on $*Y$ (the given adjusted consumption and savings schedules and the taxation schedules), then either equilibrium condition reduces to an equation in one unknown, $*Y$. The solution to

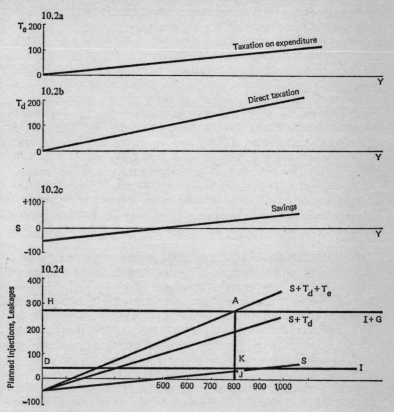

Figure 10.2 Equilibrium income with governmental activities

the equation is the equilibrium level of income, since this value will cause each side of the equation to be equal and thus satisfy either equilibrium condition. This will now be shown.[1]

Let us assume in Table 10.2 a given amount of planned investment

1. In the first version of the equilibrium condition it will be noted that direct taxation does not appear. However, as the working shows, it is there implicitly since $*C = *Y - *S - *T_d$. The same can be said for saving.

(40) and given governmental spending (230), a given propensity to consume schedule, and given taxation schedules together with the associated savings function in columns (1) and (5). Planned spending at factor cost is composed of planned investment *plus* consumption *plus* governmental spending *minus* taxation on expenditure and is shown in column (9). Planned consumption, investment, tax receipts, and governmental spending are all realised.

At a planned output and income of 800, it will be seen from Table 10.2 that planned spending at factor cost amounts to 800. Likewise at this income level planned injections of 270 are matched by planned leakages. The equilibrium output and income position is 800. At lower levels of output, planned spending exceeds planned output and Y would rise up to 800. At higher levels of output (than 800) planned spending falls short of planned output and Y would fall back to 800. The same conclusions can be reached by comparing planned injections and leakages of columns (10) and (11) in Table 10.2. It will be noted that at equilibrium income of 800 planned investment exceeds planned savings by 10, while planned governmental spending falls short of planned tax receipts by 10. At equilibrium income there is no inherent necessity for the budget to be balanced (in the sense of $T_e + T_d = G$) from the viewpoint of equilibrium income.

Figure 10.2 represents these relations graphically, where the taxation on expenditure schedule is plotted in part (a), the direct tax schedule in (b), and the adjusted savings schedule in (c). The combined 'leakages' schedule in (d), has been obtained by adding the tax schedules to the adjusted savings schedules in such a way that the vertical distance between the savings schedule and the direct tax schedule at any income level represents the direct taxes paid. Likewise the vertical distance between the direct tax schedule and the taxation on expenditure schedule represents indirect tax receipts. The total leakages function can be thought of as a graphical presentation of columns (1) and (11) in Table 10.2. OD represents the given amount of planned investment and DI is drawn horizontally. DH is planned governmental spending and $(HI + G)$ is drawn horizontally to show the value of planned injections at each level of income. The equilibrium income position is at A, with income of 800, and planned injections equal to planned leakages. Tax receipts are AJ, while governmental spending is $AK (= DH)$ so that there is a budget surplus of JK.

Stability

In the previous chapter we asked under what conditions the level of output would return to its equilibrium position after a temporary disturbance, or under what conditions a situation of planned spending in excess of planned output would set forces in motion to cause the discrepancy to be eliminated and equilibrium income attained. The same conclusions are applicable here. (In the case in Table 10.2 the situation is such that if planned spending does not equal planned output there are forces at work causing them to converge.) The requirement is that a change in planned output should produce a smaller change in planned spending at factor cost.

Again, fluctuations in output can now occur for a wider group of reasons than in the simple economy of Chapters 3 and 4. Variations in governmental spending as well as variations in investment can affect spending; shifts in the taxation schedules as well as shifts in the propensity to consume schedule can cause disturbances to equilibrium.

The multiplier

We must now ask the question that has been put before in Chapters 4 and 9. What will happen to the equilibrium income position if either investment or governmental spending change? Suppose within the context of Table 10.2 governmental spending rose by 40 from 230 to 270. At the old equilibrium income level of 800 planned injections of 310 would now exceed planned leakages by 40, while planned spending at factor cost would now amount to 840. A rise in planned output would occur until the new equilibrium level of 900 was reached at which planned leakages of 310 now matched the new planned injections, and at which planned spending at factor cost now amounted to 900. A primary rise in spending of 40 has brought a change in income and output between the two equilibrium positions of 100. The multiplier effect is $100 \div 40 = 2.5$. This will now be examined more closely.

We are assuming a straight-line adjusted savings schedule with a constant slope s' $\left(= \dfrac{\triangle S}{\triangle Y} = \right.$ marginal propensity to save out of national income $\Big)$; a straight-line taxation on expenditure schedule with a constant slope t_1 $\left(= \dfrac{\triangle T_e}{\triangle Y} = \right.$ marginal propensity to pay indirect taxes $\Big)$; and a straight-line direct tax schedule with a constant

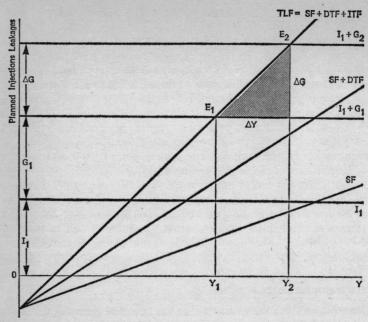

Figure 10.3 The multiplier with governmental activities

slope t_2 $\left(= \dfrac{\triangle T_d}{\triangle Y} = \text{marginal propensity to pay direct taxes} \right)^2$. These

are shown in Figure 10.3 in which they have been added together to form a total leakages function which is a straight-line also. This

2. It is important to relate the marginal propensity to save out of disposable income $\left(s = \dfrac{\triangle S}{\triangle Y_d} \right)$ to this 'adjusted' marginal propensity to save out of national income $\left(s' = \dfrac{\triangle S}{\triangle Y} \right)$.

We have $\triangle S = s \, \triangle Y_d$

But $\triangle Y_d = \triangle Y - \triangle T_d = \triangle Y - t_2 \triangle Y = (1 - t_2) \triangle Y$

$\therefore \triangle S = s(1 - t_2) \triangle Y$

But $\triangle S = s' \triangle Y$ so that $s' = s(1 - t_2)$

Likewise $\triangle C = c \, \triangle Y_d$

$\therefore \triangle C = c(1 - t_2) \triangle Y$

But $\triangle C = c' \triangle Y$ so that $c' = c(1 - t_2)$

In each case the marginal propensity out of disposable income is multiplied by $(1 - t_2)$, which takes account of the direct tax leakage, to convert it to the 'adjusted' basis out of national income.

has a constant slope which is the sum of the slopes of the individual components and equals $s' + t_1 + t_2$ or $s(1 - t_2) + t_1 + t_2$ since $s' = s(1 - t_2)$.

A given amount of planned investment (I_1) and given governmental spending (G_1) yield an equilibrium position for output of Y_1. Governmental spending then rises to G_2 where $\triangle G = G_2 - G_1$, and raises the planned injections line to $I_1 + G_2$. A new equilibrium output position is established at Y_2 with $\triangle Y = Y_2 - Y_1$. The multiplier here is $\dfrac{\triangle Y}{\triangle G}$ or:

$$\frac{1}{\dfrac{\triangle G}{\triangle Y}} = \frac{1}{\text{slope of total leakages function}}.\ \text{Now}\ \frac{\triangle G}{\triangle Y} = \text{the slope of total}$$

leakages function $= s' + t_1 + t_2 = s(1 - t_2) + t_1 + t_2$ so that the multiplier $= \dfrac{\triangle Y}{\triangle G} = \dfrac{1}{s' + t_1 + t_2} = \dfrac{1}{s(1 - t_2) + t_1 + t_2}$

It will be recalled that earlier in this chapter we said that the sum of the adjusted marginal propensities to consume and save out of national income, and the marginal propensity to pay direct taxation was one. We have, then:

$$c' + s' + t_2 = 1$$
$$\therefore s' = 1 - c' - t_2$$

If we substitute this in the multiplier formula above we get:[3]

$$\frac{\triangle Y}{\triangle G} = \frac{1}{s' + t_1 + t_2} = \frac{1}{1 - c' - t_2 + t_1 + t_2} = \frac{1}{1 - c' + t_1}$$
$$= \frac{1}{1 - c(1 - t_2) + t_1}$$

Precisely the same formula would apply to a change in planned investment.

3. Alternatively, recall that the sum of the marginal propensities to consume and save out of disposable income is one. That is, $c + s = 1$ so that $s = (1 - c)$. This may be substituted into the slope of the total leakages schedule $s(1 - t_2) + t_1 + t_2$ to give:

$$(1 - c)(1 - t_2) + t_1 + t_2 = 1 - c - t_2 + ct_2 + t_1 + t_2$$
$$= 1 - c + ct_2 + t_1$$
$$= 1 - c(1 - t_2) + t_1$$
$$= 1 - c' + t_1$$

The multiplier can then be derived as:

$$\frac{1}{1 - c' + t_2} = \frac{1}{1 - c(1 - t_2) + t_1}$$

The same formula may be derived algebraically from the requirement that between two equilibrium positions the change in planned spending at factor cost must equal the change in planned output at

Table 10.3 **Multiplier reactions**

	Case 1		Case 2	
t_1	0·10		0·05	
t_2	0·20		0·05	
c	0·75		0·84	
$c' = (1 - t_2)c$	0·60		0·80	
s	0·25		0·16	
$s' = (1 - t_2)s$	0·20		0·15	
Multiplier	2·0		4·0	
	(a)	(b)	(a)	(b)
$\triangle I$	100	0	100	0
$\triangle G$	0	100	0	100
$\triangle Y$		200		400
$\triangle T_d$		40		20
$\triangle Y_d$		160		380
$\triangle C$		120		320
$\triangle S$		40		60
$\triangle T_e$		20		20
$\triangle T_e + \triangle T_d - \triangle G$	60	−40	40	−60

factor cost. Assume that investment changes while governmental spending is unchanged. We have:

Change in planned spending at factor
cost   = change in planned output

$$\triangle G + \triangle I + \triangle C - \triangle T_e = \triangle Y$$
$$\text{But } \triangle T_e = t_1 \triangle Y$$
$$\triangle G = 0$$
$$\triangle C = c\triangle Y_d = c(1 - t_2)\triangle Y$$
$$= c'\triangle Y$$
$$\therefore \triangle I + c(1 - t_2)\triangle Y - t_1 \triangle Y = \triangle Y$$
$$\triangle I = \triangle Y - c(1 - t_2)\triangle Y$$
$$+ t_1\triangle Y$$
$$= \triangle Y(1 - c(1 - t_2) + t_1)$$

whence the multiplier $= \dfrac{\triangle Y}{\triangle I} = \dfrac{1}{1 - c(1 - t_2) + t_1} = \dfrac{1}{1 - c' + t_1}$

Table 10.3 provides two examples of the multiplier under different numerical values of t_1, t_2, c, and s. In each case the reactions of income, consumption, and taxation are the same whether the stimulus has come from a change in investment or a change in governmental spending. In case 1 the budgetary position improves by 60 when investment rises by 100, while it worsens by 40 when governmental spending rises by 100. In the 1(b) case 60 per cent of the rise in public spending has been financed by this rise in tax receipts. This implies that a governmental programme of increased spending does not require an equivalent increase in the rate of taxation to pay for it—provided that it causes incomes to rise. Cases 1(a) and 2(a) indicate scope for a government with a fixed spending programme to reduce taxation rates when incomes rise and when it does not wish to see an increased budget surplus. Case 2 indicates the different sizes of reaction when the marginal propensities are different.

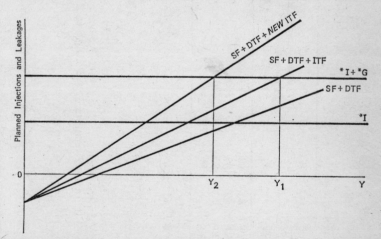

Figure 10.4 Equilibrium income when the taxation on expenditure schedule shifts

In summary, fluctuations in governmental spending will have multiplier effects on the economy in the same way as fluctuations in investment. However, the introduction of taxation which varies directly with income reduces the size of the multiplier for a given marginal propensity to save by introducing fresh leakages. Further, if governmental spending rises by a given amount, the budget position does not deteriorate to the same extent since the rise in income via the multiplier provides increased tax receipts.

Table 10.4 Section A: Old equilibrium

(1)	(2)	(3)	(4)	(5)	(6)	(7)	(8)	(9) Planned spending at factor cost $*I+*G+*C-*T_e$	(10) Planned injections $*I+*G$	(11) Planned leakages $*S+*T_e+*T_d$
$*Y$	$*T_d$	$*Y_d$	$*C$	$*S$	$*T_e$	$*I$	$*G$			
400	40	360	330	30	40	80	110	480	190	110
500	50	450	400	50	50	80	110	540	190	150
600	60	540	470	70	60	80	110	600	190	190
700	70	630	540	90	70	80	110	660	190	230

Notes:

(i) Planned consumption is derived from

$$C = 50 + 0.78\, Y_d$$

or in adjusted form

$$C = 50 + 0.7\, Y$$
$$= 0.78 \times 0.9 = 0.70$$

where $c = 0.78$ and $c' = c(1 - t_2)$

(ii) Planned saving is derived from

$$S = -50 + 0.22\, Y_d$$

or in adjusted form

$$S = -50 + 0.2\, Y$$
$$= 0.22 \times 0.9 = 0.20$$

where $s = 0.22$ and $s' = s(1 - t_2)$

(iii) Planned direct taxation is derived from

$$T_d = 0.1\, Y \text{ whence } t_2 = 0.1$$

(iv) Planned taxation on expenditure is derived from $T_e = 0.1\, Y$ whence $t_1 = 0.1$

(v) The multiplier $= \dfrac{1}{s(1 - t_2) + t_1 + t_2} = \dfrac{1}{s' + t_1 + t_2} = \dfrac{1}{0.4} = 2.5$

Section B: New equilibrium following change in indirect tax rate

(1) $*Y$	(2) $*T_d$	(3) $*Y_d$	(4) $*C$	(5) $*S$	(6) $*T_e$	(7) $*I$	(8) $*G$	(9) Planned spending at factor cost $*I+*G+*C-*T_e$	(10) Planned injections $*I+*G$	(11) Planned leakages $*S+*T_e+*T_d$
400	40	360	330	30	72	80	110	448	190	142
500	50	450	400	50	90	80	110	500	190	190
600	60	540	470	70	108	80	110	552	190	238
700	70	630	540	90	126	80	110	604	190	286

Notes:
(i) Planned consumption, savings, direct taxation as above
(ii) Planned taxation on expenditure is derived from $T_e = 0.18\ Y\ \ t_1 = 0.18$
(iii) The new multiplier $= \dfrac{1}{s(1-t_2)+t_1+t_2} = \dfrac{1}{s'+t_1+t_2} = \dfrac{1}{0.48} = 2.08$

Tax-rate changes

In the analysis so far we have assumed given tax rates and hence given taxation schedules. It is important to consider what will happen to the equilibrium income position if the government alters a tax rate as an act of economic policy.

Let us suppose that the government increases the rate at which taxation on expenditure is levied. The slope of the indirect tax schedule thus increases and so will the slope of the total leakages schedule. This is illustrated in Figure 10.4, where total planned injections remain unchanged. The old equilibrium income position is Y_1, and the new equilibrium is lower at Y_2. Further, it should be noted that the value of the multiplier has changed. It is now smaller because t_1 has increased and has made the denominator in the formula bigger.

This is also set out in more detail in Table 10.4 where the old equilibrium income is 600 with the original taxation on expenditure schedule, as shown in section A. In section B the tax rate has been increased and a new equilibrium income position of 500 emerges. Furthermore, the increase in the tax rate has been accompanied by a fall in the multiplier from 2·5 to 2·08. It is this alteration in the multiplier which makes it so difficult to apply the multiplier directly to tax-rate changes. However, it will be noted in Table 10.4 that as a result of the tax-rate change at a planned output of 600, planned spending at factor cost falls by 48. If the new multiplier of 2·08 is applied to this we get a fall of 100 in planned output to the new equilibrium position.

If we consider a rise in the rate of direct taxation such that t_2 increased, we could handle this diagrammatically in much the same way as a rise in the expenditure tax rate with an upward twist in the total leakages function, and a fall in equilibrium income would result with unchanged planned injections.[4] From an initially un-

---

4. Care is needed in this analysis, for if we assume the marginal propensities to consume and save out of disposable income remain unchanged, both the 'adjusted' marginal propensities will fall. For $c' = c(1 - t_2)$ and $s' = s(1 - t_2)$ so that if t_2 rises, $(1 - t_2)$ must fall. Now the slope of the total leakages schedule is $s' + t_1 + t_2$ or $s(1 - t_2) + t_1 + t_2$, and it is by no means clear at first sight that it will rise as t_2 increases because s' falls. However, a little rearrangement of the slope of the total leakages schedule settles the matter:

$$s(1 - t_2) + t_1 + t_2 = s - st_2 + t_1 + t_2 = s + t_1 + t_2(1 - s)$$

Now s, t_1, $(1 - s)$ each remain unchanged while t_2 rises, so that unambiguously the expression $s + t_1 + t_2(1 - s)$ increases.

Suppose t_2 rises from 0·2 to 0·3, while $s = 0·2$ and $t_1 = 0·1$. s' was 0·16 and it

changed national income, the increased direct taxation would re-duce disposable income so that planned consumption spending would fall through the given marginal propensity to consume, and a fresh equilibrium would be attained. If households reacted to this increase in direct taxation by altering their economic behaviour, and main-taining consumption spending while cutting saving, then in the extreme case no fall in spending and in equilibrium income would take place. How the economy reacts to a change in direct taxation is very important for a government when framing its economic policy.

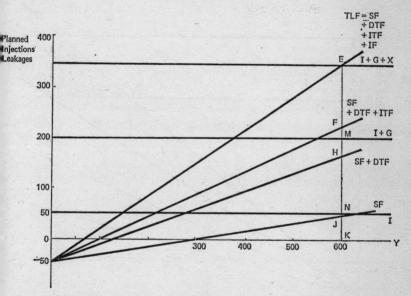

Figure 10.5 Equilibrium income with trading and governmental activities

International trade and the government

The analysis of Chapter 9 can now be combined with this chapter to produce the equilibrium income and output position, and the multi-plier, when both international and governmental transactions are incorporated. To find equilibrium income and output we must find

---

falls to 0·14, so that the slope of the total leakages schedule rises from 0·46 to 0·54.

that level of income which satisfies either version of the equilibrium condition. We have:

Planned spending at factor cost = planned output at factor cost

$$*I + *G + *X + *C - *T_e - *F = *Y$$
$$\text{now } *Y = *S + *T_d + *C$$
$$\therefore *I + *G + *X + *C - *T_e - *F = *S + *T_d + *C$$
$$\text{whence } *I + *G + *X = *S + *T_d + *T_e + *F$$

i.e. planned injections = planned leakages

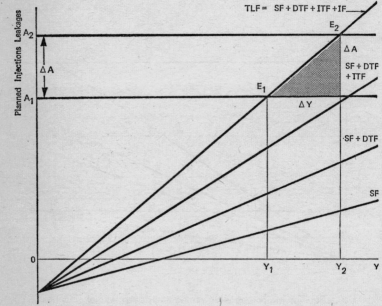

Figure 10.6 The multiplier with trade and governmental activities

If planned investment, exports, and governmental spending are given and if there are given propensity to consume, propensity to save, propensity to import, and given direct and indirect tax schedules, then either of these equilibrium conditions will yield the value of equilibrium output.

This is shown graphically in Figure 10.5 where the propensity to import schedule has been added to the adjusted savings schedule and the taxation schedules to produce the total leakages schedule.

Planned injections now incorporate export sales, and equality between planned injections and leakages produces equilibrium income and output position of OK. Imports are FE, while exports are ME, so that there is a balance of payments current account surplus of MF. Total tax receipts are JF while governmental spending is NM so that there is a budget surplus of $JN + MF$.

Overall equilibrium between planned injections and leakages, once again, does not necessarily imply equality in the individual sectors of international and budgetary transactions. For convergence on to the equilibrium to result (if planned spending at factor cost is not initially equal to planned output) requires the same condition as before. A change in planned output at factor cost should produce a smaller change in planned spending at factor cost if convergence is to take place.

The multiplier again

The multiplier has been discussed in detail in earlier chapters as well as this one so a brief treatment will suffice here. A graphical version is presented in Figure 10.6 where an existing equilibrium at Y_1 is disturbed by a rise in planned injections from A_1 to A_2 to bring a fresh equilibrium at Y_2. The multiplier is $\triangle Y \div \triangle A$, which is the reciprocal of the slope of the total leakages schedule.[5] Now:

$$\frac{\triangle Y}{\triangle A} = \frac{1}{s' + t_1 + t_2 + f} = \frac{1}{s(1 - t_2) + t_1 + t_2 + f}$$

$$= \frac{1}{1 - c' + t_1 + f} = \frac{1}{1 - c(1 - t_2) + t_1 + f}$$

5. The same formula can be derived from the requirement that, between two equilibrium positions, change in planned spending at factor cost equals change in planned output at factor cost. We have:

Change in planned spending at factor cost =
$\qquad\qquad\qquad$ change in planned output at factor cost

$$\triangle A + \triangle C - \triangle T_e - \triangle F = \triangle Y$$
$$\triangle T_e = t_1 \triangle Y$$
$$\triangle C = c \triangle Y_d = (1 - t_2)c \triangle Y = c' \triangle Y$$
$$\triangle F = f \triangle Y$$
$$\therefore \triangle A + c' \triangle Y - t_1 \triangle Y - f \triangle Y = \triangle Y$$
$$\triangle A = \triangle Y - c' \triangle Y + t_1 \triangle Y + f \triangle Y$$

Whence the multiplier $= \dfrac{\triangle Y}{\triangle A} = \dfrac{1}{1 - c' + t_1 + f} = \dfrac{1}{s' + t_1 + t_2 + f}$

$$= \frac{1}{1 - c(1 - t_2) + t_1 + f} = \frac{1}{s(1 - t_2) + t_1 + t_2 + f}$$

Table 10.5 **Multiplier reactions to different stimuli**

	Case 1			Case 2		
t_1	0·15			0·10		
t_2	0·20			0·10		
f	0·30			0·10		
s	0·15			0·11		
$s' = s(1 - t_2)$	0·12			0·10		
c	0·85			0·89		
$c' = c(1 - t_2)$	0·68			0·80		
Multiplier	1·30			2·50		
	(a)	(b)	(c)	(a)	(b)	(c)
$\triangle X$	100	0	0	100	0	0
$\triangle I$	0	100	0	0	100	0
$\triangle G$	0	0	100	0	0	100
$\triangle Y$	130	130	130	250	250	250
$\triangle T_d$		26			25	
$\triangle Y_d$		104			225	
$\triangle C$		88			200	
$\triangle S$		16			25	
$\triangle T_e$		19			25	
$\triangle F$		39			25	
$\triangle T - \triangle G$	+45	+45	−55	+50	+50	−50
$\triangle B$ of P	+61	−39	−39	+75	−25	−25

Table 10.5 presents two cases of multiplier reactions to different changes in planned spending. In case 1 the values of f, t_1, t_2, s, have been chosen to bear some resemblance to their current values in the United Kingdom, and the important point to note is the small size of the multiplier on account of the substantial taxation and import leakages. In case 2 the sizes of these marginal leakages coefficients are more modest but the multiplier, nevertheless, is still only 2·5. The figures of case 1 would suggest that the weight of a change in spending would be borne by the initial recipient—for example, export industries or investment good industries—and less proportionally by the consumer good industries in subsequent rounds of spending, while the multiplier process would soon converge within 5 per cent of equilibrium values and peter out. The multiplier may not be as efficacious and strong as it might have seemed when there were only savings leakages to take account of.

Multiplier processes can also be started from shifts in the functions as well as from changes in injections.

Let us suppose that the consumption functions rises bodily but that its slope does not alter as the 'constant term' (the intercept with the spending axis) in it gets bigger. This is an autonomous increase in planned spending and is equivalent to a downward movement of the savings function and hence a depression of the total leakages function as indicated in Figure 10.7. Equilibrium income rises from Y_1 to Y_2 as a result of the fall in leakages of Z so that the multiplier is $\triangle Y \div \triangle Z$ and is represented by the usual triangle.

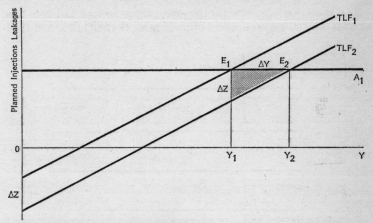

Figure 10.7 Shifts in total leakages function

It must be stressed that some lapse of time is necessary for these multiplier processes to work themselves out through rounds of successive spending, and the path of income converging on its new equilibrium level can be shown in a similar fashion to the simple case in Chapter 4 (p. 72), but it is not done here. Furthermore, it has been assumed that one can apply the same marginal propensities to each round of spending irrespective of the fact that different economic units or groups may have different marginal propensities. Clearly it can make a difference whether an initial change in spending is directed to the rich with low marginal propensities to consume, or to the poor with high marginal propensities to consume; whether it is directed to the products of firms with high import content or with low import content. These differences have been ignored in our aggregate treatment, but can be important in particular cases.

This treatment has tacitly assumed that extra output can always be supplied with no change in price in response to a rise in spending, so that our multiplier is relating changes in spending at constant prices to changes in output at constant prices. However, if the supply of output becomes less elastic, rising demand brings rising prices and this real output multiplier becomes restricted. An alternative approach is to operate in money terms regardless of price changes, and to relate changes in money incomes to primary changes in spending in monetary terms to derive a money income multiplier. This would assume that the various schedules are expressed in monetary terms (irrespective of price changes).

The low value suggested for the multiplier in Britain earlier in this chapter is by no means a recent phenomenon. Between 1870 and 1914

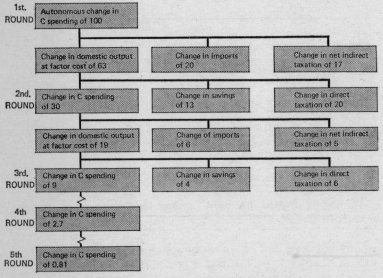

Figure 10.8 The multiplier process in the United Kingdom 1965

the marginal propensity to import was of the order of 0·35, the combined marginal tax leakage 0·10, and the marginal propensity to save perhaps of the order of 0·15 to 0·25. These would yield a multiplier of the order of 1·4 to 1·7.

This is supported by some direct estimates the author has made for 1870–1914 of the money income multiplier. This relates annual absolute changes in money incomes (at current prices) to annual absolute changes in injections (at current prices) and thus could embrace price as well as output effects. It involves the assumption that the propensity schedules are given in monetary rather than in real terms. If prices are unchanged, the money income multiplier would amount precisely to the real output multiplier, otherwise its value would approximate to it. By comparing annual changes in money income ($\triangle Ym$) with annual changes in injections ($\triangle Am$), which were taken as the sum of exports and investment, a figure of 1·44 emerged for the ratio of $\triangle Ym$ to $\triangle Am$, which forms an approximation to the multiplier.[6]

An estimate of the multiplier in Britain in the 1960s is provided by Hopkin and Godley in *The National Institute Economic Review*, May 1965. This is deduced from their estimates of the various marginal propensities, and the implied value of the multiplier is 1·43. It should be pointed out that this multiplier relates primary change in spending at market prices to total change in spending at market prices. Hence it is somewhat different from the multiplier as developed in this chapter. Their detailed estimates are consolidated and the process presented in Figure 10.8. An autonomous rise in consumption spending of 100 at market prices starts the process. In the first round, 17 leaks into extra taxation in expenditure, 20 into imports, so that domestic product at factor cost rises by 63. In consolidated terms this brings a rise in direct taxation of 20, a rise in disposable income of 43, a rise in saving of 13, and a secondary rise in consumption of 30. This starts another round of spending.

The main point to emphasise is the low values in each estimate rather than their almost identical numerical values, and the conclusions to be drawn from this for economic policy that the multiplier effect is likely to be weak.

The *IS* curve yet again

Under the assumptions of given planned governmental spending, transfers, exports and given taxation, consumption (or saving), and import schedules, it is possible to derive the *IS* curve which relates interest rates and the corresponding equilibrium income and output positions. To a given interest rate, with a given investment schedule, there will correspond a particular amount of planned investment. *With the above assumptions* this will provide a determinate equilibrium income and output position. If the rate of interest falls, planned investment will rise and the equilibrium income level will rise. The *IS* curve will still slope downwards, but it has been derived under such a large number of assumptions that it must be handled carefully.

6. By using different estimating equations, a range of values from 1·2 to 1·5 was obtained for this ratio.

Summary

This chapter has shown how an equilibrium income and output position can be derived when governmental transactions are included. It has suggested that both direct and indirect taxation depend on income, and has indicated that these influence the earlier consumption and savings propensities. To arrive at a determinate equilibrium income position, it is necessary to assume planned investment, public spending and transfers at given levels, and given taxation and consumption (or savings) schedules. Then the equilibrium position would follow from the equilibrium conditions of planned spending at factor cost equalling planned output at factor cost, or planned injections equalling planned leakages. The stability of this position and its requirements were discussed.

The multiplier in these changed circumstances was then investigated. Changes from one equilibrium position to another could be prompted by changes in planned injections of investment or governmental spending on which attention has been centred. Equally, changes could come from shifts in the various schedules.

The trade analysis of the previous chapter is then incorporated with the governmental analysis to provide both an analysis of equilibrium and the multiplier in these more realistic circumstances and the basis for short-run management of the economy. As more planned leakages which are dependent on income have been introduced, so the multiplier has fallen in size. What looked a very large effect has now been more severely limited in size.

Nevertheless, the multiplier is to be seen as an important ingredient in the pervasive spread of economic fluctuations, such as the trade cycle, in which cyclical fluctuations in income and output are immediately attributable to cyclical fluctuations in planned injections, not only investment but also export variations. It is also an important tool of policy in understanding how to manipulate an economy.

APPENDIX TO CHAPTER 10

Transfer payments

For simplicity these have been assumed zero in the main text to this chapter, but it was clear from the introduction to the chapter that they are an important constituent of disposable income in the United Kingdom. Disposable income, to repeat, has been defined as

Table 10.6

(1) *Y	(2) *T_d	(3) *B	(4) *Y_d	(5) *C	(6) *S	(7) *T_e	(8) *G	(9) *I	(10) Planned spending	(11) Planned leakages	(12) Planned injections
400	80	50	370	346	24	40	136	50	492	144	236
500	100	50	450	410	40	50	136	50	546	190	236
600	120	50	530	474	56	60	136	50	600	236	236
700	140	50	610	538	72	70	136	50	654	282	236

Notes:
  (i) All planned magnitudes
  (ii) Direct taxation is derived from $T_d = 0.2\,Y$
  (iii) Indirect taxation is derived from $T_e = 0.1\,Y$
  (iv) Consumption is derived from $C = 50 + 0.8\,Y_d$
  (v) Saving is derived from $S = -50 + 0.2\,Y_d$
  (vi) $Y_d = Y - T_d + B$

national income minus direct taxation plus transfer payments. If transfer payments are a given value, all we have to do is to insert a fresh column entry for them in our table for determining equilibrium income and to incorporate transfer payments (B) into our equilibrium conditions.

We have the equilibrium conditions:

Planned spending at factor cost = planned output at factor cost

$$*I + *C + *G - *T_e = *Y$$
$$\text{now } *Y_d = *Y - *T_d + *B$$
$$\text{whence } *Y = *Y_d + *T_d - *B$$
$$= *C + *S + *T_d - *B$$
$$\therefore *I + *C + *G - *T_e = *C + *S + *T_d - *B$$
$$*I + *G + *B = *S + *T_d + *T_e$$

planned injections = planned leakages

As before, it follows that if $*I$, $*G$, and $*B$ are given, and $*C$, $*S$, $*T_d$, $*T_e$ are all dependent on $*Y$ in definite ways, we can find equilibrium income from either equilibrium condition.

This is briefly demonstrated in Table 10.6 where planned investment is 50, planned governmental spending 136, transfer payments 50. There are given consumption and taxation schedules, as specified in the notes to the table, and the equilibrium position is 600.

What, then, will happen if transfer payments rise? Clearly, disposable income will be greater as will consumption spending via the marginal propensity to consume. Planned spending in total will rise and lead to a fresh equilibrium position with higher national income.

Within the context of Table 10.6 suppose that transfer payments rise by 57·5 from 50 to 107·5. This will cause disposable income (column (4)) to be greater by 57·5 and planned consumption spending to be greater by 46 (= 57·5 × 0·8), while planned savings will rise by 11·5. The planned spending column figures will each be 46 greater so that the old equilibrium at 600 is destroyed, and a new one established at a planned output of 700. For at this level of planned output, planned spending will amount to 700. The reader should construct a new table equivalent in form to Table 10.6 to demonstrate the equality of planned injections and planned leakages at this income level.

Chapter 11

The Economic System

In this chapter we shall put together the various pieces of economic analysis which have been built up in the earlier chapters to make a self-contained economic model which in a simplified way gives insights into the operation of an economy. Initially our discussion will be conducted in terms of a given set of prices, but later variations in the price level will be permitted.

The *IS* curve

In Chapter 5 we briefly mentioned the *IS* schedule, which related the equilibrium output position corresponding to each interest rate. This is derived under the assumption of a given investment schedule, propensity to consume schedule, and equilibrium between planned spending and planned output. To each interest rate there corresponds a certain planned investment spending, which with the

Table 11.1

(1) Rate of interest	(2) Planned investment	(3) Planned saving	(4) Equilibrium income	(5) Planned consumption	(6) Planned spending = (2) + (5)
2	80	80	650	570	650
3	70	70	600	530	600
4	60	60	550	490	550
5	50	50	500	450	500
6	40	40	450	410	450
7	30	30	400	370	400
8	20	20	350	330	350
9	10	10	300	290	300
10	0	0	250	250	250

Notes: Planned investment $(I) = 100 - 10\,R$
Planned saving $(S) = -50 + 0{\cdot}2\,Y$
Planned consumption $(C) = 50 + 0{\cdot}8\,Y$

propensity to consume schedule yields an equilibrium income position. The schedule is downward sloping because a fall in the rate of interest brings a rise in investment, and thence a multiplier-induced rise in income and output.

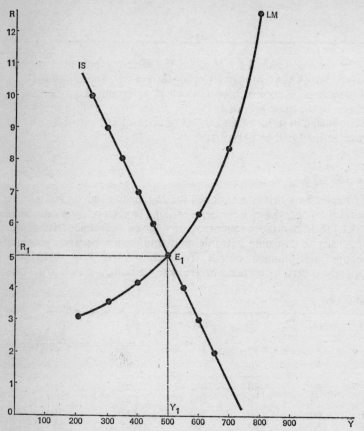

Figure 11.1 Equilibrium in product and money markets

The same results can be obtained if we use the propensity to save schedule which corresponds to the given propensity to consume schedule. To each interest rate there corresponds a given planned investment, and the equilibrium income level is that value which yields planned savings equal to the given planned investment. If the rate of interest is higher, then planned investment will be lower, and equilibrium income must fall to a lower position to yield lower planned savings to match the lower investment.

The same point is illustrated in Table 11.1 in which columns (1) and (2) represent the investment schedule relating planned investment to the rate of interest, while columns (3) and (4) are derived from the given savings function or propensity to save schedule, and columns (4) and (5) from the corresponding propensity to consume schedule.

If the rate of interest is 2 per cent, planned investment is 80. We then ask what level of planned output and income will yield planned savings of 80. The given savings schedule tell us that it will be 650. Hence, corresponding to an interest rate of 2 per cent will be an equilibrium output position of 650.

As a check, this level of output brings planned consumption of 570 which with planned investment of 80 yields planned spending of 650. Columns (1) and (4) thus provide the *IS* curve which is plotted in Figure 11.1, and they indicate that as the rate of interest rises, equilibrium income falls as a result of the multiplier effects of falling planned investment. In the appendix to this chapter an alternative derivation is provided.

If the investment schedule should shift outwards, then to each interest rate the corresponding value of planned investment would be greater. Hence each corresponding equilibrium output and income position would be greater, so that the whole *IS* schedule would move outwards to the right.

International and governmental transactions

In Chapters 9 and 10 it was suggested that the *IS* curve could still be derived when international and governmental activities were involved. If we assume given planned exports, given public spending, given consumption, investment, import and taxation schedules, then one can obtain the *IS* curve which relates interest rates and the corresponding equilibrium income and output positions.

To any given interest rate, there will correspond a certain value of planned investment. This will be sufficient (with the above collection of assumptions) to provide a determinate equilibrium output position (see Chapter 10, p. 211). If the rate of interest falls, planned investment spending rises and income expands to a fresh equilibrium position. The *IS* curve will still slope downwards, and a rise in exports or in public spending will shift the whole schedule outwards to the right. This makes for a much more complicated mechanism which underlies the deceptively simple appearance of the *IS* curve.

The *LM* curve

A second relationship between income and the rate of interest was derived in Chapter 6, which dealt with money and the rate of interest. Under the assumptions of a given stock of money, and given liquidity preference schedules, it was shown that with a given real income and price level (that is, a given money income) the M_1 demand for money was determined. Equilibrium in the money market then required a particular rate of interest to equilibrate the demand for money for speculative purposes (M_2) with the available supply.

Table 11.2

(1) Stock of money	(2) If Y	(3) then M_1	(4) then supply of money available for M_2 purposes	(5) therefore equilibrium interest rate per cent
400	200	80	320	3·125
400	300	120	280	3·571
400	400	160	240	4·167
400	500	200	200	5·000
400	600	240	160	6·250
400	700	280	120	8·333
400	800	320	80	12·500

Notes:
The M_1 demand is calculated from $M_1 = 0.4\ Y$

The M_2 demand schedule is $M_2 = \dfrac{1,000}{R}$

The equilibrium interest rate is calculated by setting the available supply of money of column (4) equal to $\dfrac{1,000}{R}$

The *LM* curve is derived from columns (2) and (5)

To each level of income there will be an equilibrium rate of interest. If income rises, the M_1 demand for money will rise and reduce the supply available for speculative purposes so that the equilibrium rate of interest rises. Hence the *LM* schedule between real income and the rate of interest will be upward sloping. Every point on it corresponds to equilibrium in the money market, with total planned demand for money to hold being equal to the total stock of money. It must be remembered that a particular *LM* curve is drawn up on the assumption of a given price level, and later we shall see what happens if the price level varies.

The *LM* curve can be demonstrated numerically as in Table 11.2, if there is a given stock of money, given demand schedules for money and equilibrium in the money market. For example, with a given stock of money of 400 and Y of 600, the M_1 demand is 240, thereby leaving 160 for speculative purposes. For the M_2 demand to be 160, and thus yield equilibrium in the money market, the rate of interest must be such that $1,000 \div R$ is 160. It must be 6·25 per cent. Hence, corresponding to the value of 600 for Y an equilibrium value for the rate of interest of 6·25 per cent results. This will be one point on the *LM* curve. By choosing other values of Y, the corresponding equilibrium interest rates can be derived, and other points on the *LM* curve deduced. The *LM* schedule represented by columns (2) and (5) of Table 11.2 is plotted in Figure 11.1.

If the stock of money were to rise to 500, then within the context of Table 11.2 all the figures for column (4) would be greater by 100. In other words the supply of money available for speculative purposes would have risen, and all the interest rate figures would be lower. Hence the *LM* curve would shift downwards on Figure 11.1, since to each level of Y the corresponding equilibrium interest rate would fall.

Again, if people wanted to hold more money for M_1 purposes at each level of income, this would diminish the supply available for M_2 purposes (all the figures in column (4) would fall), and all the interest rate figures would be higher. This increase in liquidity preference would shift the *LM* curve upwards, and a higher interest rate would correspond to each income level. The same upward shift would result if people wanted to hold more money for speculative purposes at each interest rate. (The derivation of the *LM* curve is also discussed in the appendix to this chapter.)

Equilibrium

Can we then find a joint equilibrium position for the economy by putting together the *IS* schedule, with its product market equilibrium at a series of interest rates, and the *LM* schedule with its money market equilibrium at a series of real income levels? As *LM* is upward-sloping and *IS* is downward-sloping, it seems certain that they will cut as indicated in Figure 11.1 at E_1 and produce the required joint equilibrium position for the economy as a whole. At E_1 we have a pair of values of 500 for income and 5 per cent for the rate of interest, which are such as to give (i) planned aggregate demand equal to planned output and (ii) planned demand for money to hold equal to the stock of money. There is equilibrium in both product and money markets jointly with this pair of values Y and R.

Our economic analysis, or our economic model of the economy, has provided a unique short-period equilibrium position for the economy as a result of an *interacting* complex of forces which are summed up in a deceptively simple way by the *IS* and *LM* curves. Underneath lies a mass of assumptions and schedules which we have worked through in earlier chapters. (A derivation of the *IS* and *LM* curves is shown in the appendix to this chapter.)

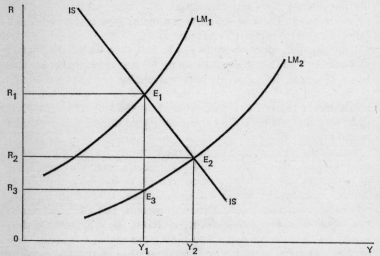

Figure 11.2 Changes in the stock of money

The analysis also makes it clear that we should not think about the determination of income without being concerned about money market and interest rate repercussions, nor about the determination of the rate of interest without incorporating income effects. The rate of interest is *not* a purely monetary phenomenon.

This analysis can be used to show the effects of changes in the stock of money, or in the liquidity preference schedules, or in the positions of the investment schedule or the consumption function. In Figure 11.2 a given *IS* schedule and LM_1 schedule, product equilibrium position E_1 with income OY_1 and the rate of interest OR_1. If now the stock of money is increased, this causes a downward displacement of the *LM* curve to LM_2. With an unchanged income the interest rate would have fallen to OR_3, but the falling interest rate causes investment and income to rise, which increases the transactions demand to hold money, and absorbs some of the increased stock of money.

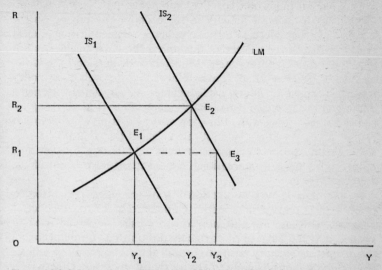

Figure 11.3 Changes in equilibrium position when the desire to invest increases

This prevents the interest rate from falling so far. A new equilibrium is established at E_2,[1] with a rise in income of $Y_1 Y_2$ as well as a fall in interest rates of $R_1 R_2$. As suggested earlier, a rise in liquidity preference would shift the *LM* curve upwards. This would result in a higher rate of interest and a lower level of real output in the new equilibrium.

In Figure 11.3 a given *LM* schedule and IS_1 schedule produce an equilibrium position E_1. If the investment schedule shifts outwards as expected future earnings estimates are revised upwards, this causes an outward displacement of IS_1 to IS_2. With an unchanged rate of interest the multiplier process would have caused income to rise to OY_3, but rising investment and rising income increase the transactions demand for money, thereby lessening the available supply for speculative purposes and forcing the interest rate up. This has the effect of checking the rise in investment and incomes, until a fresh

1. It is assumed that this new equilibrium will be established smoothly. There may be difficulties. See appendix.

equilibrium is established at E_2, with higher incomes and higher interest rates, so that the rise in incomes is less than with unchanged interest rates. The same analysis could be applied to a rise in export sales or a rise in public spending which shifted the *IS* curve outwards.

This has an important corollary for public policy: if a government seeks to increase activity in the economy by relying on the simple multiplier effects of a rise in public investment, rising interest rates may lessen the efficacy of this unless the government expands the money stock appropriately. Monetary repercussions, therefore, need to be borne in mind. It also follows that if purely fiscal policy is used to expand spending, rising incomes are associated with rising interest rates; whereas, if monetary policy alone is used, rising incomes are associated with falling interest rates. It may be important to take account of these interest rate effects if the country has considerable international banking and financial interests, for they may influence the flow of international capital funds into or out of the country.

Furthermore, when international transactions are involved, a position of *IS* and *LM* intersection could correspond to a balance of payments surplus. For this position to persist we would need to assume that the balance of payments position has no influence on the domestic monetary position, or that the central bank so adjusts the domestic money supply to ensure that it does not. Otherwise a balance of payments surplus should bring an influx of gold and cause the money supply to rise; a balance of payments deficit should cause the loss of gold and a restriction in the money supply. Then the *LM* curve would move about in response to the balance of payments position. This is only a summary argument. These matters are outside the scope of this volume and are dealt with thoroughly in *International Trade and The Balance of Payments* by H. Katrak.

The price level and equilibrium

The price level can also be introduced, for it will be recalled that the demand and supply of money were measured in monetary units and that the M_1 demand for money was taken to depend on the money value of spending, output, and income, so that it would change if either real output or the price level, or both, varied. Up to now we have concentrated on the 'output' effect in the money market, but equally if real output Y was unchanged and the price level rose, the M_1 demand would increase and bring a rise in the interest rate as the supply available for M_2 purposes declined from a given stock of

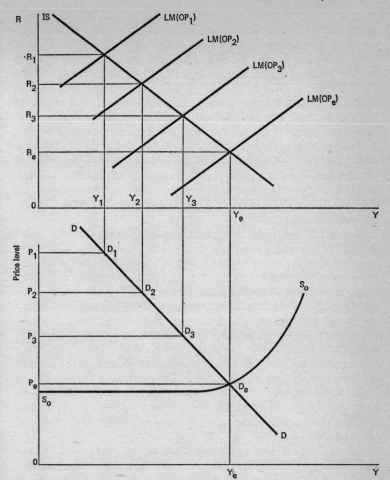

Figure 11.4 Equilibrium income and interest rate when the price level can vary

money. For a given real income, the higher the price level the higher the equilibrium rate of interest with given liquidity preference schedules and a given stock of money. Hence an *LM* curve constructed under the assumption of one given price level (OP_2 in Figure 11.4) will lie below one constructed with a higher price level (OP_1), if the stock of money and liquidity preference schedules are unchanged. There is, then, a different *LM* curve for each price level.

On the other hand it is assumed that the IS curve's position is unaffected by variations in the price level—that planned aggregate spending in real terms is insensitive *directly* to variations in the price level. However, it may be affected indirectly so that the schedule relating planned aggregate spending in real terms to the price level (DD of Figures 7.6 and 7.7 in Chapter 7, pp. 133 and 135) may no longer be vertical but may exhibit some sensitivity. For a rise in the price level would bring an increased M_1 demand for money, a fall in the supply available for M_2 holdings, and a rise in the rate of interest unless the economy was on the perfectly flat part of the M_2 schedule (the 'liquidity trap'). This rise in interest rates would reduce planned investment spending in real terms, unless the investment schedule was vertical, and thus lead to a lower equilibrium real income. On the same lines, a fall in the price level would bring a rise in equilibrium real income and output.

This can be illustrated in Figure 11.4 where the upper part presents the IS/LM apparatus and the lower part the total supply schedule of real output with respect to the price level (S_0S_0), and the equilibrium real output schedule (DD) which is constructed from IS/LM intersections. At price-level OP_1 the relevant LM curve is $LM(OP_1)$, which yields OY_1 as the equilibrium real income (product and money markets in equilibrium).

This may be plotted on the lower diagram against price level OP_1 as D_1 (with $P_1D_1 = OY_1$). At the lower price level of OP_3 the lower LM curve of $LM(OP_3)$ produces equilibrium income of OY_3, which is plotted as D_3 (with $P_3D_3 = OY_3$). Points such as D_1, D_2, D_3 are linked up to form DD. The point where this cuts S_0S_0 yields the price level, and is an equilibrium position in which real output, the interest rate, and the price level are all determined together at OY_e, OR_e and OP_e in Figure 11.4.

A qualification to our earlier analysis of changes in money wages (see p. 134), the position of the total supply schedule, and their effects on real output and employment, is thus introduced. So long as DD is not vertical (this implies that changes in the price level influence the interest rate and that the interest-rate changes influence real investment spending), general cuts in money wages would lower S_0S_0 and increase equilibrium real output and employment, while general rises would lift S_0S_0 and check real output and employment. This point should be kept in mind when thinking about the persistence of cost inflation or of deflationary conditions. (The other possible influences of the price level on planned effective demand which were mentioned in the Appendix to Chapter 7 would involve a separate *IS* curve for each price level so that, as the price level varied, both *IS* and *LM* would move and a *DD* curve could be derived in a more complicated way.)

Summary

This chapter has sought to indicate the interdependence in equilibrium of the various main sectors of the economy and the equilibrium configuration of real output, interest rates, and the price level. Further, it has presented the *IS/LM* apparatus, which can be used to predict the likely qualitative consequences of shifts in schedules and of policy measures when repercussions of immediate effects are taken into account. However, it is essentially concerned with short-term equilibrium and ignores the growth of the economy. This must form part of any longer-term analysis.

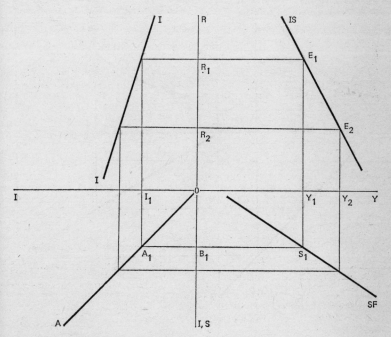

Figure 11.5 Derivation of *IS* curve

APPENDIX TO CHAPTER 11

1. Derivation of the *IS* and *LM* schedules

Derivation of IS schedule. Given:

    (i) savings function (south-east quadrant of Figure 11.5)
    (ii) investment function (north-west quadrant of Figure 11.5)
    (iii) OA line drawn in south-west quadrant at 45° to each axis so that $OI_1 = I_1A_1 = OB_1$

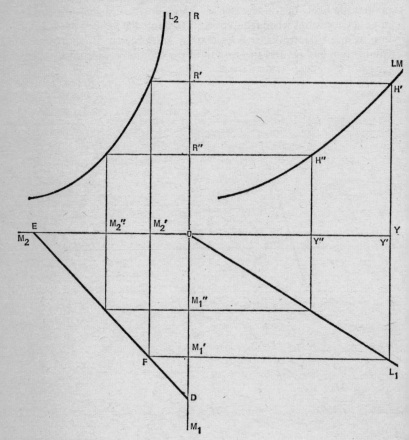

Figure 11.6 Derivation of *LM* curve

At interest rate OR_1 planned investment is $OI_1 = OB_1$. This equals planned savings of S_1Y_1, at income level OY_1 which is therefore equilibrium income corresponding to interest rate OR_1.

The point where the horizontal line through R_1 and the vertical through Y_1 meet in the north-east quadrant, yields E_1, a point on the IS curve. Other points can be derived similarly to yield the whole schedule (for example, E_2).

If the investment schedule moves outwards the new IS schedule is displaced outwards. Shifts in the savings schedule could be handled in the same way.

Again, in the case of an economy with governmental and international transactions, II could be interpreted as the investment schedule, to which had been added the given amount of governmental spending and export sales. (A change in these would be equivalent to a displacement of II.) SF would be interpreted as the leakages function allowing for import and taxation leaks as well as savings, and requiring given savings, import, and taxation functions

Derivation of LM schedule. Given:

(i) M_1 demand for money function dependent on real income as price level is assumed constant (south-east quadrant of Figure 11.6)

(ii) M_2 demand for money dependent on the rate of interest (north-west quadrant of figure 11.6)

(iii) Given stock of money OD measured on OM_1 axis and OE measured on OM_2 axis with DE drawn in south-west quadrant. A property of this line which cuts each axis at 45° is that DM'_1 equals FM_1', equals OM_2'; and OM_1' equals FM_2', equals $M_2'E$

At income level OY_1', the M_1 demand for money is OM_1' which leaves DM_1' available for speculative M_2 holdings. With equilibrium in the money market this yields interest rate OR', since $DM_1' = FM_1' = OM_2'$. Where the horizontal line through R' cuts the vertical line through Y' in the north-east quadrant yields H', a point on the LM curve. Other points (for example, H'') can be derived similarly to yield the whole schedule.

If the stock of money is increased, a new LM curve can be derived which is pushed outwards from the old one.

2. The move from one equilibrium position to another

It was suggested in the main text to this chapter that the transition from one equilibrium to another, when either the IS or the LM

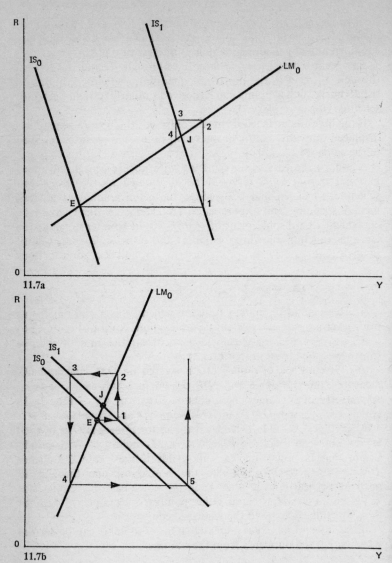

Figure 11.7 Convergence and divergence after a disturbance

curve shifted, might not be as smooth or straightforward as dia-grammatic analysis would suggest if there were lags in the response of the interest rate to disequilibrium in the money market, or lags in the response of investment to changes in the interest rate.

For example, suppose the economy is at an equilibrium position E in Figure 11.7 where IS_0 intersects LM_0, and that (because of a shift in the investment schedule) the IS curve moves out to IS_1 with a potential new equilibrium position of J. If all reactions are instan-taneous, J will be achieved speedily, but if the rate of interest reacts sluggishly (with a lag of a time period, say) investment will expand sufficiently to cause output to be greater than the new equilibrium level. Then the rate of interest will react and rise above its new equi-librium level, which will reduce investment and income below its new equilibrium level J.

Subsequently, the rate of interest will fall below the new equili-brium level and investment will expand. . . . Hence a process de-velops with income and the rate of interest oscillating about their new equilibrium position. What is vital for economists is whether the oscillations grow smaller, so that Y and R converge on their new equilibrium, or whether they grow larger so that Y and R diverge from their new equilibrium.

Part (a) of Figure 11.7 illustrates convergence on J in a 'cob-web' fashion, whereas part (b) illustrates divergence in an 'explosive cob-web'. Crudely, they converge if the slope of IS in the relevant area is steeper than the slope of the LM curve, and diverge if LM is steeper than IS. Similar results follow if LM shifts and IS remains constant. Failure to converge on the new equilibrium is the more likely, the more sensitive is investment to interest-rate changes, and the more sensitive is the interest rate to income changes. In practice such explosive possibilities seem remote, but they do illustrate the importance for economists of looking not only at equilibrium posi-tions but also at dynamic processes by which the economy may move from one to another.

Chapter 12

Epilogue on Growth

Introduction

Much of the economic analysis in this book has concentrated on the short run, to discover equilibrium positions, to discuss shifts from one equilibrium to another, and to use this analysis for short-run policy adjustments of the economy by manipulating effective demand. There has been no systematic analysis of the factors making for the economic growth and fluctuation of societies and no discussion of why some economies grow faster than others. To tackle these topics adequately would require another volume, and even then no settled theory of economic growth would emerge, such is the current state and spate of growth theories. All that is attempted here is to draw out a few of the growth implications of our earlier analysis.

Certainly our analysis had growth in mind for, in Chapter 5, dealing with investment decisions, it was stressed that net investment was largely motivated either by the expectation of future growth in sales, or by current growth in sales pressing on inadequate productive capacity so that business undertook net additions to capital stock to expand productive capacity. In terms of the acceleration theory of investment decisions—in which net induced investment was equal to the accelerator multiplied by the expected (or actual) growth in sales and output—growth was necessary to get any investment: zero *growth* in output meant zero induced investment. On the other hand, to get growth in the supply of output in a full capacity situation, more capacity (and hence net investment) were essential.

The U.K. record

The growth of real gross domestic product in the United Kingdom has proceeded at various rates over the past 100 years. Between 1856 and 1899, the calculations presented in Table 12.1 indicate an annual percentage growth rate of 2 per cent. When this is adjusted to allow for the growth in the labour force, the annual growth rate in real gross domestic product per man-year amounts to roughly 1 per cent. The years 1899–1913 provide an instance of growth in output matching growth in labour force so that product per man-year virtually stagnates. In the inter-war period 1924–37, despite the heavy unemployment, we find a substantial annual percentage growth rate in gross domestic product of 2·3 per cent, and a recovery in the growth in output per man-year to the 1856–99 rate of just over 1 per cent a year. Then, in the post-war period, we find a modest rise in the growth rate of gross domestic product to 2·5 per cent a year, and an acceleration in the growth rate of output per man-year to almost 2 per cent.

Table 12.1   **Growth in United Kingdom 1856–1962**

| | Annual percentage rates of growth | |
	Real gross domestic product	Real gross domestic product per man-year
1856–1899	2·0	1·1
1899–1913	1·1	0·1
1924–1937	2·3	1·1
1948–1962	2·5	1·9

Source: R. C. O. Matthews, *Transactions of Manchester Statistical Society*, 1964.

Clearly in the post-war period the British economy has been growing more rapidly than at any other period in the past 100 years, and this is reflected more noticeably in the 'per man-year' figures. Nevertheless, this has not been the subject of pleasure but of disquiet, because the post-war U.K. growth rate has compared very poorly with the much more rapid rate of growth of similar European economies, to say nothing of the phenomenal Japanese performance.

Growth in supply

How may growth in output supplied be achieved? If, with a given capital stock, more men are employed, increases in output can be expected; but gradually diminishing returns to labour will prevail as the capital stock is more intensively utilised. We will then find the labour force growing more rapidly than output, so that output per man-year falls.

If, then, we seek to produce more output by increasing all factor inputs, we may well find that 5 per cent more capital *and* labour inputs produce 5 per cent more output. This would be a case of constant returns to scale, and output per man-year would remain unchanged as output and the labour force grew at the same rate. If, however, there was scope for increasing returns, or economies of scale, as the size of enterprises grew, then 5 per cent more of each input might produce 6 per cent more output. Here output per man-year would grow (unless the number of hours worked per year fell).

These methods of achieving growth broadly rely on unchanged methods and factor qualities. A lesson of economic history is that, frequently, episodes of growth have involved *changed* methods and *changed* products as a result of inventions, innovations, technical progress, and better education. There is an important role here not

Table 12.2 **Annual growth rates 1950–62 (in percentages)**

	United Kingdom	*W. Germany*
Real national income	2·29	7·26
explained by:		
(i) growth in labour input	0·60 ⎱ 1·11	1·37 ⎱ 2·78
(ii) growth in capital input	0·51 ⎰	1·41 ⎰
Leaving growth in output per unit of input	1·18	4·48
explained by:		
(i) advances of knowledge	0·76	0·76
(ii) economies of scale	0·36	1·61
(iii) improved allocation of resources	0·12	1·01
(iv) other	−0·06	1·10

Source: E. F. Denison, *Why Growth Rates Differ*, pp. 308 and 314.

only for the spectacular inventions, but also for the more humdrum and slow improvements in the abilities of the labour force, and for the many minor but steady improvements in the design and capacity of machines. These various improvements in the quality and productiveness of labour and capital inputs have come as a result of technical progress and education, and have been immensely important elements in achieving the growth in output per head which has raised our living standards so greatly. A second important feature has been the willingness of labour and management to adapt and accept changed methods, for lack of willingness to adapt, and innate conservatism, have undoubtedly retarded growth in some societies.

A further source of growth in output is provided by the re-allocation of factors of production from occupations of lower productivity to occupations of higher productivity. For example, a shift in factors of production from agriculture to manufacturing industry has often had this effect. More generally, this increase in output per man-year as a result of greater economic efficiency, may well take the form of a once-and-for-all rise in the level of output rather than provide the source of continuing growth in output.

An attempt has been made by the American economist, E. F. Denison, to measure the contribution of various factors to the actual growth rates of European and North American economies. In Table 12.2 are presented his estimates for the growth rates of the United Kingdom and West Germany for the period 1950 to 1962. It will be seen for the U.K. that growth in labour and capital inputs explained 1·11 percentage points of the 2·29 per cent annual growth rate in real national income (or 48 per cent of this actual growth rate). In Germany growth in such inputs explained 2·78 percentage points of the 7·26 per cent annual growth rate in real national income (or 38 per cent). In the U.K., of the 1·18 per cent growth in output per unit of input, advances in knowledge (0·76 percentage points) and economies of scale (0·36 percentage points) provide the chief explanation. However, in West Germany, besides advances in knowledge (0·76 percentage points) and economies of scale (1·61 percentage points), improved allocation of resources (1·01 percentage points) provided an important source of growth. (Re-allocation of resources from low productivity agriculture to high productivity industry was a major element here.)

Precisely why British and German growth rates should differ so much for the period 1950–62—and continue to differ—is a fascinating problem in applied economics, as well as a vital influence in the relative growth in living standards in the two economies. For the basic method of obtaining more goods and services for each inhabitant is by increases in output per unit of input, at which Germany has been notably more successful than the U.K.

A growth model

So much then for growth in *supply*. Our analysis in the preceding chapters has emphasised the role of *planned spending* in determining output and employment. What part has this to play in the growth process? Let us consider growth in output in a macroeconomic system such as we developed earlier (particularly in Chapters 3, 4, and 5).

From the method of analysis two key points emerge. To get growth:

(i) planned spending must grow;
(ii) capacity to produce must grow.

The former aspect has been somewhat neglected in discussions on growth both past and present, yet our emphasis on the importance of planned spending should be carried over into a growth context. For it is of no use producing increasing quantities when the market for the output is not growing. This is a lesson economies seeking economic growth and development may have to learn the hard way. Again, in historical reviews of past growth, of 'industrial revolutions' and the like, more attention should be paid to the 'market' or 'demand' aspects. Where did the growing spending come from, which absorbed the growing output, and why?

Again, growth in demand without growth in capacity is a perfect recipe for excess demand inflation, so that growth in capacity is a vital element. Partly this can come from increasing stocks of factors of production (population growth expanding labour, and net investment increasing capital) in a duplicative fashion, and partly by better methods and by better or improved qualities of factors of production in which aspects the application of technical progress and the role of education are of crucial importance. The key role of real capital formation or net investment hardly needs stressing here in accomplishing growing capacity to produce, while population growth is best treated as an 'outside' variable, although it may be influenced by economic forces.

Can we marry together growing effective demand and growing capacity to produce over time to yield an equilibrium full-capacity growth path? And, if so, will this yield steady growth at a constant equilibrium growth *rate*?

From earlier analysis one condition must hold over time: planned effective demand must always equal planned production at full capacity. Secondly, let us assume a given consumption function, which for simplicity is of the form $C_t = cY_t$ so that it goes through the origin, and the average and marginal propensities to consume are both equal to c. Thirdly, let us recognise the dual role of investment: while projects are being constructed, spending on them constitutes an injection into the flow of income. Once completed, they add to capital stock and to capacity to produce in a definite way.

Assume that each £1 worth of net real investment (also written as $\triangle K$ where K is capital stock) undertaken in this year adds in the succeeding year £n worth of extra capacity to produce ($\triangle Y$) to existing annual capacity (Y). n can be thought of as a productivity ratio of investment to extra annual capacity, and

$$n = \frac{\triangle Y}{I} = \frac{\triangle Y}{\triangle K} = \frac{1}{\text{marginal capital-output ratio}}$$

We further assume constant prices, no governmental nor international transactions, and that initially (in time period 1) the economy is operating at full capacity.

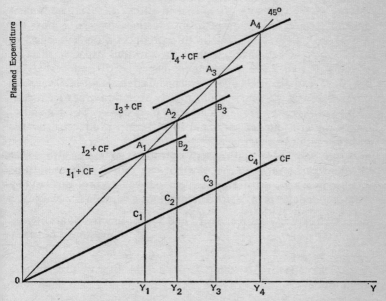

Figure 12.1 Growth in investment and income for full-capacity equilibrium

Hence, in time period 1 net saving will be taking place and must be offset by an equivalent amount of net investment in order to ensure that planned effective demand fully absorbs planned full-capacity production. This net investment adds to capacity to produce in time period 2, so that if full-capacity operation is to be maintained, planned investment must be greater than in the previous period, since full-capacity planned savings will have grown, to ensure that planned effective demand grows sufficiently. This investment of period 2 increases capacity in period 3 by a greater amount than it was increased in period 2 and a further increase in investment will be needed in period 3. Hence if an equilibrium growth path is to be interpreted as a full-capacity growth path with full utilisation of a growing capital stock, this analysis indicates that this is a distinct possibility, provided that net investment grows as required.

This is illustrated diagrammatically in Figure 12.1. Here OY_1 is full-capacity income in year 1, Y_1C_1 consumption and C_1A_1 savings which must be offset by an equivalent amount of net investment I_1 to generate sufficient effective demand to match OY_1. This investment will add nI_1 to capacity to produce in year 2, which is denoted by Y_1Y_2, thus making full capacity output in year 2 OY_2. Planned full-capacity saving rises to C_2A_2 so that to offset this saving and maintain full-capacity operation planned investment in year 2 must rise by B_2A_2 to C_2A_2 $(= I_2)$. This in turn produces a capacity effect of nI_2 $(= Y_2Y_3)$ which is bigger than the previous capacity effect of nI_1 $(= Y_1Y_2)$ so that investment in year 3 must rise above I_2 by B_3A_3 to C_3A_3 to maintain effective demand equivalent to full capacity output in year 3. To achieve full-capacity operation over time investment has to grow to provide a growing planned effective demand to absorb the growing capacity, and in its turn it produces a further growth in full-capacity output.

The requirement for full-capacity operation can be seen also in that between year 1 and year 2 the growth in capacity to produce must be matched by the growth in effective demand, which is brought about by the multiplier effects of the rise in investment between the two years.

Increase in capacity between year 1 and 2 = productivity ratio $\times$ investment of year 1

$$= nI_1$$

Increase in effective demand between year 1 and 2 = increase in investment $\times$ multiplier

$$= (I_2 - I_1) \times \frac{1}{(1 - c)}$$

Setting these equal as an equilibrium requirement:

Increase in investment $\times$ multiplier = productivity ratio $\times$ investment of year 1

$$\frac{I_2 - I_1}{(1 - c)} = nI_1$$

whence

$$\frac{I_2 - I_1}{I_1} = n(1 - c) = ns$$

$$\frac{\text{increase in investment}}{\text{investment of year 1}} = \frac{\text{productivity ratio}}{\text{multiplier}}$$

In other words, the growth in investment between the two periods (and it will apply to any two successive periods) should equal the productivity ratio times the marginal propensity to save, and this means that investment must grow at a constant (percentage) rate, provided that n and s both remain constant. For example, if $n = 0.5$ and $s = 10$ per cent, the required growth rate in investment will be 5 per cent, and this will also be the growth rate in full-capacity income, provided that the average and marginal propensity to consume are equal.[1]

A numerical example will help to illustrate these points. Suppose:

(i) $C_t = 0.9 Y_t$ so that m.p.c. = a.p.c. = 0.9
(ii) Increment in capacity in $= \triangle Y = 0.5 I_t$
   next time period
(iii) Full capacity income in period 1 (Y_1) is 2,000 and investment in period 1 onwards is such as to ensure planned effective demand matching full capacity output
(iv) There are no problems about shortage of labour limiting output

Period	Full capacity real income	Full capacity real consumption	Full capacity real savings	Required real investment	Capacity effect $(= 0.5 I_t)$
1	2,000	1,800	200	200 ⟶	100
2	2,100	1,890	210	210 ⟶	105
3	2,205	1,984·5	220·5	220·5 ⟶	110·25
4	2,315·25				

In period 1 the investment of 200 required to offset full-capacity saving creates extra production capacity of 100 in period 2, thus raising full-capacity output to 2,100. This necessitates a growth in required investment in period 2 to 210, which adds 105 to productive

1. From the multiplier $(I_2 - I_1)\dfrac{1}{1 - c} = (Y_2 - Y_1)$

whence $(I_2 - I_1) = (1 - c)(Y_2 - Y_1)$ 1

In period 1 $\quad I_1 + C_1 = Y_1$

$\therefore I_1 + cY_1 = Y_1 \quad$ since $C_t = cY_t$

whence $\quad I_1 = (I - c)Y_1$ 2

Divide 2 into 1 $\quad \dfrac{I_2 - I_1}{I_1} = \dfrac{(1 - c)(Y_2 - Y_1)}{(1 - c) Y_1} = \dfrac{Y_2 - Y_1}{Y_1}$

i.e. growth rate in investment = growth rate in income

capacity in period 3 and so on. From the figures given above, required investment is growing and at a constant rate of 5 per cent per time period (210 is 5 per cent greater than 200, 220·5 is 5 per cent greater than 210). Also full capacity income is growing at the same rate of 5 per cent, which squares with the earlier formula rate of ns or $n(1 - c)$, since n is 0·5 and s is 10 per cent.

With the marginal propensity to consume at 0·9, the multiplier is 10 so that the rise in investment of 10·5 between periods 2 and 3 causes effective demand to rise by 105, which just matches the extra productive capacity of 105 being made available in period 3.

Clearly, then, it is possible to obtain an equilibrium growth path which ensures full-capacity use of a growing capital stock, and which grows at a constant rate—provided that we stick to the earlier assumptions, and provided that investment grows at the appropriate rate. However, it should be noted that this growth path may not be attainable if the labour force is not growing sufficiently rapidly, while if attained it might not guarantee full employment of a growing labour force.

Let us consider the growth path of investment, which we have asserted must grow at a particular rate and whose motivation has been ignored. Can businessmen be induced to undertake such investment outlays? Here the underlying assumptions of the accelerator theory of investment decisions can come to our aid, in particular the desire of businessmen to keep a fixed capital–output ratio and to undertake investment to bring the actual capital stock into equality with the desired capital stock.

For example, if they are currently operating at their desired capital–output ratio but have good reason to believe that demand for output will rise next year by £n, then they will currently undertake £1 worth of net investment to ensure that their capital stock and productive capacity next year will be adequate to meet the extra demands without strain. n is, of course, the productivity ratio we met earlier and here an expected increment in output of £n is inducing net investment of £1 so that the accelerator (v) is $\frac{1}{n}$.

For $I = v \triangle Y$ (Accelerator)

but $nI = \triangle Y$

$\therefore I = \frac{1}{n} \triangle Y$

$\therefore v = \frac{1}{n}$

In this way the productivity ratio and the accelerator are linked, and in our numerical example $n = 0.5$ so that $v = 2$.

In this example in period 1 we have to suppose that (to justify their investment of 200) they are operating at full capacity currently with their desired capital stock; and that they confidently expect in period 2 that demand for output will grow by 100 to 2,100, or by 5 per cent, and so they need to invest 200 in period 1 in order that the extra productive capacity will be available. Strictly, this is a 'forward looking' accelerator relationship in which the $\triangle Y$ in the equation relates to the difference between the current period's planned output and next period's expected output.

For net investment to take place on the appropriate scale businessmen must believe that growth at x per cent (5 per cent in this example) is a permanent feature of their future economic environment, for it is the prospect of future economic growth of a particular size which is inducing an investment outlay of the requisite size in the current period. Indeed, in such an economy economic growth takes place because *businessmen believe in growth*: once they cease to believe in growth, growth ceases because investment collapses and with it effective demand. The same conclusions would follow if our model incorporated a 'currently based' accelerator where $\triangle Y = Y_t - Y_{t-1}$.

In reality continuous growth at the particular rate and exact stability of n and c would seem highly unlikely, while many chance occurrences could cause actual investment outlays to differ from required investment outlays. Let us suppose that in time period 2 of our earlier example, actual investment spending was 208 instead of the 210 required to achieve effective demand of 2,100. In these circumstances effective demand would be lower and 'equilibrium' income would be 2,080 as compared with capacity to produce of 2,100 so that excess capacity of 20 would have emerged and capital stock would be larger than desired.

The normal entrepreneurial reaction, even if a 5 per cent growth in sales were still expected, would be to cut investment in period 3 to 200, say. A further reduction in effective demand would bring 'equilibrium' income down to 2,000 in period 3 as compared with capacity output of $2,100 + 0.5 \times 208 = 2,204$, so that excess capacity has widened to 204. Normal business reactions will aggravate this situation, so that a (temporary) discrepancy has brought a self-aggravating divergence from the growth path. However, if businessmen took a different view and were prepared, despite excess capacity, to increase investment in period 3 to 220, effective demand would be sufficiently high to eliminate excess capacity. But is it reasonable to expect them to behave in that way? This may indicate an important role for public investment in promoting steady growth by being allowed to grow steadily despite fears of excess capacity.

Again, let us suppose that in time period 2 actual investment was 212 instead of the required value of 210, so that effective demand was higher than full-capacity output, and 'equilibrium' income of 2,120 indicated a shortage of capacity of 20. The normal entrepreneurial reaction to this shortage of capacity and capital stock would be to expand investment in period 3 by yet more to 230, say. This would cause effective demand to rise yet more and 'equilibrium' income would be 2,330 as compared with a full capacity output of $2,100 + 0.5 \times 212 = 2,206$ and an even greater excess demand (or shortage of capacity). Aggravating effects to the initial discrepancy similar to these in the previous example can be expected to follow.

Given the entrepreneurial reactions underlying the accelerator theory of investment decisions, any divergence from the equilibrium growth path will initiate self-aggravating divergent tendencies. This provides some insight into the way that growth and instability have been inextricably linked in private enterprise economies, and may help us to recognise sources of instability. Further, it explains the paradox that to cure a capacity shortage one should invest *less*, and to cure a capacity surplus one should invest *more*! Yet, in the real world these self-aggravating instabilities have not emerged on the scale that theory might suggest.

Upward movements may be checked in real terms by a 'full employment' ceiling to growth in output, which is set by the growth in the labour force and any increase in its productivity, after which they will spread themselves into price increases of 'excess demand' inflation with real growth slackening and the shortage of capacity declining. In a downward direction we may find that a floor is provided to effective demand because not all kinds of investment may be reduced despite excess capacity. Long-range autonomous investment and innovational investment will tend to be more stable than induced investment, while governmental spending may also remain steady. A 'safety net' may thus be provided for the economy if it falls from its tight-rope path of equilibrium growth. Lastly, businessmen may not react so slavishly and rigidly as the strict accelerator theory would suggest.[2]

2. Other stabilising factors can be adduced, but they are really beyond the scope of this epilogue and can only be treated satisfactorily at much greater length.

Besides providing a view of growth this approach would suggest that economic fluctuations, such as the trade cycle, might be treated as unsteadiness about a growth path which is limited by the bounds of a full employment ceiling and a floor to effective demand. The proximate cause of fluctuations was variations in investment (or variations in exports or governmental spending in more complex economies) which might have come about accidentally or might have reflected variations in the confidence of businessmen or in the firmness of their expectations. Economies can be subject to waves of optimism and pessimism which feed on themselves and which may underlie the unsteadiness of investment and effective demand.

Our treatment has been in real terms and attention has centred on investment, savings, and output decisions. Nothing has been said about monetary factors which implicitly have been assumed not to matter. The real approach is equivalent to the *IS* curve shifting steadily outwards—but what of the *LM* curve? If monetary adjustments are not made, the growth in output should slow down in real terms as monetary stringency and rising interest rates check spending decisions. One cannot for ever be on the flat part of the *LM* curve, nor can one assume that planned spending is insensitive to the interest rate, whatever level it reaches. For an equilibrium growth path in real terms one must assume that the stock of money is so adjusted as to keep interest rates unchanged and to permit desired spending to take place. Otherwise, monetary forces could impose a brake on the real forces of growth.

Another limitation has been imposed by the view taken of production. Extra output is obtained in fixed proportion to extra capital stock, and little has been said about the role of labour except to assume that the labour requirements are met. The possibility of substituting capital for labour in a more comprehensive production function has been ignored, as has the possibility of steady improvements in capital equipment over time so that the productivity ratio (of investment) n rises. These supply-oriented developments need to be incorporated into any full treatment of growth.

Summary

Once again, it must be stressed that this equilibrium growth path is one which ensures full use of a growing capital stock in an economic environment of a given consumption function and a given productivity ratio for investment, or a given capital–output ratio. It does not necessarily produce full employment of a growing labour force, nor is it one which is necessarily attainable. The fundamental forces of growth in the labour supply and the growth in productivity may only permit real output to grow by 4 per cent a year when the equilibrium rate is 6 per cent. These are crucial points to bear in mind when looking at growth analysis. Further, the analysis of this chapter would suggest (i) the importance of businessmen believing in growth; (ii) the high risk of instability in growth in a private enterprise economy; (iii) the need to look for stabilising features, since in practice such economies have rarely been wildly unstable.

Suggestions for Further Reading

Readers who wish to advance their knowledge of macroeconomics beyond the basic outline presented in this volume will find *Macroeconomics* by F. S. Brooman and *Output, Inflation and Growth* by D. C. Rowan useful general textbooks which are clearly and concisely written. Topics which have here only been touched on are pursued in more detail. Somewhat more difficult and advanced treatment is provided in *Macroeconomics* by T. F. Dernburg and D. M. McDougall and in *Macroeconomic Theory* by G. Ackley. This latter book provides an excellent discussion and comparison of Keynesian and Neo-classical macroeconomics as well as much other useful material and can be strongly recommended.

Much more advanced (and mathematical) in content is *Macroeconomic Theory* by R. G. D. Allen, as is *Readings in Macroeconomics* by M. G. Mueller which should be used once the student has a firm grasp of such a book as Ackley.

Every student of Economics should read the classic work by J. M. Keynes—*The General Theory of Employment, Interest and Money*. This laid the foundations of modern macroeconomics and will be found both brilliant in style and content and in places difficult and confusing. Help will be provided by consulting *Guide to Keynes* by A. H. Hansen, while *The Keynesian Revolution* by L. R. Klein provides an advanced but illuminating reference.

For those who wish to pursue national income accounting further, *National Income and Social Accounting* by H. C. Edey and A. T. Peacock and *National Income Analysis* by W. Beckerman can be confidently recommended at the elementary level. Still one of the best introductions to banking is given by R. S. Sayers, *Modern Banking*, while monetary matters are admirably dealt with in *Theory of Money* by W. T. Newlyn and *The Demand for Money* by D. Laidler (more difficult).

Economic fluctuations and instability which have occupied the attention of so many economists in the past and which have plagued the lives of working people through involuntary unemployment are handled well in *The Trade Cycle* by R. C. O. Matthews. Economic growth has currently been the focus of much activity in macroeconomics but no really satisfactory textbook has yet emerged. Books which can be recommended here are W. Baumol, *Economic Dynamics*; Sir Roy Harrod, *Towards a Dynamic Economics*; J. E. Meade, *A Neo-Classical Theory of Economic Growth*; W. Eltis, *Economic Growth*; while *Economic Growth in Britain*, edited by P. D. Henderson, provides a more practical approach. As a corrective for those who have the impression that economic management is an easy affair for a government, we recommend strongly *The Management of the British Economy 1945–1960* by J. C. R. Dow.

Index